Practising Social Work

Meeting the professional challenge

NEIL THOMPSON

palgrave
macmillan

First published 2009 by
PALGRAVE MACMILLAN
Houndmills, Basingstoke, Hampshire RG21 6XS and
175 Fifth Avenue, New York, N.Y. 10010
Companies and representatives throughout the world

PALGRAVE MACMILLAN is the global academic imprint of the Palgrave Macmillan division of St. Martin's Press, LLC and of Palgrave Macmillan Ltd. Macmillan® is a registered trademark in the United States, United Kingdom and other countries. Palgrave is a registered trademark in the European Union and other countries.

ISBN-13: 978-0-230-20192-7
ISBN-10: 0-230-20192-X

This book is printed on paper suitable for recycling and made from fully managed and sustained forest sources. Logging, pulping and manufacturing processes are expected to conform to the environmental regulations of the country of origin.

A catalogue record for this book is available from the British Library.

A catalog record for this book is available from the Library of Congress.

Printed in China

For Helen

Contents

Tables and figures

Tables

Figures

Preface

I have been delighted with the very positive feedback I have received in relation to my book, *Understanding Social Work* (Palgrave Macmillan, 2000, 2nd edn, 2005). The very clear message such feedback has given me is that the book succeeds in its aim of laying the foundations for social work practice by giving readers a good understanding of what social work is all about and what they can expect from a career in social work. This book now builds on those foundations by exploring some of the key issues and challenges that social workers face. It covers a wide range of aspects of the very complex world of social work and, as such, should provide a helpful guide to practice.

The book should be of particular interest to social work students and those in the early stages of their career. However, many very experienced social workers and practice teachers (and even a few managers) have told me that they found my *Understanding Social Work* book useful as a means of 'revisiting their roots' and thereby reaffirming their commitment to the goals and values of social work. I anticipate that the same will apply to this book too, and that many people who are further down their career path will welcome, and benefit from, the opportunity to revisit some key themes and issues relating to social work.

My aim has been to provide a blend of theory and practice, but with the emphasis very clearly on the actual challenges of practice. However, this does not mean that this is a 'how to do it' type of book, as I feel that prescriptive approaches are unhelpful – partly because they tend to paint too simplistic a picture of the complexities of practice, and partly because they go against the grain of reflective practice by giving the misleading impression that effective practice can be carried out in a formulaic way. The subtitle of the book, 'Meeting the Professional Challenge' is very significant in two ways. First, there is the emphasis on professionalism, and this term tells us that what is involved is not simply following rules, procedures or orders, but rather developing an informed picture of the situation and deciding (in partnership) how best to proceed in the circumstances. A 'how to' approach cannot prepare us for that. Second, the word 'challenge' emphasizes that social work is not a simple or straightforward set of activities. Rather, it is a set of quite complex challenges that require us to have a well-informed, highly skilled approach based on clear values that will help to guide us through the intricacies involved.

This book will not provide simple answers, but what it will do is help to guide readers towards effective, rewarding and high-quality practice. Social work plays an important role in 'humanizing' society by seeking to help those people who, for a variety of reasons, are distressed, disadvantaged or otherwise experiencing difficulties. I see this book as making a contribution to making sure that our efforts are well informed, well targeted and as effective and rewarding as they reasonably can be.

Neil Thompson

Acknowledgements

This book is in many ways a culmination of over 30 years' experience in social work and so I am indebted to far too many people for me to list them individually here. It is none the less important for me to acknowledge the gratitude I owe to the various colleagues over the years that I have learned so much from, the managers who have also played a part in shaping my understanding and development and, importantly, the people I have been privileged to help and support over the years: clients and carers, students, practice teachers and other professionals. Giving is also about receiving, and so I have been very fortunate indeed to have had so many people I could learn from, so many people to enrich my understanding.

More recently I have had the benefit of being a member of two excellent teams. At Avenue Consulting I have been ably supported by Anna Thompson and Sharon Brimfield-Edwards and, of course, Sue Thompson has continued to be such an important bedrock and inspiration. At Liverpool Hope University, John Bates, Liz Brooksbank and Vassilis Ioakimidis have proven to be excellent colleagues in laying the foundations for a centre of excellence for social work.

I am grateful to Professor Bernard Moss of Staffordshire University for his helpful comments on my ideas and their development. As usual, his insights and understanding were a great resource to be able to draw upon.

Catherine Gray and Sheree Keep at the publishers have built on their long-standing track record of being an excellent source of support. Similarly, Margaret Holloway's excellent audiotyping proved a great help in producing this work. I am very grateful to Penny Simmons not only for her excellent copy-editing work, but also for the very helpful and supportive way she has been involved in this project.

The book is dedicated to ex-colleague and current friend, Helen Keaney-Cheetham, whose commitment to social work values and standards, and skill in upholding them, are an inspiration.

Tragically, Jo Campling is no longer with us, but she was part of the original discussions in planning this book and so her influence is very much to be felt in the present work. I am very grateful for that and for all the other help and guidance she gave me over the years.

About the author

Neil Thompson is a Director of Avenue Consulting Ltd (www.avenueconsulting.co.uk), a company based in Wales offering training and consultancy services in relation to social and occupational well-being.

He has previously held full and honorary titles at four British universities and has over a hundred publications to his name, including best-selling textbooks, papers in learned journals and training and open learning materials. His recent books include:

People Problems (Palgrave Macmillan, 2006)

Promoting Workplace Learning (Policy Press, 2006).

Power and Empowerment (Russell House Publishing, 2007)

The Palgrave Social Work Companion (with Sue Thompson, Palgrave Macmillan, 2008)

The Critically Reflective Practitioner (with Sue Thompson, Palgrave Macmillan, 2008)

Loss, Grief and Trauma in the Workplace (Baywood, 2008)

Neil has over thirty years' experience as a practitioner, manager, educator, consultant and expert witness in the human services. He is very well respected for his ability to communicate complex ideas in an accessible way without oversimplifying them.

He has been a speaker at seminars and conferences in the UK, Ireland, Greece, the Netherlands, Norway, Spain, Italy, Hong Kong, Canada, the United States, Australia and India, and has qualifications in social work, management (MBA), training and development, mediation and dispute resolution, as well as a first-class honours degree in Social Sciences and a PhD.

Neil is a Fellow of the Chartered Institute of Personnel and Development and the Royal Society of Arts (elected to the latter on the basis of his contribution to workplace learning). He is also a Fellow of the Higher Education Academy and a Life Fellow of the Institute of Welsh Affairs. He is the editor of the US-based international journal *Illness, Crisis & Loss*, and currently also edits the *Well-Being* quarterly e-newsletter (www.well-being.org.uk). In addition, he is a member of the International Work Group on Death, Dying and Bereavement.

He is now a sought-after workshop facilitator, consultant and conference speaker. His website is at www.neilthompson.info.

Introduction

There is a huge and growing literature relating to social work, so why another book? And why this one in particular? First, it is important to realize that social work is a vast subject and so it merits a vast array of published literature to help us make sense of it. It is also a subject that is changing over time in response to changes at the political and social levels and in terms of how it is conceived and put into practice by each new generation of practitioners, how it is managed by each new generation of managers, and taught by each new generation of educators. In that respect, there is always room for fresh comment and new insights about the subject as a whole or about particular aspects of it. What this book seeks to offer in particular is a guide for students or beginning practitioners to help them appreciate the complexities of professional practice and provide a foundation for being able to wrestle with them in what Schön (1983) famously referred to as the 'swampy lowlands of practice'.

In my work as a trainer and consultant and in my university-based work, I have encountered a great deal of uncertainty among students, practitioners and managers about how best to respond to the challenges of social work practice. Some might even call it a lack of professional self-confidence, a certain reservation about what and how social work can contribute to the broader field of promoting social well-being. My plan in writing this book has been to do something positive and constructive about this by presenting a text that stimulates further discussion, analysis and understanding of the professional foundations of social work practice – so that we can, individually and collectively, be better equipped for the challenges involved by being better informed. There is no shortage of literature on the subject matter covered by the book (see the *Guide to further learning* at the end of the book), but what this book offers is a synthesis of important insights based on much of that literature plus my own experience of practice, management and education in social work over the past thirty years. It can therefore be seen as useful foundation for understanding plus a gateway to the wider literature.

While, as the book's title indicates, the emphasis is on *practising* social work, this is none the less a theoretically informed book. I would certainly not wish to give the impression that this is a book about practice *as opposed to* theory. Rather, it is a case of linking theory to practice by discussing practice in ways that are informed by theoretical understandings. The companion book, *Theorizing Social Work* (Thompson, forthcoming) addresses similar concerns and issues, but with more of a focus on theory – not for its own sake, but as an important set of underpinnings for practice. Effective social workers need to have a good understanding of both theory and practice (Thompson and Thompson, 2008a), and this book is devoted to helping in that regard, with a particular focus on the professional challenges involved.

As I have argued elsewhere (Thompson, 2005), social work is a contested concept – that is, different factions have different ideas about the nature and purpose of social work and the direction it should be going in. This book is part of my contribution to establishing social work as a *professional* enterprise, but one that is grounded in promoting social justice and well-being through an emphasis on problem-solving activities and empowerment, rather than a bureaucratic activity based on rationing services. The significance of conceptualizing social work in this way should become very clear in the course of the book.

The text is divided into four parts. Part 1 is concerned with the idea of the social worker as a problem solver. It s unfortunately the case that in some areas, some forms of social work have become reduced to providing or commissioning services without a clear analysis of what problems such services are intended to address or indeed whether there are other ways of responding to the concerns identified without the need for services (and the danger of creating dependency that is associated with them). Part 1 therefore begins by exploring important questions relating to problem solving and the unmet needs that give rise to such problems. From this, we move on to note how the problems individuals and families experience have their roots in the wider social context. Next comes a consideration of the importance of change in social work and how we can be involved in both promoting and preventing change. The last chapter of Part 1 focuses on the need to work in partnership – that is, to be able to work alongside others so that we can appreciate the various perspectives involved and thereby gain a more holistic view of the situations we are dealing with.

Part 2 builds on the work of Part 1 by examining the significance of the social worker as a thinker. This is to emphasize that social work is an intellectual activity in the sense that, while it is very much a practical concern, good practice none the less relies on the ability to think clearly and to be able to work with complexity. The first chapter is concerned with what has come to be known as 'reflective practice'. This involves developing critical analysis skills and being able to make sure that our practice is based on professional knowledge (rather than guesswork or habit, for example) and professional values (rather than simply expediency or responding to pressures from others). Next comes a discussion of the role of the social worker as an educator – that is, someone who helps people with their problems by promoting learning and understanding. This leads on to a discussion of the relationship between thinking and feeling. In particular, the important topic of emotional intelligence is explored. The final chapter is concerned with the central role of meaning in people's lives. It looks at how we develop stories or 'narratives' as part of a process of meaning making and how social work can be helpful in assisting people in developing more empowering narratives or frameworks of meaning where this is needed.

Part 3 is concerned with the role of the social worker as a manager – not in the sense of a practitioner who has been promoted to a managerial position, but rather in relation to these aspects of the social worker's duties that have managerial characteristics. The first of these to be considered is self-management. This involves self-care (making sure that we do not allow ourselves to be harmed by the pressures of the job) and also being sufficiently well organized to make the most of the limited time and resources available to us. The next chapter examines what is involved in managing processes, tasks and outcomes and gives particular attention to the importance of being clear about what we are trying to achieve and not allowing pressures from others or from our workload as a whole to distract us from the focus of what our work is about. Unfortunately, there are many ways in which we can be distracted from our goals and thereby lose focus, and so this chapter has some important messages about how to avoid this problem.

Managing risk and resources is the subject matter explored next. Here we are concerned with how issues of risk and resources can both be oversimplified, and can then lead to very poor or even oppressive practice. The last chapter in Part 3 addresses the important process of managing expectations. This refers to the need to be clear in our dealings with other people about what we can and cannot do. This is a very important activity, as many people will try to influence us in a direction that is in some way inappropriate. Skills in negotiating realistic and appropriate expectations are therefore vitally important in social work practice.

Part 4 concentrates on the issues arising from the professional nature of social work. It begins with a consideration of traditional forms of professionalism and discusses significant problems historically associated with such approaches – and how the legacy of such problems is still with us in some regards. This is followed by an account of how traditional professionalism was largely displaced by an ethos of anti-professionalism. Once again, the historical problems are identified and their unfortunate legacy for present practice is discussed. The third chapter in Part 4 puts forward arguments in favour of a new, emerging form of professionalism based on principles of partnership and empowerment rather than elitism. Finally, the steps necessary for tackling the challenges of professional practice are explored by way of summary and conclusion.

Each of the four parts ends with a conclusion that contains some brief concluding comments plus a set of 'points to ponder' questions and an exercise for each of the four chapters. These are intended as aids to reviewing understanding of the key issues in each of the chapters in that part of the book before moving on to the next part (in the case of Parts 1 to 3) or completing the book as a whole (in the case of Part 4). These questions at the end of each part are not intended as essay questions to be answered in detail or as seminar questions for discussion in class (although some tutors or trainers may wish to adapt some of them in this way). Rather, they are simply intended to provoke further consideration of the important issues discussed.

Throughout the book there are practice examples (indicated by the heading 'Practice focus'). These are drawn from my experience over 30 years as a practitioner, manager and educator. Some are direct practice examples (with the names changed to preserve confidentiality), while others are 'composite examples' – that is, they represent very typical situations that I have encountered over the years. All of them are therefore drawn from real-life social work situations.

Also to be found throughout the book are 'Voice of experience' examples. These are comments made by practitioners and managers that I have worked with in my role as trainer and consultant, and so they too are drawn from real-life social work situations. As such, they can offer important and valuable insights into the professional challenges of practice that this book is all about. We can also learn a great deal, of course, from the voices of experience that come from the people we serve – the clients and carers that are at the heart of our practice. There is now a growing literature that is helping us to appreciate the perspectives of those we seek to help, and so it is a very wise move to pay close attention to this growing body of work and the lessons we can learn from it (see the *Guide to further learning* at the end of the book).

Underpinning all four parts of the book are some important messages that are worth spelling out explicitly before we move on to begin making our way trough the various chapters. These are:

- Social work is difficult and demanding work, and so we need to be well informed about, and alert to, the challenges involved.
- Social work is potentially very effective in achieving its aims and very rewarding for its personnel. Practitioners, individually and collectively, have an important role to play in maximizing this potential.
- Social work is more than providing or commissioning services. Problem solving can make a major contribution to empowerment which, in turn, is an important foundation for promoting social justice and well-being.

> Being able to think clearly and handle complexity is an important foundation for good practice, as is the ability to deal effectively with emotional issues and to be able to help people make sense of their lives. Thinking, learning and understanding are therefore essential components of good practice.

> Being able to take effective responsibility for ourselves and our work is a fundamental part of maximizing our potential in social work practice.

> Being committed to social work as a *profession* (in terms of professional knowledge, skills, values and accountability) without returning to elitist forms of professionalism is a major challenge that we now face. We all have a part to play in rising to that challenge, in terms of both our individual efforts and the contribution we can make to support one another as part of a collective endeavour.

The social worker as problem solver

Introduction to Part 1

People come to the attention of social workers when there is some sort of problem (or set of problems) they are encountering or causing. So, problems and efforts to tackle them are at the heart of social work. However, the situation is more complex than this for (at least) three main reasons. First, social work is not concerned with just any problem, whatever it may be. We are not there to duplicate the problem-solving efforts of others. For example, although housing issues may often feature in social work cases, we are not housing providers, and cannot therefore solve housing problems directly, although we may have a role at times in supporting people in their efforts to address their housing needs. Similarly, we are not health professionals, and cannot therefore be involved directly in addressing health care needs. However, given that health and social well-being are so closely intertwined, there will often be situations where health issues are to the fore, especially for social workers based in hospitals, clinics or health centres. So, we are problem solvers, but we are not the only problem solvers. This means that (i) we have to be clear about our professional boundaries to make sure that we are not taking on responsibilities that belong elsewhere (to avoid duplication of effort, for example); and (ii) we need to work in partnership with other professionals in order to try and ensure that the people we serve receive the best help they can as a result of co-ordinated efforts where these are needed.

'We are problem solvers, but we are not the only problem solvers.'

Second, as England (1986) made clear quite some time ago, we tend to deal mainly with people who not only have problems (everyone has problems from time to time), but who also have difficulty resolving those problems unaided for some reason (as a result of illness, disability, social deprivation or other such factors). In order to understand this, it can be useful to distinguish between first-level problems – the challenges, demands and issues that everyone has to face – and second-level problems, which are the sort of things that can get in the way of addressing the first-level problems. Consider the following examples:

> *First-level problems:* financial difficulties; relationship tensions; social isolation; grief; and so on.
> *Second-level problems:* stigma; discrimination; poverty; trauma; lack of confidence; and so on.

This is one of the reasons why empowerment is so important in social work: it involves helping people to solve their own problems as far as possible, rather than doing it *for* them, and thereby risking making them dependent and therefore *less* well equipped to deal with the problems life throws up, rather than in a better position to do so.

Third, there is the added complication that relatively recent developments in the history of social work have tended to de-emphasize the problem-solving nature of social work and have emphasized in its place a focus on (i) risk management; and (ii) service provision. Risk management will be discussed in more detail in Part 3 (Chapter 11). The undue focus on service provision will feature in Chapter 1 in this part of the book. The discussion of managerialism in Part 4 will also be relevant in this regard.

The four chapters

Chapter 1 focuses on the important concept of needs and argues that, if certain needs go unmet, then this will produce problems. This is the territory of social work: helping people to meet their needs so that problems can be avoided or dealt with, and, by the same token, dealing with problems that are getting in the way of needs being met can help to ensure that those needs are then met. This chapter therefore explores some of the important issues connected with needs, unmet needs and related problems.

Chapter 2 is concerned with the social nature of the problems social workers are charged with addressing. A key point established is that so many individual or personal problems are, in fact, reflections of wider social problems (poverty and social exclusion, for example). Trying to address individual or family problems without understanding this wider social context can leave us very ill equipped for the challenges involved.

Chapter 3 explores the vitally important topic of change. This is because so often social work is geared towards bringing about positive change in problematic circumstances. However, there is also the important topic of preventing change to consider. This is because many aspects of social work involve trying to prevent deterioration – for example, in working with people with debilitating conditions, such as dementia.

Chapter 4 concludes Part 1 of the book. Its focus is on working in partnership. This is a key topic as so much of what we do in social work involves relying on the co-operation of others, whether clients and carers directly or indirectly through our dealings with other professionals. It is quite a complex topic and one of many that has tended to be oversimplified over the years. This chapter therefore discusses some of the intricacies and challenges involved.

Links with the other parts of the book

Part 1 sets the scene for the other three parts of the book. In particular, the emphasis on problem solving prepares the way for a discussion of the social worker as thinker in Part 2. This is because problem solving relies on analytical skills and the ability to draw on a professional knowledge base – in effect, what we shall refer to in Chapter 5 as 'critically reflective practice'.

Part 1 links well with Part 3, where the emphasis is on managements skills (it is not only managers that need management skills – practitioners need them too). We will struggle to be successful in our problem-solving efforts if we are not able to manage our time and pressures properly, manage the processes and tasks and so on.

Part 1 also fits well with Part 4, as the focus on professionalism in the final four chapters offers important insights that are very relevant to our efforts to meet needs and address problems.

Needs, unmet needs and problems

Introduction

The concept of need is a fundamental one in social work. It underpins so much of what we do. This chapter therefore explores what is meant by the term 'needs', how they are significant, and other related matters. In particular, it focuses on the concept of *unmet* needs and the problems that such unmet needs can generate. In doing this, I am setting the scene for the chapters that follow, in so far as they will all relate back in one way or another to the question of needs, unmet needs and problems. The significance of the concept of need should therefore not be underestimated.

We begin by looking at the central question: what are needs? This is followed by a discussion of the significance of situations in which a person's needs are not being met and what can arise as a result of this. This in turn sets the scene for a discussion of the problems that people may experience that are likely to bring them to the attention of social work personnel.

What are needs?

This is a more complicated question than it immediately appears to be. For example, there are different types and levels of need. We can begin with survival needs – those fundamental needs that have to be met if we are to stay alive. These are primarily biological – for example, in relation to food, drink and shelter. More complex issues arise when we consider the psychological dimension of needs in relation to such matters as identity, for example. This involves knowing who we are and where we fit into the world. Related to this are esteem needs – our need to feel valued. The picture gets even more complex when we add to this the significance of social needs. These include, among other things, being part of a community and citizenship (see Table 1.1).

One well-known theory of need is associated with the psychologist, Maslow (1973), who wrote of a hierarchy of needs, with physiological needs as the most fundamental, followed by safety, belongingness and love, esteem and self-actualization:

> The basic principle underlying Maslow's theory is that we cannot progress from one level to another without our needs first being met at the lower level. That is,

we cannot be safe unless our physiological needs (air, food, water and so on) are satisfied; we cannot experience love and belongingness unless we feel safe. The ultimate 'pinnacle' of this hierarchy is 'self-actualisation', the realisation of our full potential through finding or constructing a coherent framework of meaning and value which allows us to achieve a sense of personal fulfilment.

(Thompson, 2004, p. 20)

Table 1.1 Types of needs

Biological needs	Food, drink, warmth and shelter; medicine at times of illness and so on.
Psychological needs	Self-esteem; identity: a sense of who we are; stimulation and learning; achievement; sense of security; play/relaxation.
Social needs	Citizenship; social contact/being part of a community

However, this approach has been criticized for being too narrow and individualistic and for not taking enough account of the social circumstances and how these can change over time. It has also been criticized for being too fixed and rigid and thereby not allowing for the diversity and flexibility of human experience. None the less, despite these limitations, it is a useful starting point for understanding the complexity of the concept of need.

It is unfortunately the case that oversimplified conceptions of need have been adopted by many people over the years. These oversimplified conceptions can be criticized for being 'essentialist' – that is, they seem to regard need as something that is a fixed essence, an essential part of an individual or the human condition. For example, it is often stated that sex is a basic need, and yet many people live happy and fulfilling lives without sex. Above and beyond basic survival needs, this conception can be seen to be far too narrow and oversimplified. It is important to recognize that needs are, to a large extent, culturally defined. That is, what is perceived as a need in one culture may not be perceived as a need in another. Another way of putting this is to say that needs are socially constructed. They are defined within the context of a set of social relations and social processes as well as social institutions. What is considered a need by, for example, a wealthy westerner in a highly industrialized country, may be very different from someone living in a rural, agricultural, underdeveloped part of the East. Clearly, then, a more sophisticated understanding of need is called for.

Practice focus 1.1

Karen was excited to begin her placement with the older people team. When she received her first referral to deal with, her practice teacher explained that she would be expected to visit the client, Mrs Peters, and carry out an 'assessment of need'. She was very anxious about this as she wasn't 100 per cent sure what was meant by 'need' – what sort of needs? Need for what? However, she was reassured when she realized that she would be able to 'shadow' her practice teacher on a number of assessments she would be doing before she was called upon to do it herself. As a result of this 'shadowing', she had a much clearer picture of what was involved. The discussion she had with her practice teacher about what constituted a need, how serious it needed to be before it became a social work matter, and so on, was also very helpful for her. She realized that defining and assessing need are not necessarily straightforward matters, but she could see what some of the key issues were that she would need to give attention to. She could now understand why there was so much emphasis on this important concept of need.

It can be helpful to understand need as being related to purpose or desired outcome. That is, it makes more sense to understand need as need *for*, or need *in order to*. Such needs can also be seen to be layered, in the sense that one need is likely to be embedded in another. Figure 1.1 illustrates this.

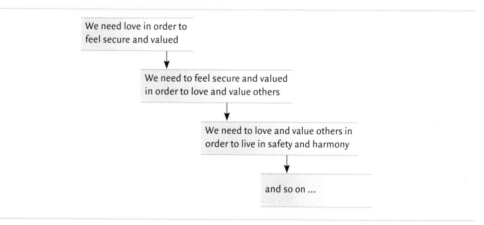

Figure 1.1 Layered or embedded needs

Source: Thompson, 2004.

This concept of purpose can be linked to the significant concept of well-being. A person's well-being can depend on purpose, in the sense of what goals they are aiming for and whether they are able to achieve those goals by having the associated needs met. We shall return to the important topic of goals later in this chapter.

What can also help us to develop a more sophisticated understanding of need is the question of negotiation, as this is involved in identifying and addressing needs. For example, in social work, needs are very relevant to the process of assessment. It has long been recognized that assessment needs to be done in partnership (Lymbery, 2003). It is not simply a matter of a professional making a unilateral expert diagnosis of the situation (see Chapter 14 for a critique of a medical model approach to social work). Assessment involves gathering information to form a picture of the situation, so that needs can be identified, and ways of meeting those needs can be explored as part of an action plan.

Voice of experience 1.1

Sometimes it's hard to get people involved in the process of assessment. They tend to see the social worker as the 'expert' and are waiting for us to come up with magic answers to their problems. But, it is certainly worth persevering and using your negotiation skills to get people involved. Once you get past that initial barrier you get a much better picture of the situation, and you get a lot more commitment on clients' part to moving forward on the important issues.

Andrea, a social worker in an adult learning disability team

Need also has to be understood in relation to the specific circumstances that apply at the time. For example, if somebody is grieving after a significant loss or is undergoing a period of recovery after a trauma, then their needs will be different from when they are not in such a situation. Attempts to understand need that do not take account of such circumstances are likely to be superficial and misleading – and can therefore be very dangerous at times.

Fook also emphasizes the importance of seeing situations in context when she argues that:

> Reframing our practice as contextual therefore means we reframe our practice as working *with* environments, rather than working *despite* environments. We see ourselves as part of a context, ourselves responsible for aspects of that context.
> In this way, we see possibilities for change, for *creating different microclimates within broader contexts.*

(2002, p. 162)

Understanding the context is an important theme that we will revisit from time to time. This is because social work is a *psychosocial* enterprise, not simply a psychological matter of dealing with individuals. The social context – at both micro and macro levels – is therefore very important (this is the subject matter of Chapter 2).

Unmet needs

By definition, our survival needs have to be met if we are to continue to exist. We cannot last very long without the basics of food, drink and so on. However, once we go beyond this basic level, we have to recognize that it is not uncommon for some people to have many of their needs go unmet, while it is also the case that all of us at some time will be in a position where our needs are not met. There is an important sociological dimension to this, in so far as whose needs are met and when is not simply a matter of random distribution. There will be significant social patterns that shape to a large extent whose needs are met and whose needs are not (see Table 1.2). For example, while there is no guarantee that a very wealthy person will be able to meet his or her needs, the chances of being able to achieve many of those needs will be significantly higher than for a person who is living in poverty and debt. As Rogers and Pilgrim put it:

> Although all social classes experience distressing negative life events, poorer people experience fewer positive life experiences to buffer them against these ubiquitous existential challenges.

(2003, p. 26)

Table 1.2 Social influences on meeting needs	
Finance	Income levels affect purchasing power and thus ability to buy assistance (for example, private health care or legal assistance). Debt can produce additional needs in terms of psychological pressures and feelings of loss of control. Access to savings can be helpful in some circumstances, and so people without savings will be disadvantaged in many situations.
Gender	The media are very powerful in shaping consumer behaviour and what is perceived as normal and desirable. This is often 'gendered' – that is, follows gender-specific lines. What is perceived as a problem owes much to gender, as does how people characteristically respond to problems. See, for example, Martin and Doka's (1999) work on gender differences in grieving.
Race/ethnicity	Racism can both generate needs (for protection, for example) and stand in the way of some needs being met. There will also be considerable diversity relating to needs in connection with religious beliefs and cultural practices. There may also be language needs that are relevant to social work issues.
Disability	How physical and/or mental impairments are conceived and dealt with owes much to dominant social perspectives on disability that reflect a discourse of dependency and pity. See, for example, the work of Michael Oliver (Oliver and Sapey, 2006).
Culture	Culture relates not only to ethnicity, but also region, class, occupation and other social categories. People's needs will be shaped in part by their location within this complex network of cultural formations.

Where needs are not met, there can be significant implications. At its simplest, where survival needs are not met, there is clearly a risk to life. In less extreme cases, there can be issues of neglect in relation to children and/or vulnerable adults. That is, while survival needs may be met to a sufficient degree to ensure that death does not ensue, they may be met to such a poor level that the individuals concerned suffer significant consequences – malnutrition at a physical level and psychological harm at the level of how individuals experience neglect as a very detrimental process.

Practice focus 1.2

Steven was expecting it to be a difficult case when he was asked to work with Callum, a 15-year-old boy who had been in foster care for about two years. Callum had experienced extensive neglect over the years that had remained undetected because his parents kept moving from area to area. However, Steven was taken aback at how much damage the experience had done to Callum in terms of his low self-esteem, his self-destructive behaviour and his unwillingness to trust adults. It soon became apparent that these problems presented major difficulties for Callum, as his lack of trust and his acting-out behaviour had jeopardized his foster placement on several occasions and had also seriously held back his education. To begin with, it made Steven feel quite distressed to think about just how detrimental the neglect had been, not only at the time it was happening, but also on a much longer-term basis. It made him determined to do his best to help Callum get over the ordeal and, as far as possible, to recover from the trauma that he had experienced. It was the sort of case that helped Steven to appreciate how demanding social work can be, but also how potentially rewarding it can be too.

Where identity needs are not met, dignity can suffer. A person's identity can be undermined in certain circumstances where who they are is not respected or valued. The result of this can be a damaging effect on confidence and self-esteem. These, then, can begin a vicious circle, in so far as a person with low self-esteem may encounter a range of other difficulties – for example, problems in securing employment. Such difficulties in turn can lead to financial problems, problems in acquiring suitable accommodation, and so on. These in turn can leave the individual concerned feeling inadequate and incompetent, thereby reinforcing a sense of low self-esteem. In social work, it is unfortunately not uncommon to meet many people who have suffered from this. Some people are more prone to this than others as a result of the sociological patterns mentioned above. For example, many older people encounter ageism which has the effect of treating them in a disrespectful way that in turn undermines dignity and associated identity.

Voice of experience 1.2

I came into social work with the intention of working in child care. However, on my first placement I worked in an older people team and that really opened my eyes to how appallingly so many older people are treated in our society. I was so shocked to see the extent of discrimination against people who should be respected and looked up to – sometimes it was quite overt and shameless the ways some people treated elderly people, but very often it was very subtle. It made me decide to work in the field of elder care so that I could play a part in promoting more respectful and dignified attitudes towards the older generations.

Kim, team manager of an older people team

In relation to social needs, where these are not met there can be significant problems associated with isolation, alienation and disaffection. The possible result of this (and the actual result in very many circumstances) is anti-social behaviour. That is, if people are not having their needs met, they may have little motivation to feel any sort of commitment to the broader social good. An important concept here is the notion of social capital (Putnam, 2000). There is a parallel between financial capital – that is, 'money in the bank' – and social capital. The latter refers to the resources we draw on as individuals within our social circumstances. Those who are rich in social capital will have, for example, a large number of friends and associates. They will be members of various organizations, clubs and networks. They will have lots of interests and activities that they enjoy engaging in. A person who is socially poor, by contrast, will perhaps have a much smaller network of human contacts, in some cases limited to one or two people only, or even in a minority cases, no contacts at all with the outside world in any meaningful way.

There will also be many people who are not members of any sort of club, society or association, and have little by way of interest which will enable them to engage with other people in their community and in life in general. Social capital is therefore an important issue to consider in relation to people's needs. Rogers and Pilgrim offer helpful comment when they make the point that:

> Resources, such as social capital, entail a form of psychosocial rather than economic wealth – the ability and opportunity to be involved in community networks and activities. As with economic wealth, it can be present in abundance or it can be depleted, with predictable consequences.

(2003, p. 63)

Practice focus 1.3

Bindhu was an experienced social worker in a 'gateway' team that dealt with all the new referrals in the area. One day she was allocated the case of an elderly man who was said to be living 'hand to mouth' in a semi-derelict building. As she drove to the address she had been given she wondered what she would come across, as the referral was very vague. It seemed to suggest that this man possibly had mental health problems, but there was very little to go on. What she actually found was an 82-year-old man who lived in a single room at the back of a long-disused shop. He had no electricity or running water and relied on calor gas for heat, light and what limited cooking he did. Bindhu was shocked to find that he had no family, friends or other social contacts. He spent his life in this very dirty room and his only excursions from it were to the public toilets about five minutes' walk away where he would use their facilities and fill up his bottle of water while he was there. She discovered that he had been living like this for approximately 15 years since his wife died and he had to sell their family home because of debts. Bindhu realized that he had managed to survive on a very small works pension he had, but his 'social capital' was even more meagre than his financial position. It was as if he had been living in a trance-like state for many years. She began to wonder where to begin when it came to helping him.

The embeddedness of needs, as discussed above, means that where one need is not met, this can lead to the collapse of the whole network of needs. It is like a house of cards; if one of the lower cards is absent, then there is nothing to support the cards laid above. This interrelationship of needs is very significant, as it means that, if our assessment is skimpy and does not take adequate account of the range of needs a person faces, such an assessment may be superficial and of little value when it comes to making a positive difference to that person's life.

Unmet needs, then, are a significant factor in social work. Indeed, they are a fundamental basis of our work. Preston-Shoot goes so far as to state that:

> It is possible to argue that a failure to satisfy need, and the tendency to construct and present complex social problems as an individual pathology, are acts of injustice, abuses of power.

(1996, p. 30)

This is a very important and valid point. The discussions in Chapter 2 about the importance of recognizing the *social* basis of social work concerns will reflect this perspective. We have to make sure that we adopt a broad psychosocial perspective on need and do not fall into the trap of 'atomism'. This is a philosophical term that refers to the tendency to focus narrowly on individuals and neglect the wider social context of people's lives, as if people live in a social vacuum, uninfluenced by the cultural and structural circumstances they grew up in and find themselves in currently.

Realistically, however, we have to accept that we are not able to meet everybody's needs all of the time. This is partly a matter of scarcity of resources and also partly a matter of circumstances changing, with new needs developing all the time, as we make our way through our life course. Hugman captures the point well when he argues that:

> By definition, social workers are concerned with situations in which someone, either the individuals or groups in question, or else the state, considers that ordinary social relations or arrangements are not meeting needs. (As England expressed it, 'social work is provided not for people with problems but for people who have difficulty in dealing with their problems unaided' [England, 1986, p. 13].)
>
> (1998, pp. 18–19)

This is a significant passage, as it underlines not only the significance of unmet needs as a fundamental basis of social work, but also the role of problems in people's lives. It also relates to the point made in the Introduction to this part of the book that it is important to distinguish between first-level problems that will affect the population in general some or all of the time, and second-level problems, the latter being the type of problems that can make it difficult to deal with first-level problems. For example, we all have to contend with the problem of grief from time to time, but for someone who has a drink problem, this might prove an insurmountable problem that plunges them into a deep, long-term depression or exacerbates their drink problem to the point where their level of alcohol consumption becomes life threatening. It is therefore to the link between unmet needs and problems that we now turn.

Voice of experience 1.3

I suppose I was a bit naive when I first came into social work. I thought that those people who needed social work help were in some way not up to life's challenges. 'Inadequate' sounds too strong a word, but I suppose I was making assumptions about what I saw as their limited capabilities. But I soon had that illusion shattered. The more clients I met and got to know, the more I realized how significant their social circumstances and previous life experiences were. If I had had to deal with the social barriers and disadvantages that so many of my clients had faced in their lives, I'm sure I would have struggled to cope too – probably more so. I have learned to admire so many of the clients I have dealt with for their strengths and resilience, often in extremely difficult circumstances, rather than see them as 'charity cases'.

Kevin, a social worker in a mental health team

Problems

There is a close interrelationship between unmet needs and problems. Where there is an unmet need, a number of problems can arise. Where problems arise,

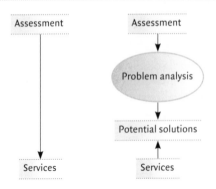

Figure 1.2 The importance of problem analysis

this can lead to unmet needs. The two can mutually reinforce one another. It is important to be alert to the fact that a key part of a social work role is being a professional problem solver (Thompson, 2006a). There is a danger that, if we lose sight of this problem-solving feature of our role, we become reduced to rationers of services (see Figure 1.2).

In fulfilling our role as professional problem solvers, it is important to recognize that our primary concern is the problem *situation*. It is an easy mistake to make to think in terms of the problem *person* or problem *family*, rather than the problem situation. Where there are difficulties, there is often a person at the heart of these difficulties who may be acting in such a way that makes his or her life more difficult or may be causing difficulties for other people. It is therefore understandable that many people see the individual concerned as the problem. This is, however, a superficial and misleading view. It is also a judgmental view that is in conflict with social work values, in so far as it attaches a label to an individual that, in the vast majority of cases if not all, will be unjustified. When we look at the problem situation in greater depth and detail, we will start to realize that the behaviour of the individual, however problematic for him- or herself or for others, is part of a wider matrix of problem factors and not simply down to a 'bad' or 'inadequate' person. As Jack puts it: 'The problem is always the problem: the person is never the problem' (2005, p. 179).

Similarly, it is easy to apply the label of 'problem family' to those families that have significant difficulties or present problems in terms of, for example, anti-social behaviour. However, it is simplistic to assume that there is an entity known as a 'problem family' that is somehow a different species from other gatherings of humans. A social worker will need to take account of the wide range of significant factors, such as family dynamics and power relations; wider sociopolitical issues to deal with poverty and deprivation; and other such concerns. Simply dismissing a group of people as a 'problem family' is not an acceptable approach to social work, although it may be one that in our work we encounter in others from time to time. This can bring us into conflict with such people, and we may have to use our conflict management skills to good effect to be able to manage such situations effectively (see Chapters 4 and 10). The key point, then, is that it is not a matter of oversimplifying and reducing complex sets of issues to the notion of a problem person or a problem family. In other words, we need a more holistic approach that takes account of the wider picture of how and why such problems are emerging.

Part of this will be a recognition of the social context of the problems that people encounter. Indeed, there is a strong link between the personal problems that individuals and families encounter and the wider social milieu. This is such an important set of issues that there is a whole chapter devoted to these concerns (Chapter 2).

Problem solving is an important part of empowerment. Given that empowerment is a central role of social work intervention, then the links between it and problem solving are significant. Empowerment is not simply a matter of 'giving' power to people in any direct way, as it is clearly not possible to do that. Power is a much more complicated set of issues than this. As Beckett helpfully puts it:

> Empowerment, in a social work context, means working in a way that is aimed at increasing people's sense of power and control over their own lives, rather than diminishing it. It is not a single method or technique and, perhaps partly because of this lack of specificity, it is a word (like 'partnership') which can easily be used in rather a cosmetic and superficial way to give a warm glow to a social worker, to include in the publicity literature of a social work agency, or to provide a social work student with a named 'theory' to include in an essay or a placement report. Just as the word 'partnership' is often misused in social work to describe work in which the client is in *no* sense an equal partner, so the word 'empowerment' can unfortunately be used to put an acceptable face on practice which in truth is anything but empowering. 'Empowerment' as Brandon and Brandon (2001:20) observe, can 'become a method used to reconcile people to being powerless. Our systems are extremely seductive and manipulative.'
>
> (2006, p. 126)

Empowerment can therefore be seen to involve helping people to develop greater control over their lives and circumstances. This will often involve helping them to remove barriers to progress, and this is where problem solving can be a key part of the empowerment process. If we can play a key role in addressing the problems that people encounter, we may be well placed, then, to help them move forward in terms of having a more fulfilling life and a greater sense of well-being by being better equipped to tackle any problems they encounter in future. Problem solving, then, is not simply a technical matter of providing a quick fix but, rather, of working in partnership with the people we are seeking to help to enable them to address their problems in a more confident, better informed and more effective way.

Talking about empowerment at a general level without being able to pin it down to processes by which it can occur is of limited benefit and may actually be counterproductive, as it can add to the vagueness and superficiality that have tended to haunt this term (see Thompson, 2007a, for a discussion of this). Without clarity about what we mean by empowerment and what can be helpful in promoting it, we also run the risk, as Beckett (2006) rightly points out, of using the term to describe actions that are far from genuinely empowering.

A key part of empowerment is avoiding falling into the trap of seeing people's problems in narrow, atomistic terms by regarding them as signs of inadequacy or 'pathology'. Reference was made earlier to England's (1986) idea that it is not simply people with problems who need a social worker, but rather those people who (for whatever reason) have difficulties in dealing with their problems unaided. Folgheraiter makes a similar point but also emphasizes the significance of moving away from the idea of 'pathology' – that is, the judgemental tendency to see the problem as arising from a personal inadequacy rather than a complex interplay of a range of psychosocial factors:

> Elsewhere (Folgheraiter, 1998), I have defined (in)capacity for action to be the subject matter of social work. By this I mean that a problem of interest to social workers is not a *pathology*, or a static state of affairs, but a dynamic difficulty: an impediment against the achievement of goals.
>
> (2004, p. 44)

This helps us to appreciate the significance of goals in people's lives – that is, their aspirations for progressing from their existing situation. In terms of empowerment, we can see that personal goals have an important part to play, in so far as they are a significant source of motivation. Having a goal to aim for can help people address their problems and thereby develop greater control over their lives.

In a similar vein, Rogers and Pilgrim link goals to mental health when they argue that: 'Blocked or absent personal goals are consistently associated with poor mental health outcomes' (2003, p. 52). By this, what they mean is that people may struggle to cope with their life pressures if there are factors that are preventing them from achieving their goals or if they have lost sight of the benefits of goal setting (or have never learned the value of goals for giving life shape and meaning – an important aspect of spirituality; see Moss, 2005).

 Practice focus 1.4

As Bindhu got to know Mr Jameson, she began to appreciate that, when his wife had died and he had to give up his home because of their debts, he had been so overwhelmed by cumulative grief that he had, in effect, been traumatized by the experience. She therefore decided to do some background reading on the subject of trauma and, from this, she realized that an important part of the healing and recovery process was the development of new frameworks of meaning (the previous sense of normality having been shattered by the traumatic experiences). She therefore decided that a useful way to move forward might be to talk to Mr Jameson about what he had previously held dear by way of beliefs and values before adopting his hermit-like lifestyle. It had become clear that he was desperately unhappy living like he had been doing, but she was aware that trying to do too much too soon before he was ready for it could traumatize him further. She therefore decided to focus on issues of meaning to begin with, while also looking at the practical help she felt he needed. This seemed to work well, and she was quickly able to gain Mr Jameson's trust and thereby be in a strong position to support him in moving forward.

Conclusion

We all have needs: that is part of the human condition. Those needs will vary from person to person, culture to culture, situation to situation. Some people are more likely than others to have unmet needs as a result of a complex combination of personal, cultural and structural reasons. Unmet needs create a number of problems for the people so affected. As we have seen, those problems in turn can lead to further needs going unmet and having a knock-on effect in terms of creating a highly problematic situation for some people. It is often at this point that social work comes into play. We will often find ourselves drawn into situations where unmet needs and problems have begun to develop a vicious circle that leads to a highly unsatisfactory situation where one or more people are distressed or otherwise suffering. The role of the social worker in so many situations, then, can be seen as that of a skilled helper who, working in partnership, (i) identifies needs, particularly unmet needs; and (ii) then sets about assisting the person concerned to develop a plan of action based on problem-solving principles that can have the effect of addressing the unmet needs. In many cases, part of that problem-solving process will be the provision or commissioning of social services of some description (for example, day services and/or home care). However, we should not allow ourselves to fall into the trap of seeing a direct link between assessment and services that misses out the crucial stage of problem analysis and the implementation of problem-solving strategies (see Figure 1.4). Where problem solving is a key part of the process, the result can be, potentially at least, a very empowering one. Where there is no involvement of problem solving in terms of a direct connection between assessment and service, then the result is often one of dependency creation – the exact opposite of empowerment.

| See page 58 | for some questions about what you have just read. |
| See page 223 | for some pointers to useful further reading. |

chapter

2

The social context of personal problems

Introduction

Social work is part of the branch of social policy known as 'personal social services'. This is an important term, as it connects the personal problems of individuals and families to the wider context of social services, with the emphasis on the *social* dimension. This is because it is essential to be aware that, what are generally perceived as personal problems or family problems are closely linked to the wider social context. It can therefore be misleading and potentially dangerous to adopt a superficial approach to personal and family problems that does not take account of wider social issues. As Davis puts it:

> Social work is concerned with achieving negotiated change in the lives of people who face difficulties. Most people who receive social work services are members of disadvantaged, stigmatised and socially excluded groups.
>
> (2004, p. 7)

This chapter, then, is concerned with exploring how personal problems need to be understood in relation to the social context. In many ways, personal problems are a reflection of wider and deeper social problems and concerns.

In this chapter, we first address the feminist adage that the personal is political, based on the important idea that an individual's circumstances are inevitably connected to the wider sociopolitical context – they do not occur in a vacuum (see the critique of atomism in Chapter 1). This helps us to understand that individual or family problems need to be understood by reference to the wider sphere of social and political influence. This discussion in turn leads on to an exploration of various forms of social problems and social issues, such as poverty, deprivation and social exclusion; discrimination and oppression; crime and disorder; illness, disablement and mental disorder; and, finally, homelessness and poor housing.

The personal is political

This statement has now been closely associated with the development of the feminist movement, which was helpful in highlighting how the experiences of women that prove to be quite problematic in many ways were not purely of a personal nature and owe more to the wider sociopolitical context of patriarchy and gender inequalities. This is an important principle, but it is one that can also be extended to include not only women in relation to feminist concerns, but also to men, children and, indeed, all people who encounter difficulties of one sort or another. There are very strong and important links between what one person experiences as an individual problem and the wider context of power relations, cultural formations, social structures, processes and institutions, and so on. And so, in saying the personal is political, we are also saying the personal is social. Personal problems therefore have significant resonances in terms of social problems.

We often speak or write about 'the person in society'. Strictly speaking, however, the phrase 'in society' is redundant, as it is not possible to have a person separated from society – as if he or she can live in isolation from wider society. What makes each of us an individual in our own right, ironically, is largely a social matter, in the sense that individuality is a dimension of the social world (society is made up of individuals) and the social world is a dimension of the individual (individuals are social beings). It is how and where we fit into society that gives us so many parameters of our sense of self. In using the phrase 'the person in society', we are therefore emphasizing the significance of society, but we have to take cognizance of the fact that there is no person without society (just as there would be no society if there were no people). It is for this reason that social work is so often referred to as a *psychosocial* enterprise – an activity (or set of activities) that encompasses both personal (or psychological) factors and social ones. Indeed, it could be said that social work is located at the point where the individual and society meet. In this regard, Hamer makes an important point when he argues that: 'For a social worker being able to perceive interconnectedness is a vital skill' (2006, p. 62).

It can be helpful to understand the individual in terms of the interaction between two sets of factors: biography and society. Biography refers to those factors that are unique to an individual. Each of us will have had experiences and encounters that are unique to us, or at least the combination, intensity or interrelationships between aspects of those experiences are unique to us. There is no getting away from the fact that each individual is a unique person in his or her own right. That is what is meant by the notion of biography. However, such biographical developments do not occur in a vacuum. The other side of the coin in terms of what makes an individual an individual is the social context – society. The influence of, and interaction with, social factors (both cultural and structural) is a primary shaper of human experience and the development of identity. It is therefore fair to say that identity, while being, by definition, about the uniqueness of an individual (what is it that makes me, me?), identity is also sociopolitical. It is a matter of how each of us, as a unique individual in our own right, is interrelated with the complex processes that go on in society. This means that, as unique individuals, we are not fixed entities. We are constantly interacting with other people and with social processes and institutions.

Practice focus 1.1

When Hilary started her degree in social work she was surprised to find how much emphasis there was on social factors. She had expected to be focusing more on the specific circumstances of the individuals needing social work help. At first, she thought the social emphasis was misplaced and that there was too strong a focus on the general social level and not enough on the narrower, more specific concerns of each individual or family. However, when she went on her first placement, she had a very good practice teacher who was able to help her understand that the individual factors were so strongly influenced by the wider social issues (for example, she came across instances of how poverty and deprivation, stigma and disablism were all highly significant in the lives of many of the people the team dealt with). Her practice teacher explained that it was necessary to consider the specific, individual circumstances of each case, but also pointed out that it would be a dangerous distortion to try to understand the personal level without taking account of the cultural and structural factors that were so significant in shaping people's life experiences. She could see now why one of the course tutors had said on more than one occasion: 'Never forget that the term, "social work" begins with the word social.'

Understanding the individual in these terms can help us to appreciate how personal problems are therefore linked to social problems. This can be seen to apply in a number of ways. Consider the following aspects:

- **Society** *shapes* **what we see as a problem.** Problems are in large part culturally defined – for example, what is generally recognized as a problem these days in terms of anorexia nervosa can be linked to cultural images. There has been much debate about the portrayal of emaciated young women as glamour models having an effect on adolescent girls, who may then eat less than they require for full nutrition in a misguided attempt to maintain an unhealthily slim body shape. This issue would not arise for the individuals concerned if not for the wider social context that influences what is perceived as a 'desirable' body image.

- **Society** *defines* **what we see as a problem.** An example of this would be sexual abuse. The age of consent for engaging in sexual intercourse is different in different countries. In some countries, therefore, something that is considered sexual abuse (for example, sexual intercourse between an adult and a minor of, say, 15 years of age) may in many cases not be considered abuse in a society where the age of consent is lower. What this means is that there are historically changing definitions of problems that are linked to how particular societies construct the notion of what is acceptable and what is unacceptable. A further example would be the drinking of alcohol. This is unacceptable in some societies today (Saudi Arabia, for example) and has been in other countries at other times (the prohibition years in the United States, for example).

▹ **Some social interventions can in themselves** *cause* **problems**. For example, imprisonment as a result of criminal offences can result in significant problems for the children of prisoners. They may be deprived of a parent at a key time in their development, with significant consequences for their future life experiences. In this sense, then, trying to address one social problem (that of crime) can lead to other problems. Similarly, removing an abused child from their home or their own society may do more harm than good – for example, as a result of the potentially traumatizing experience of being separated from one's familiar surroundings and relationships that normally provide a sense of security and rootedness. For many children, being abused in an otherwise loving family can be the lesser of two evils when compared with being uprooted, especially when the move also entails a change of school. Such matters therefore have to be handled very sensitively and weighed up very carefully.

▹ **Society has the potential to** *resolve* **social problems**. As Rogers and Pilgrim argue:

> The interconnection between low income, financial hardship, unemployment, poor housing and lack of education, which we can collectively call 'socio-economic adversity', could be corrected by political action.

> (2003, p. 25)

It should be clear, then, that individual problems and social problems overlap to a considerable extent. Space does not permit a detailed analysis of the complex interactions between these two sets of factors. We shall therefore have to limit ourselves, in the space available, to examining a number of social problems and considering how they relate to the experiences of individuals how, in effect, social problems become experienced as personal problems. The examples of social problems that follow should therefore help to establish that a key part of the social work role is to play a part in addressing social problems: (i) minimizing, removing or cushioning their detrimental effects where possible; and (ii) making a contribution, however small, to tackling those social problems (for example, by challenging discrimination). Community work, as a now sadly unpopular and much reduced branch of social work, can be particularly effective in identifying the social nature of people's individual problems and trying to address them collectively at a community level (Jordan, 2007).

Voice of experience 2.1

I worked in a child care team for two years, but never felt entirely comfortable there as I wanted to deal with things at a broader level. My current post involves a very strong focus on community development and that gives me much more scope for dealing with the wider issues that lead so many people to struggle when it comes to bringing up children – things like inadequate housing, poor facilities, constant fear of crime as a result of a lot of drugs problems in the area and no sense of community solidarity or support.

Jan, a community worker in an urban regeneration project

Poverty, deprivation and social exclusion

These significant social factors can cause problems in their own right. That is, to suffer from poverty, deprivation and/or social exclusion is sufficient in itself to make for a considerable amount of distress and unhappiness. However, there is much more to it than this, in so far as these factors can also exacerbate other problems. For example, there are close links between poverty and crime (Jones and Novak, 1999). This is not to oversimplify the matter and say simplistically that poverty causes crime in any direct way, but it would be naive not to acknowledge that a shortage of funds and crimes such as theft or deception are not unconnected. There are also established links between poverty and deprivation on the one hand, and mental health problems on the other (Barnes and Bowl, 2001). The strain of financial pressures can understandably be seen as a key factor in exacerbating any underlying mental health needs. Poverty can also have a detrimental effect on self-esteem and can therefore be very significant in relation to such problems as depression. This can then lead to the development of a vicious circle, as having mental health problems and the associated stigma can lead to social exclusion which, in turn, is part and parcel of poverty and deprivation. There are also issues relating to abuse to consider. While it is not simply a matter that abuse occurs only in poverty-stricken households, poverty is none the less a key factor in the development of abuse and how it is dealt with (Parton et al., 1997)

In terms of recognizing the significance of poverty in social work, Garrett sums up the situation well when he argues that: 'current approaches, focused on notions of diversity and difference, are failing to produce a rounded analysis because the impact of poverty and material hardship is not acknowledged' (2002, p. 187).

Discrimination and oppression

Much has been written about prejudice, as if it were primarily a personal characteristic, but it is important to recognize that discrimination is embedded in cultural and structural formations (Thompson, 2003a, 2006b) – that is, cultural norms, values and assumptions (stereotypes, for example) and structural relationships across different social categories (gender, 'race' and so on) are also highly significant. While some discrimination does arise as a result of personal prejudice, the reality is far more complex than this in terms of how discrimination is often embedded or 'institutionalized', to use the technical term, in social practices, processes and institutions. This means that much discrimination is unintentional, in so far as someone acting in a discriminatory fashion may be doing so in ways that reflect wider cultural and structural factors (unquestioned assumptions about age or disability as socially significant issues, for example) without any intention of being unfair or oppressive. However, even unintentional discrimination has the potential to be highly oppressive and is therefore unacceptable – hence the importance of self-awareness in social work. We need to be 'tuned in' to issues of discrimination to ensure that we are not unwittingly being unfair or oppressive (see Chapters 5 and 9).

Who is affected by discrimination is not a matter of chance or random distribution. Sociological analysis has established that patterns of discrimination are embedded in society in terms of how our social arrangements are structured and organized (Payne, 2006). For example, while some white people may in certain circumstances experience racial discrimination, it is clearly the case that racism is a matter predominantly affecting people from ethnic minorities. There are complex social, political and historical reasons for this development, but it would be naive not to recognize that such matters are firmly ensconced in the social fabric and are not simply matters of individual prejudice.

How people are affected by discrimination is also socially *channelled*, in the sense that different people will experience discrimination in different ways at different times, but these issues will none the less follow social channels or pathways. For example, there is the well-established notion of the glass ceiling that prevents women from rising to senior management positions in so many organizations (Itzin and Newman, 1995). While this is indeed a well-established phenomenon, it is not uniform across all organizations or types of organization. There will be significant differences from work sector to work sector in terms of the extent to which a glass ceiling operates (Hayward, 2005).

How discrimination and oppression persist over time is also fundamentally a social matter. For example, the media play a significant role in perpetuating stereotypes and other distorted views of groups that are stigmatized or otherwise subject to discrimination. A clear example here would be asylum seekers who are often 'demonized', and the complex circumstances surrounding their decision to enter a particular country are often reduced to a matter of assumed greed or a wish to rely on state benefits. In addition to the media, we can see that other social institutions, such as the education system, play a part in keeping the wheels of discrimination turning – not necessarily in any intentional way, but as a result of the institutionalized patterns of inequality that have come to be part of these systems historically.

Practice focus 2.2

Colleen welcomed the opportunity of a new challenge when she joined the asylum seeker support team. She was an experienced and highly respected social worker with a background in family support work and felt she had a lot to offer this recently established project. She was aware that there was a certain amount of 'tabloid' disapproval of asylum seekers, and so she was expecting to encounter some degree of resistance from some people. However, what she hadn't realized was just how much hostility towards asylum seekers she would come across on the part of so many people. What struck her as such a stark contrast was the immense suffering and pain, the traumatic experiences, the fear and persecution that so many of the asylum seekers had encountered in their homeland, only to be met with, in many cases, an additional layer of hostility, rejection, stigma and discrimination in the country where they were seeking refuge. The harsh reality was so far removed from the simplistic and judgemental assumptions that so many people were making about asylum seekers. At first she felt angry about this, but she was able, with the support of her supervisor, to channel this anger positively into an even stronger commitment to being as helpful as she could in supporting asylum seekers to find safety and, as far as possible, the basis for a new life.

How discrimination and oppression are tackled will also owe much to social organization and systems. For example, much of the effort geared towards tackling discrimination has come through governmental measures, such as anti-discrimination legislation. While there have been many individuals who have made concerted efforts to tackle discrimination and oppression, the main thrust of opposition has come through social movements rather than isolated individuals. For example, Crossley (2006) presents a very helpful analysis of how users of mental health services have, as part of the user involvement movement, have influenced policy and practice in the mental health field. In this regard, too, social work can be seen as being in an important position, as it has, in many ways, led the field compared with other professional groups when it comes to promoting practices that are geared towards addressing the problems of discrimination and oppression (Thompson, 2002a).

Crime

Crime is clearly recognised as a significant social problem, although it has to be recognized that its impact is quite significant for very many individuals at a personal level, whether we are thinking of the victims of crime or the perpetrators who may suffer significantly as a result of their involvement in criminal activity (consider the harm to child development that can occur as a result of youth offending). Another group of people adversely affected by crime whose needs tend to receive less attention are the families and, to a certain extent, friends and other associates of people who are imprisoned (Howard League, 2006), as mentioned earlier in this chapter. Crime is, by definition, a social problem, as it relates to social order. A further aspect of this is that what constitutes a crime is socially defined. That is, if we did not have a society to label something as a crime, then the concept of crime would not apply. This is illustrated by the fact that different societies have different definitions of particular criminal acts. Some things will be considered a criminal offence in some countries, but not in others, and it is even the case that, in some nations, what constitutes a crime differs from state to state or province to province. Prostitution would be a good example of this variability. This clearly shows that crime is not simply a matter of personal factors shaping criminal behaviour but, rather, crime being part of a wider social understanding of how societies regard and deal with particular behaviours. Again, it is a *psychosocial* matter, a combination of personal or psychological matters, on the one hand, and broader social and political factors on the other.

Crime is also socially influenced in other ways. For example, the combination of significant poverty with consumerism can lead to pressures towards crime. That is, where people are living in very restricted financial circumstances, but are constantly exposed to advertisements and other pressures towards a consumerist ethos, then it is clear that the conflict between the two is likely to be a factor in many crimes (see Merton's, 1938, classic work on this subject for a discussion of the complexities involved in this).

In addition, sentencing in relation to criminal offences can also be seen to be influenced by a range of social factors. Despite strenuous efforts on the part of many within the criminal justice system to challenge racism, there is still evidence of racial bias in some aspects of how sentencing works (Smith and Natalier, 2005). Similar issues can be seen to apply in relation to gender. For example, women offenders are far more likely to be channelled in the direction of psychiatric help than in the direction of punitive measures (Hedderman and Gelsthorpe, 1997). Finally, in relation to the social context of crime, we can see that criminal behaviour has significant consequences for other sectors of society. Even where people are not directly affected by crime, the fear of crime can be a significant source of distress. In addition, victims of crime, especially where violence and/or violation of a person's home are involved, can experience a traumatic reaction as a result of the events they have experienced (Brewin, 2003; Rosen, 2004). These factors can have a very significant detrimental effect on people's lives.

Voice of experience 2.2

I find the whole field of crime quite fascinating. I had known I wanted to be a social worker for some time but wasn't sure what area to specialise in. However, when I studied criminology and youth offending as part of my degree, I was hooked. The complex ways in which psychological issues interrelate with sociological processes and institutions was a bit mind-boggling at first, but once I got my head round it, I really loved studying this area of social work. My work is quite hard-going – it's quite demanding really – but I still find it really interesting and enjoyable.

Mari, a social worker in a youth offending team

Clearly, then, the interlinking of personal and social problems when it comes to crime is a major consideration for anyone who seeks to have an adequate understanding of what is involved.

Illness, disablement and mental disorder

Issues of disability and physical and mental health can have profound consequences for the people directly affected by them and, indeed, for others closely associated with them, such as family members. However, it is vitally important to be aware that there are significant social dimensions to these concerns. For example, the social model of disability is now well documented in its challenge to traditional medical models than can be seen to be pathologizing and patronizing towards disabled people (Oliver and Sapey, 2006). Similarly, there is an immense literature now in relation to the sociology of health and related matters (Nettle, 2006). This includes both physical and mental health issues. The work of Tew reflects a growing commitment to moving away from pathologizing approaches to mental distress towards more person-centred, holistic ones:

> Working within a holistic model implies a very different language from that of the medical model – one that situates the user as someone who is active and responsible, and draws on the terms that have been proposed and negotiated by service users themselves. A shift from a discourse of 'mental illness' to one of 'mental distress' signals a move away from an emphasis on some objective disease entity (and the tendency to conflate the person with their hypothetical disease) to a more 'full-on' appreciation of the subjective pain, unhappiness or confusion that a person may be experiencing.
>
> (2002, p. 146)

What is of particular significance when it comes to linking personal and social aspects of this subject matter is the question of inequalities in health. It has long been established that social factors are crucial in relation to health (Jones, 1994; Nettle, 2006). The influence of social factors cannot now be denied. It is worth considering these in a little more detail:

- What is defined as an illness, especially a mental illness, is shaped by social factors. There is a growing literature on the critique of medicalized models of mental distress that can be seen to pathologize and disempower people who are experiencing problems relating to their mental well-being (see, for example, Tew, 2002). This is discussed in more detail in Chapter 13.
- There will be significant contributing conditions that apply across the board that are very much of a social nature. This will include poor nutrition (often as a result of poverty), dampness in housing, stress and working conditions.
- There will, in addition, be contributing conditions that apply to some members of the community at least, but not to all. A key example here would be alcohol and drug abuse that have their roots in the social context, but are also very significant in relation to health (Orford et al., 2005).
- There is also the question of inequality of access to health care. There are two dimensions to this. First there is the question of the more affluent sectors of the community having the purchasing power to obtain private health care in circumstances where national health service provision is not sufficient – something that is denied those members of the community at the lower levels of the income range. Second, there is evidence to suggest that quality of health care provision has some degree of a postcode lottery attached to it. For example, it can be seen that, in many parts of the United Kingdom, there are discrepancies in health care provision within particular communities, with more deprived communities generally having the highest rates of sickness and lowest levels of life expectancy (Jones, 2001).

Practice focus 2.3

Morag had worked as a nursing auxiliary for three years before deciding to train as a social worker, with the intention of becoming a hospital social worker. She had been aware from her previous experience that people came from very different social backgrounds, but she had just tried to do her best for each of them, regardless of their social circumstances. However, studying for a degree in social work gave her a much greater opportunity to explore the social influences on health and illness in more depth. From this she was able to see just how significant social factors were and that it wouldn't do for her to ignore them or simply rely on 'treating everybody the same', regardless of their background. She started to see that issues like the strain of poverty and debt could be very significant aspects of their health experiences. She realized that there was a lot more to the significance of people's social circumstances than she had originally understood. She felt positive, though, that this deeper level of understanding would help to offer a better standard of service to the people she was trying to help.

Homelessness and poor housing

For many people, a vicious circle of homelessness develops. There may be problems at home relating, for example, to family conflicts or to abuse or other traumatic experiences which can lead people to leave home, perhaps without the wherewithal to obtain adequate alternative accommodation. This can produce a situation of homelessness, with the attendant difficulties that so often arise. That is, homelessness will have implications in terms of the ability to hold down a job or to claim benefits, with poverty as a likely result. Homelessness can lead to health problems, as well as exacerbating existing health concerns. Being homeless can also leave people open to violence and crime due to the lack of security involved. The pressures of being homeless could also lead to increased alcohol consumption or reliance on other drugs. All these problems then add up to a reduction in opportunities to obtain housing. This means that, for many, it will not be possible to break out of this cycle of homelessness, and for those who do, the housing they obtain is likely to be of a low quality, often within stigmatized and highly disadvantaged areas. Problems people have in relation to housing can therefore be seen to be social as well as personal.

Voice of experience 2.3

What has troubled me for a long time is that housing issues are often a key part of the stresses and strains our clients experience, and yet we have so little influence over what happens in this regard. We can write to the housing department or housing association in some cases, but even that has little impact most of the time. It's something that the Government should pay more attention to, as housing issues can add a significant layer of extra pressure to what are often already very fraught situations.

Andy, a social work team leader

There will also be people who, while not actually homeless, have significant problems in relation to housing. This can be as a result of the physical quality of the housing in terms of such factors as dampness, lack of adequate facilities, and so on. However, there can also be other significant problems related to housing in terms of overcrowding, problems with aggressive or disruptive neighbours, and so on.

It is clear, then, that problems experienced by individuals can be severely exacerbated by the social problem of our inability as a society to provide adequate housing provision for our citizens. The result can be a wide range of problems, not least a deterioration in people's mental health. As Rogers and Pilgrim comment:

> residents of disadvantaged neighbourhoods have shown a greater propensity to report symptoms of depression, independently of the effects of socio-economic and demographic characteristics (Ross, 2000). Similarly, in recent studies, *neighbourhood* income has been significantly related to the prevalence of diagnosed schizophrenia and of substance abuse (Goldsmith, Holzer and Manderschied, 1998). Independently of personal characterisitics, such as sex and socio-economic opportunities, poorer neighbourhoods have been shown to provide fewer 'opportunity structures' for health-promoting activities than more affluent ones (Ellaway *et al.* 1997).
>
> (2003, p. 47)

Practice focus 2.4

Penny was a social worker in a multidisciplinary team working with adults with learning disabilities. The team had come to adopt quite a strong medical model, as was reflected in the terminology commonly used (for example, the team's interventions were generally referred to as 'treatment'), even though the medical component of the team's work was minimal. She realized that there were problems in adopting such an individualistic, disempowering approach and wondered about how she could get her colleagues to take a broader focus and take more account of social issues as they affected the team's clients. She realized it would be an uphill struggle as the team had such a long-established culture of focusing on individuals, with little or no attention paid to the wider social side of people's lives. She decided to speak to social work colleagues in other multidisciplinary teams to see if they had any ideas about how to take matters forward. Despite the size of the challenge she was determined not to give up on making sure the social basis of personal problems was not neglected.

Conclusion

It should be clear from these discussions that when we, as social workers, are engaging with individuals or families in relation to the problems they are experiencing, we are in effect connecting with a wider world of social problems. While it is important to understand people's circumstances as a unique set of situational concerns that must not be overgeneralized, the understanding of individuals and their specific 'biographical' issues must be complemented by a recognition of the fact that those personal and family problems have significant roots in the wider social sphere in terms of such factors as the distribution of wealth and power and so on.

It is, of course, not simply a matter of social problems directly leading to personal or family problems in any simplistic way. What we have to recognize is that there is a matrix of significant and complex interrelationships between personal and family matters on the one hand, and wider social and political factors on the other. If we attempt to practise social work without recognition of this wider picture, then we run the risk of being at best ineffective by failing to grasp the reality of the circumstances we are dealing with and, at worst, we may make the situation considerably more problematic for the people we are seeking to help. As I have already stressed, we must not forget that social work is a *psychosocial* enterprise.

See page 58   for some questions about what you have just read.

See page 223   for some pointers to useful further reading.

3 Promoting and preventing change: developing versus sustaining

Introduction

Social workers are often described as change agents. That is, they are seen as a group of professionals with a remit to play an important part in bringing about social amelioration. This is clearly a central part of the social work role. Promoting positive change in people's lives is a significant part of the value social workers can bring to their day-to-day activities. However, there is also an important role in many circumstances for social workers to prevent change, in the sense of preventing deterioration in an individual's or family's circumstances. Either way, change is a significant factor for social workers, and so this chapter is devoted to considering the relationship between social work services and change.

We begin by exploring the importance of change in social work. From this we move on to a discussion of how social work can be involved in promoting change. This is then followed by a consideration of how preventing change can also be a significant activity for us in many ways. As Brechin helps us to understand:

> What is required increasingly is a capacity to handle uncertainty and change, rather than simply operating in prescribed ways in accordance with professional skills and knowledge. Practitioners must, in a sense, face both ways, to be seen as appropriately knowledgeable and competent but at the same time be continually aware of the relative and contextual basis of their practice.
>
> (2000b, p. 26)

This chapter is therefore intended to provide a foundation for dealing with the challenges of responding to change and handling the uncertainties involved.

The importance of change in social work

In Chapter 1 we saw the importance of unmet needs and problems and the interrelationships between the two. These present us with a significant need for change. Where people are in situations in which their needs are not being met and problems are arising because of this, social work intervention can be seen as an activity geared towards bringing about positive changes in the circumstances concerned.

Change can bring about positives in people's lives – for example, growth and development and a movement away from problematic situations.

However, in doing so, change can also produce anxiety and uncertainty. As a result of this, understandably people can often be resistant to change. There can also be an element of giving up control in a change process. That is, even where somebody's circumstances are far from ideal, but they are familiar with those circumstances, changing to new circumstances that may be in the longer term of great benefit can, none the less, be resisted, especially if the ceding of control through the change process is experienced as threatening.

In some circumstances, change can also bring about a grief reaction. As I have argued previously (Thompson, 2002b) grief is not only a reaction to a significant bereavement (that is, a loss arising as a result of a death); it can also be a meaningful reaction to any form of significant loss in our lives – as a result of such factors as: divorce or other relationship breakdown; being abused or violated in some way; or having to give up our home. Change situations, even positive changes, involve a degree of loss and may therefore evoke a grief reaction. In some circumstances, there may be an accumulation of losses leading to what is known as 'cumulative grief', and this can be a very difficult form of grief indeed to endure. Any form of grief is painful, of course, but cumulative grief can be especially so. Another form of grief that is significant is what is known as 'disenfranchised grief' (Doka, 1989). This refers to types of grief that are not socially recognized or sanctioned, that are perhaps stigmatized in some way (for example, death by suicide – Lukas and Seiden, 2007). Where changes occur in a person's life that are not related to a death, this too can be a form of disenfranchised grief, in so far as many people will not be alert to the grief being experienced in the middle of such a transition and will therefore not recognize it as a grief reaction.

Practice focus 3.1

Emma was a little wary when she met Tim, a 24-year-old with learning disabilities, as he was known to display challenging behaviour – especially when meeting people he didn't know. However, over the coming weeks and months she got to know Tim very well and felt much more confident in being able to predict and deal with instances of 'difficult' behaviour. The more she got to know him, the more she realized that his life had been characterized by so many losses. His mother had died when he was 16. Soon after this he was placed with his aunt and uncle, as his father could not cope with the pressures of looking after him. However, this placement did not last very long, as his behaviour became increasingly aggressive. He was therefore placed with foster carers who had had special training, but they too found his behaviour unmanageable. As a result of this, he was placed in a residential school where he settled quite well. At the age of 19, he had to leave that school and transfer to an adult residential placement, which was quite an upheaval for him. At no point in the case file was there any acknowledgement of his losses – it seemed that no one had taken account of his experiences of cumulative grief. If I had had so many losses without anyone even beginning to address them with me, then *my* behaviour would be pretty challenging too, thought Emma to herself.

In certain extreme cases, change can even be traumatic. That is, it can cause a psychological wound. Just as the medical profession uses the term trauma to refer to physical wounds, social workers and others in the helping professions use the word trauma to refer to a psychosocial wound – that is, an event that has the effect of doing harm to an individual's psychological and social well-being. People who have a history of trauma may be resistant to change because they have experienced such hurtful circumstances in the past and they are loath to enter into situations that may reproduce such painful feelings. For example, a new change situation may open up old wounds that are associated with previous traumatic experiences.

However, change is not entirely negative in its side effects. It brings with it the potential for what is referred to as 'post-traumatic growth' or 'transformational grief' (Calhoun and Tedeschi, 1999; Schneider, 2000). These terms both refer to the ways in which a painful process of grieving in response to a trauma or other loss results in positive growth. For example, someone whose parents are killed in a road traffic accident may be devastated at first by the loss but may, as a result of the transitions involved, become a much more confident and independent individual when he or she is forced into making the necessary changes to enable him or her to exist without parental support. This is not to say that the experience will not have been a difficult or painful one, and that there will not be significant negatives involved, but it is none the less important to take account of the fact that positives can emerge from trauma and loss. Note, however, that, from a social work point of view, it would be extremely dangerous to try and provoke a trauma in order to attempt to evoke a positive transformational response but, equally, it would be a significant failure on our part if we did not take the opportunity to help people to capitalize on the positive potential of the negative circumstances they have been forced into as a result of some sort of significant loss or traumatic incident.

This notion of growth or transformation is consistent with the theoretical approach known as crisis intervention (Gibson, 2006; Roberts, 2006; Thompson, 1991). A crisis is a turning point in someone's life, and so intervening in a crisis should not be seen as simply trying to re-establish a state of equilibrium (homeostasis, to use the technical term), but rather as an attempt to capitalize on the positive potential of the crisis:

A crisis is the 'point of no return', the pivotal point at which a situation changes. To understand a crisis, we first need to understand its opposite, 'homeostasis'. This refers to the state of psychological equilibrium or balance that characterizes most people most of the time. It is when we are coping with the demands being made upon us without experiencing a significant strain. Homeostasis incorporates a continuum of coping – from a low level (when we are having a bad day, for example) to a high level (when things are going well for us). Provided our level of coping remains within this broad continuum, we can be said to be 'in homeostasis'. A crisis, then, occurs when homeostasis breaks down, when our everyday coping resources are overwhelmed for some reason and we are forced into adopting a new approach. The new approach may be better than our previous approach or worse – hence the idea that a crisis is a turning point, a situation that is either an improvement on what went before or a worsening. In the former case we can be said to have learned and grown from the crisis – it has strengthened us and taken us in a positive direction, while in the latter case, it will have weakened us and taken us in a negative direction. The aim of crisis intervention, then, is to maximize the positive potential of the situation, to do what we reasonably can to help the client(s) involved in the crisis turn it into a point of growth, rather than a diminution of their ability to cope.

(Thompson and Thompson, 2008b, p. 248)

This is a point to which we shall return below.

Voice of experience 3.1

In the team I worked in before, people used the term 'crisis' very loosely – just to mean any situation that needed an urgent response. There was very little real understanding of crisis. It's much better in my current team – we have a much clearer focus on the idea of a crisis as a turning point in a person's life and therefore as a chance to grow and develop. We try to see how we can maximize the positive potential of the situation, rather than simply getting people back to 'normal'.

Irene, a social worker in a child and adolescent mental health team

As well as the 'situational' crises that people can face from time to time (that is, those critical events that are unpredictable and related to specific events or sets of circumstances in our lives), there are also 'developmental' crises. This refers to key transitions in our lives, such as adolescence, leaving home and so on. Such points of transition in a person's life can be very significant, creating major change for the person concerned and those close to him or her. In trying to understand the significance of change in people's lives, we therefore need to be tuned in to the significant transitions that each of us goes through during the life course.

Promoting change

As noted above, promoting change is an important part of a social worker's repertoire. One of the significant implications of this is that it places considerable weight on the role of assessment. Assessment is the process by which we gather information and form a picture of the situation in order to identify what problems there are, what unmet needs exist and how we might best respond to these. As such, assessment provides a basis from which to develop an action plan about what needs to be done, what problems need to be addressed, what strengths are there to be built upon, and so on. If we are to take promoting change seriously, then assessment needs to be characterized by considerable clarity about what needs to be done to promote such change. This will include some understanding of the required direction of change, the factors that need to be addressed in order to promote such change, and so on.

An important part of this is being able to form a picture of what factors can be helpful in bringing about change and what factors, by contrast, can be seen to be obstacles to change. One important way of understanding this is what is known as force-field analysis, derived from the work of Lewin (1947). This involves identifying what needs to change and then, in relation to this, further identifying:

1 the 'driving' forces – that is, those aspects of the situation that can be drawn upon to promote the change required; and
2 the 'restraining' forces – that is, those aspects of the situation that are likely to impede change.

This framework can be put to useful effect as a way of outlining the key factors that need our attention. Once we have this clear picture, we are then in a much stronger position to be able to maximize the positive potential of the driving forces (or 'push factors') and to try and undermine the significance of the restraining forces (or 'drag factors') – see Thompson (2006a) for a further discussion of this.

 Practice focus 3.2

Peter became quite interested in force-field analysis when he attended a course on creative problem solving. He realized it could be quite a useful tool for dealing with change situations. He was therefore keen to put it into practice. He found it difficult the first time, but he persevered and then found it got easier (and more useful) every time he did it. What soon became clear to him was that it was a useful tool for deploying in partnership – getting clients involved directly in the process meant that they brought their own ideas and insights. He also found that using the tool promoted partnership in itself, in the sense that the transparency involved promoted a greater sense of trust and security.

It was especially helpful in one particular case where a family he was working with were in quite an anxious and confused state. He discovered that the structured nature of the process helped them to settle and begin to feel more in control of the situation. As such, it was a helpful contribution to fostering empowerment. Peter was so pleased he had persevered with this tool, despite having found it difficult at first.

In promoting change, we quickly encounter the very important notion of risk. Risk is an ever-present part of human experience, but there are clearly additional risks involved in bringing about change. It is important that we set ourselves the task of balancing risks rather than simply trying to eliminate them. This is because, if we focus too strongly on removing risk, this in itself brings about other risks. This is an important and complex topic which is discussed in more detail in Chapter 11. However, for present purposes, it is important to note that we should not be reckless in bringing about change without considering the risk factors involved. It is, as Pugh (1996) argues, essential to think *through* change, rather than simply think *about* it.

What is also very important in relation to bringing about change is working in partnership. Imposed change is recognized as the least successful form of change, and so, whatever change initiatives are being explored, they need to be explored together (Kotter and Schlesinger, 1989; Kotter, 1996). It is not something that should be done in a spirit of superiority, with the professional trying to impose some form of change process on a reluctant client (although some forms of imposing change may be necessary as a last resort in extreme circumstances – for example, to protect someone from significant harm). Rather, it is a case of an empowering professional working alongside a client to identify the key change issues that require attention and to discuss how best to address them (see Chapter 4 for a more detailed discussion of the nature and importance of partnership).

It is also important to make sure that we get the pace of change right. If we are too slow in bringing about change, then momentum can be lost and, with it, motivation. Attempting to bring about change without motivation is likely to be a fruitless task, and one that can actually make the situation worse in terms of producing additional resistance and perhaps undermining somebody's confidence into the bargain. On the other hand, if we try to bring about change too fast, we can leave people feeling overwhelmed and thus destabilized, and this also can be an experience that has an adverse effect on confidence. Indeed, too fast a rate of change can prove stressful and disempowering for all concerned. This further adds weight to the importance of assessment because, in determining an agreed plan of action for bringing about change, it is important that timescales are part of that plan and that those timescales pay heed to the appropriate pace needed for change in the light of the circumstances and the wishes and needs of the individuals concerned.

In social work, the significance of crisis as a key factor in change has long been recognized. A crisis is a turning point in somebody's life; it is a situation which, by definition, will not stay the same. It will either get worse or get better. As we noted earlier, the role of the social worker in a crisis intervention situation is therefore to try and maximize the positive potential of change rather than simply to re-establish a degree of equilibrium (an approach often referred to as crisis *survival,* rather than crisis *intervention*). Unfortunately, crisis intervention is a much misunderstood practice modality. Many people reduce it to simply responding to emergencies, but this fails to do justice to the complexities involved. This is because a crisis is not necessarily an emergency, nor is an emergency necessarily a crisis. A more careful analysis of crisis intervention reveals that it is important to distinguish between the two.

The importance of empowerment has already been emphasized. It is a factor that also needs to be taken into careful consideration when it comes to seeking to promote change. If we are not careful in how we handle change situations, the effect can be one of disempowerment rather than the desired outcome of greater empowerment (that is, people end up feeling less in control, rather than more). Where we have succeeded in supporting people in a process of empowerment, then this is likely to give them greater control of their lives in terms of making the changes they feel are needed both now and in the future. However, if our empowerment efforts have failed (or we have not made efforts to bring about empowerment), then the more likely result is a feeling of disempowerment which is likely to stand in the way of further positive change.

The basis of empowerment needs to be an understanding of the complexities of power. Without an adequate understanding of power, we will fail to appreciate the significance of empowerment – for example, in terms of the different types and levels of empowerment (Thompson, 2007a). In terms of change efforts, empowerment can potentially be increased in the following ways:

- **Promoting personal growth (especially at times of crisis).** This can be done, for example, by helping to provide focus and clarity in times of confusion, and a degree of structure in times where there is a lack of understanding. The method known as task-centred practice is a good example of this approach (Marsh and Doel, 2005).
- **Bringing people together.** This can be achieved in a variety of ways – for example, through groupwork or through day services and other related approaches.
- **Advocacy and brokerage.** By acting as a go-between, a social worker can make a significant contribution to empowerment in a variety of ways and in various settings.
- **The provision or commissioning of services.** It is important that we do not have a simplistic understanding of services and are not too quick to offer a service with the possible result of dependency developing. However, it has to be recognized that, in terms of the potential solutions we are able to draw on in helping people tackle their problems (and thus to promote positive change), various services are often an important part of it.

What is also of great importance is what is commonly referred to as 'use of self'. This is a topic that used to be a major feature of social work practice and education, but over the years has tended to become seen as quite unfashionable. However, fashion should not be any determinant of what constitutes good practice. Whatever direction social work may take in its various incarnations over time, one of its underlying central themes is that it involves person-to-person work. As Hamer comments:

> It has been shown time and time again that the most therapeutic part of any therapeutic relationship is the relationship itself. Not the stuff that is done, not the therapies, but the interaction between two human beings.
>
> > The gift you offer another person is just your being
>
> > > Ram Dass
>
> You can make people feel respected, worthwhile and hopeful, you can build trust from the very moment you meet with them.
>
> > > (2006, p. 12)

Although there are key issues to be considered here in terms of the complexities involved, the importance of self interacting with another self is not to be underestimated (on this topic, see the very important work of Jordan, 2007).

 Practice focus 3.3

John was used to carrying quite a heavy caseload and enjoyed the pressures and challenges involved. However, when one colleague left and another went off on long-term sick leave, he found himself in a situation where he was significantly overloaded. The referrals kept coming and he felt the need to work faster and faster just to keep up. Before long he was working in a very mechanistic way, just trying to get through the work. He didn't feel comfortable doing it, but he felt he had to.

After about three months a new social worker had joined the team and his absent colleague had returned, and so the level of pressure steadily returned to normal. He felt so relieved. Looking back over the past three months, he could see how poor his practice had been, giving his clients a very low and ineffective level of service and gaining no real job satisfaction from the work. He vowed that if ever he was in that situation again, he would find some other way of dealing with it, as he recognized that it was a wholly unsatisfactory way of doing social work. What is the point, he thought, of trying to help people, but doing it without the human element, so that it became just a mechanical process? He could see that there was no point in being busy or hard working, if what he was doing was ineffective.

Related to this is the important distinction introduced by theologian, Martin Buber as long ago as 1923, when he wrote about interpersonal interactions as being of one of two kinds, either I-Thou, or I-it. The former refers to situations in which an individual treats the other with respect and there is a genuine reciprocity in the relationship. The latter refers to those circumstances in which an individual uses another person and, in the process, treats him or her as less than human. An example of this would be a situation where a busy practitioner regards a client with complex needs as a nuisance. Buber makes the crucial point that treating somebody in this way (that is, engaging in an I-it relationship) not only dehumanizes the other person, but also has the effect of dehumanizing the person who is behaving in this way. This is an important foundation of social work ethics, recognizing that, although other people may sometimes make our job difficult for us, we should never lose sight of the fact that our commitment is to their well-being.

Voice of experience 3.3

Sometimes the pressure of work can leave you tempted to cut corners and not really engage with people, but then you run the risk that they will feel that you are just fobbing them off, not really interested in their worries and concerns. And, once that happens, you leave yourself open to all sorts of hassles, like having complaints made against you. It can be tough at times when the pressure is on, but you have to keep coming back to the fact that social work is all about working person to person – nothing else is going to make any real difference.

Maggie, a social worker in a children and families team

Other important aspects of promoting change include such significant ideas as narrative and meaning. A narrative is literally a story, and there is increasing emphasis within social work theory on the significance of the stories that we tell ourselves in order to make sense of our lives (Parton and O'Byrne, 2000). There is a form of practice now widely used across the helping professions, including social work, that goes under the name of 'narrative therapy'. It is based on the idea that a key part of social work is helping somebody to move away from a disempowering narrative towards an empowering one (Crossley, 2000; Dallos, 2006; see also Chapter 8).

Linked to this is what has come to be known as solution-focused practice. The idea behind this is that, rather than focusing specifically on problems, it is helpful to focus our attention more on solutions (see Myers, 2007, for a clear and helpful introduction to solution-focused approaches). That is, in talking to people about their problems, if we ask them in what circumstances their problems do not apply, then that can give us avenues for looking at how to help them change the situation so that the problem situation features less in their lives and the non-problematic aspects feature more. An example of this would be somebody who is depressed much of the time. The solution-focused approach would ask this person to consider the times when he or she is not depressed and try to work out what is it about those times that are significant in terms of keeping depression at bay. Efforts can then be made to maximize those aspects of the situation that lead to the non-depressed periods of time and minimize those that lead to depressed periods of time. Solution-focused approaches have much in common with narrative therapy in terms of the fact that they both have in common an emphasis on seeking to replace an unhelpful narrative with a more positive and constructive one. What ties these approaches together, then, is the significance of meaning – a concept which, as we shall see below, is very relevant to many other aspects of social work practice.

In promoting change for individuals and families, we have to take account of the social context, as noted in Chapter 2. Some would argue that social work is of little value, tinkering with what happens at a micro level when so much arises from problems in society at a macro level. I would regard this view as having an element of truth within it, but of being an exaggeration of the actual situation. However, I do feel it is important to recognize that, as social workers, we have a part to play in contributing in whatever reasonable ways we can to promoting wider social change. If not, we are doomed to diving into the river to help people who are drowning without creating the opportunity to find out who is pushing them in and why.

Preventing change

While promoting change is clearly a fundamental part of social work activity, there are also elements of preventing change that need to be taken into account.

This relates to situations of actual or potential deterioration in a person's condition or well-being. This would include situations involving:

- **Some health conditions.** There are very many degenerative health conditions that can mean that a person needs considerable support. These are likely to be not only of a medical or nursing nature, but also relating to personal and social conditions. Hospital social workers and others involved in various aspects of health-related social care often encounter such situations.

- **Some aspects of disability.** Some people with a disability have a tendency to experience a deterioration in their capabilities. However, it is important to recognize that this relates to only a proportion of impairments associated with disability. We should beware of falling into the disablist trap of regarding disability as necessarily a situation of deterioration.

- **Old age.** It is unfortunately the case that old age is often presented as some form of illness, with older people expected to adopt the sick role. The reality is, of course, much more complex. However, it is important to note that many older people will be in situations where they are encountering a worsening situation. It may be partly as a result of health or disability conditions as mentioned above, but there may be other factors as well, not least the effects of ageism (Sue Thompson, 2005).

In such circumstances, the role of the social worker will include looking at what factors are likely to play a part in preventing negative change from occurring, or at least will contribute to slowing down the pace of negative change. Force-field analysis, as discussed above, can be used in these circumstances too, but with the reverse flow. That is, in circumstances of preventing change, instead of strengthening those factors identified as significant for promoting change and seeking to weaken those factors that are seen to hold up change, the reverse is the case. Our task is to weaken the 'driving forces' towards change and strengthen the 'restraining forces' that prevent or slow down change.

There is a considerable irony in the fact that things may have to change in order to prevent change from occurring. For example, a person's condition may be deteriorating because of their over-reliance on alcohol or other drugs. In order to prevent deterioration, therefore, a change in patterns of alcohol or drug consumption may be the goal that we need to aim for – in effect trying to change the underlying factors. We will often find ourselves trying to change those factors that are leading to deterioration. Once again though, it is not simply a matter of providing services. Some people have the distorted view that 'real' social work is about promoting change and, in circumstances of preventing deterioration, it is simply a matter of putting supportive services in place where possible. This is a very limited and limiting view that can lead to quite disempowering forms of practice. We therefore have to guard against such an oversimplification by taking account of the complexities involved in preventing change.

Practice focus 3.4

Bill was an experienced practice teacher working in a community care team. He was very impressed to begin with by the quality of work undertaken by his new student, Sam. However, as the placement progressed, Bill realized that there were aspects of Sam's approach to the team's work that were not so positive. In particular, he was concerned that, at times, Sam displayed an attitude that seemed to imply that working with adults was not 'real' social work compared with child care work.

When challenged by Bill about this, Sam's response was that the work was so often about maintaining situations, rather than about helping real change to take place. Bill was quite annoyed about this, as he felt it reflected an arrogant attitude towards adult services work. However, he managed to remain calm and professional and took the opportunity to explain that: (i) where positive change was possible, that is exactly what he and his colleagues would aim for; and (ii) even where positive change is not possible, maximizing someone's quality of life and well-being by preventing deterioration was a very worthwhile and honourable goal. He was disappointed that Sam seemed to have such an oversimplified understanding of the nature and role of change in social work practice.

In dealing with change prevention situations, there is an important emphasis on keeping situations under review. It is not enough to undertake an initial assessment to put into place a package of measures to address the situation as best we can and then leave the situation as it is. There will need to be close monitoring of the situation and periodic review to determine whether different measures are needed to respond to the circumstances as they currently stand.

In seeking to prevent change, a number of dangers arise. First, there is the important issue of dehumanization through an over-reliance on routines. There can be a considerable emphasis on routinization in terms of providing supportive services to people – that is, for situations to be treated as straightforward, routine matters with no real consideration of the individual's point of view or how this specific situation differs from similar ones. Such an approach can be very misleading and even dangerous, as a routinized outlook on practice runs the risk of failing to recognize key factors that are unique to the circumstances concerned. It is very easy for routinization to descend into practice based on I-it relationships, with inadequate attention being paid to the humanity of the person who is receiving care or support. Routinization is also problematic in so far as it can have a very detrimental effect on job satisfaction and thus morale.

Second, there is the danger of being stifling through being too 'risk averse'. That is, if there are risks involved in the situation and deterioration is likely to increase those risks, then it is understandable (but not acceptable) that some people will be unwilling to balance one set of risks against another in a carefully considered way, and will prefer to simply try and eliminate the risks perceived as threatening, even if this has the effect of reducing the quality of life of the person concerned (we shall explore these complex issues in more detail in Chapter 11).

Also of relevance to preventing change is the concept of 'preventative work'. It is an important aspect of social work that has received relatively little attention in recent years. When it comes to preventing change, there is an important connection with preventative work. This is because preventing change can be seen as a form of preventative work in itself.

Three levels of preventative work can be identified. The primary level refers to efforts that are made at a broad social policy or public health level. This relates to initiatives to prevent problems arising in the first place – for example, in seeking to improve housing and stress factors in communities. Secondary prevention refers to interventions that occur when problems are starting to occur. So, for example, when, in relation to the upbringing of children, there appear to be problems emerging, family support measures can be brought to bear in order to try and prevent the difficulties escalating as time goes by. The third level of preventative work, known as tertiary, involves interventions that have gone beyond the primary and secondary levels where clear problems, often very significant problems, have already emerged, but there is still a significant element of prevention in terms of attempting to prevent the situation getting even worse. All social work, then, can be seen to have an element of prevention within it.

The relationship, then, between promoting change and preventing change is quite a complex one. It would be a mistake to see it as a clear-cut distinction between the two. None the less, if we are going to understand the significance of change in social work, then we need to take account of change efforts in both directions: those that promote positive change and those that seek to prevent negative change.

Conclusion

In situations where the need to promote change, or the need to prevent change, is not present, it is unlikely that a social worker's input will be required. This is because the bread and butter work of a social work professional revolves around those situations that are problematic or unsatisfactory in some way. Our efforts are therefore geared towards addressing the concerns that arise. This will involve, in many cases, seeking to bring about positive change, while in others, as we have seen, the main focus will be on seeking to prevent or slow down negative change. We have also noted, though, that many situations will involve an element of both. Good practice in this area therefore relies on our having a clear understanding of the nature of change, its implications for people's lives and the various ways in which it affects our practice.

| See page 58 | for some questions about what you have just read. |
| See page 224 | for some pointers to useful further reading. |

Perspective on problems: working in partnership

1

Introduction

As noted in Chapter 1, social work is concerned with problem solving. However, my idea of what is a problem may be different from your idea, and the ideas of others may be different from both our conceptions of what constitutes a problem. Problem-solving activities therefore need to take account of a range of perspectives. This is where partnership comes in. To try and impose our own definition of the problem without taking account of the perspectives of others involved in the situation is not likely to lead to successful outcomes. Indeed, there is a very high chance that we will increase the problems rather than tackle them. This chapter is therefore concerned with exploring how we can develop systems of working that are premised on the central notion of partnership.

The chapter begins with a discussion of multiple perspectives and is based on the idea that there is no single correct way of seeing the situation. Everyone has their own perspective and discrepancies in perspective can lead to significantly different outcomes from those that we are aiming for. Next, we explore issues relating to the significant task of making partnership a reality. Simply having a commitment to the notion is not enough. We also need to have some clear ideas about how to put it into practice in a meaningful way. Here we explore what is involved in taking our ideas forward on this vitally important, but often misunderstood and oversimplified, concept.

Multiple perspectives

Phenomenology is a branch of philosophy that offers us a helpful way of under-standing the significance of multiple perspectives. Phenomenology is literally the study of perception (a phenomenon is 'that which is perceived'). This means that while people will perhaps have much in common in terms of how they perceive situations, there are also likely to be significant differences. Indeed, different perspectives on a problem situation are inevitable. For example, parents may regard their teenager who is not coming home until two o'clock in the morning as displaying problem behaviour. The teenager, by contrast, may regard having unreasonably restrictive parents as the problem. There is, then, no single correct way of seeing the situation, no definitive version. Life is not that simple. To try and practise as if there were such a correct way of seeing it is, in effect, to put ourselves in the position of a god-like figure.

One of the implications of this is that conflict can easily arise, and indeed escalate. For example, it can lead to a situation where people do not trust us, because they feel we are not listening to their point of view, that we are simply seeking to impose our own understandings. It is therefore important to have a degree of clarity about our respective understandings of what problems we are dealing with and what makes them a problem. This is an important part of assessment. To form an assessment based purely on our own views without taking account of how the situation manifests itself to other key players is likely to lead to very poor practice.

Lloyd's comments are instructive in this regard:

> The value of undertaking a user-centred assessment of need, with the user respected and involved in the process, should not be underestimated (Lloyd and Taylor, 1995). My own research demonstrated significant psychological benefits for carers of a community care assessment having been completed, independent of any ensuing service provision (Lloyd and Smith, 1998).

(2002, p. 163)

What is needed, then, are the skills involved in taking on board other people's views and perspectives. We need both the skills to do this and the willingness to do so. What we also need to prevent chaos and confusion is some degree of skill in getting our own point across, but in a non-dogmatic way. That is, we need to be assertive about such matters, rather than aggressive or submissive.

Practice focus 4.1

Gale had been struggling with certain aspects of working in partnership, as she seemed to find herself constantly in conflict with other people. She felt quite uncomfortable about this, as she had been brought up to see conflict as a bad thing and therefore as something to be avoided wherever possible. She was therefore surprised that, when she attended a course on assertiveness, the point was made that conflict is an inevitable part of everyday life, and therefore something that we should learn to manage as effectively as possible.

This gave her a whole new perspective on conflict and, because of this, on working in partnership. At first she wasn't happy when the trainer claimed that conflict is not something that we should worry about or try to run away from. However, as the day went on, and there was more and more discussion around these issues, the more she could see the value of this approach. In turn, this gave her a much clearer picture of how assertiveness skills were a fundamental basis for working in partnership. She could see that she had a steep learning curve ahead of her, as she knew it would take a big step forward for her to move away from the idea that conflict is a problem to be avoided, rather than a potentially constructive way forward.

Working in partnership is an idea that has been around for quite some time in social work now but, unfortunately, 'partnership' has achieved the status of a buzzword, in the sense that the extent of its usage is not matched by the depth of understanding relating to this important idea. Some people use it very tokenistically without actually engaging in the significant changes that are necessary from traditional forms of practice to produce a genuinely partnership-based approach to social work. Other people are committed to the term, but are not necessarily appreciative of the complexities involved, and therefore have a tendency to oversimplify it. For example, a naive approach to partnership which takes little or no account of conflict is often to be found. My view is that any attempt to work in partnership that does not recognize inherent conflicts and the need to deal with these constructively is doomed to failure. Part of the value of working in partnership is aiming for a 'seamless' service – that is, one where there are no discrepancies between what different professionals allegedly working in tandem are supposed to be doing. However, there will inevitably be degrees of difference of emphasis between professionals, and so it would be naive not to recognize the potential inherent conflicts in terms of differences of priority, approach, values and desired outcomes. As mentioned earlier, what is a problem for one person, may not be a problem for another. For example, the social worker, with a strong emphasis on the value of safeguarding rights, may enter into conflict with another professional who is more concerned with providing care for somebody and is not attuned to rights issues in the same way that a social worker may be.

Voice of experience 4.1

I've often found it a difficult call when you've got somebody who is really concerned and wants to be caring, but who perhaps doesn't realize they may be doing more harm than good. A common example of this is when people put pressure on an elderly person to give up their home and move into a care home. In the vast majority of cases the people doing this have their heart in the right place, but they forget that people have a right to live in their own home, even if this involves significant risks.

Val, a social worker in an older people team

Similarly, people who are experiencing a problem may not recognise it as such or may see it differently; for example, someone whose excessive drinking is wreaking havoc with family life, and placing their health and even life at risk, may be oblivious to the fact that there is any problem at all. They may be quite happy to continue drinking at that level. These subtleties need to be taken into consideration if our practice is to do justice to the complex reality of social work situations. It is therefore important that we clarify people's understandings of what situation we are dealing with. Simply assuming that we are all in agreement as to what the problem is and what the potential solutions are can lead to major difficulties. For example, people may be pulling in different directions, causing confusion and mistrust for the client and, because of this, quite possibly contributing to a failure to make progress in addressing the issues concerned.

Practice focus 4.2

Marta was a social worker at a children's centre. She knew that Tracy had been going through a difficult time after her boyfriend left, leaving her to care for their two children alone. Marie, aged 3, attended the centre quite regularly and was normally very chatty and cheerful. Her sister, Rosanna, aged 6, attended the local primary school.

One day, Marie arrived at the centre with what appeared to be two cigarette burns on her arm and was very quiet and withdrawn. On her manager's advice, Marta made a child protection referral, as a result of which a case conference was held. Marta attended the conference, the first one she had ever been to. She found it a good learning experience, but what surprised her most was the range of views expressed by the professionals present. The deputy head teacher from Rosanna's school was convinced that Tracy was suffering from depression, while the district nurse said she had suspicions that Tracy and her recently departed boyfriend had been using drugs. Marta was quite taken aback by this, as she felt she knew Tracy quite well, but had never considered her to be depressed (although she acknowledged she could get quite stressed at times) and had had no reason to suspect drug abuse.

From this experience she recognized the importance of working in partnership – pooling information and trying to form a consensus about what issues need to be addressed and how best to tackle them. She realized that multidisciplinary collaboration could be quite challenging, given the range of perspectives involved, and so she resolved to make an all-out effort to develop the skills she would need for working together, so that she would be as well equipped as she reasonably could to rise to that challenge.

An important part of understanding the basis of working in partnership is a recognition that all action is *interaction* – that is, an individual's behaviour does not occur in a social vacuum: it will influence, and be influenced by, other people's behaviour. Butt captures the point well when he argues that:

> What makes social life interesting and valuable is that the whole interaction cannot be simply assembled from the parts. It is the organising of the parts into a meaningful gestalt that characterises interactions in the human order. It is this formulation of the social act that Blumer (1969) and Shotter (1993) refer to as

'joint action'. The outcome of a social act cannot be traced back to the individual intentions of any of the participants.

(2004, p. 122)

This social, interactional perspective gives us a much stronger theory base for understanding partnership than a narrow focus on individual factors in isolation from the wider social field.

Lovelock, Lyons and Powell also affirm the importance of both a theoretical understanding of 'joint action' as a basis for practice and the need to understand it as part of a broader social milieu:

> Cronen wishes to emphasise the practical use of theory, and with 'practical theory' he is proposing an approach that holds on to a framework which helps the *inquirer* know where to go next, while also being committed to *joining with others* in situated action. Thereby, practical theory is 'importantly informed by data created in the process of engagement with others' (ibid). In this way the understanding of what to do next is open to change as a result of engagement with others' lived experience. It is this willingness to put our ways of thinking 'on the line' that can help us engage with the uncertainties and ambiguities that constitute social work.

(2004, p. 178)

This passage raises (at least) three important issues:

1 **Integrating theory and practice**. In Chapter 5 I shall be emphasizing the importance of linking theory to practice. Lovelock and colleagues echo this importance, but also make the point that our theoretical understandings develop through our interaction with others. It is not simply a matter of applying theory to practice in any direct or technical sense, but rather using our knowledge base to make sense of our interactions with others and, further, using our interactions with others to develop and test out that knowledge base.

2 **Engagement with others' lived experiences**. The notion of 'lived experience' is an important one for understanding partnership. It helps us to appreciate the importance of understanding a situation from the point of view of the people concerned. For example, in some situations, we encounter someone who is very frightened, even though we may recognize that what they are afraid of is highly unlikely to happen (perhaps where somebody has been traumatized as a result of being subject to a violent assault and now reads many innocent, safe situations as if they were a significant threat). It would be of little use for us to disregard his or her fear. The fact that we may think, with some justification, that the fear is misplaced does not alter in the slightest the fact that the reality of that person's situation right now is a disabling fear. In other words, effective partnership working is

premised on appreciating other people's points of view and how that shapes their sense of reality.

3 **Uncertainties and ambiguities**. Social work is one of the 'people professions', and so it involves working with considerable uncertainty and ambiguity much of the time (as does any work where *people* are to the fore). This is a topic we shall revisit in Chapter 5 when we focus our attention on reflective practice. However, for present purposes, we should note that partnership is doubly significant in relation to uncertainty and ambiguity. On the one hand, where partnership is not working or where it is being used tokenistically, it can add to uncertainty and ambiguity (for example, when professionals from different disciplines are not communicating effectively and are therefore causing confusion and uncertainty rather than clearing them up). On the other hand, effective partnership working can clear up a lot of ambiguity and uncertainty by providing a clearer, more holistic picture of the situations we are dealing with.

These are all important points we should bear in mind when we try to put a sound theory of partnership into practice, and so it is to the topic of making partnership a reality that we now turn.

Making partnership a reality

It can be seen that there is little prospect of progress in terms of pursuing social work goals without addressing the issues of partnership in general and the question of conflict management in particular. We shall return to the topic of conflict below.

One key aspect of working in partnership is the importance of 'setting out our stall'. In using this phrase I am referring to the process of making it clear what we can and cannot offer, what is and what is not our role. Chapter 12 on managing expectations explores these issues in greater detail but, for now, it is important to note that a key feature of partnership work is clarity about these matters.

Effective communication is also something that occupies a central role in partnership working. If we are to move from a situation of multiple perspectives that will often not dovetail neatly together, then communication becomes vital. Without effective communication, we are highly unlikely to reach a situation in which we have sufficient consensus to move forward or sufficient understanding of the conflicts involved to be able to address them constructively. Without effective communication, the notion of partnership becomes an unobtainable goal.

Denney gives a good example of this when he states that:

there is, as Le Grand (1997) suggests, a widespread belief on the part of service users that professionals are preoccupied with budget management and workload, rather than the need to provide good quality service in the public interest.

(2005, p. 77)

In terms of communication, this passage shows that there is a danger that we will be communicating the wrong message to clients and carers (namely, that our primary concerns are budgets and workloads, rather than *people*). This is clearly a message that we should not be giving to the people we serve, so Le Grand's comment, as reported by Denney, should prove quite sobering. A point I have made elsewhere (Thompson, 2003b) is that we cannot not communicate – that is, even silence communicates something (whether we intend it to or not). We therefore have to make sure that the messages we are communicating (whether intentionally or not) are not contrary to a spirit of partnership and shared endeavour.

Part of the communication that we need to undertake is about goals and the plans for achieving them. This brings us into the territory of systematic practice (Thompson and Thompson, 2008b), an approach to social work which emphasizes the need for clarity about what we are trying to achieve, how we are going to achieve it and how we will know when we have achieved it (that is, what success will look like). Attempting to work in partnership without having this clarity will make the task much more difficult if not impossible, as we will not be able to establish the common ground necessary if there is confusion over the goals we are aiming for and/or how we intend to achieve them. Full attention, therefore, needs to be given to the demands of systematic practice. These issues are discussed in more detail in Chapter 10, where we explore what is involved in managing processes, tasks and outcomes.

Voice of experience 4.2

I have found systematic practice to be a really helpful tool. It gives a nice clear focus to my work, and it seems to be infectious – other people, whether service users, carers or other professionals, seem to be reassured by the clarity it offers. It has really stood me in good stead.

Nicole, a social worker at a health centre

It is important to recognize that there will be differences of perspectives, not only between the worker and the individual client or between worker and colleagues in other agencies, but also perhaps key differences between clients within a family or group setting. For example, in working with a family, we will need to take account of the major role of family dynamics as these are likely to have a significant influence on the experiences of individuals within that family. This is the basis of family therapy (Barnes, 2004; Carr, 2000). While it is not necessary to engage fully in the family therapy approach, there are aspects of the insights of the theory underpinning family therapy that can be very helpful to any social worker engaged with families, whether or not a formal family therapy approach is adopted. For example, a common process in families is that of scapegoating. Where there are tensions within a family, these may manifest themselves through the least powerful member of that family being blamed for the situation. Returning to the issue mentioned above of a teenager not coming in until two o'clock in the morning, part of the reason for such behaviour may be that he or she is glad to spend as little time at home as possible due to the tensions within that family. His or her behaviour may then intensify those tensions to the point where it becomes seen by other family members as a situation in which the teenager is the source of the problem, rather than just one factor amongst many in terms of the complex dynamics operating across the family group. What can then develop is a situation where the lack of agreement about what is or is not a problem may become part of the problem itself. This may both reflect under-lying conflicts and reinforce or exacerbate them. Being tuned in to different perspectives is therefore an important part of working with families in general, but also in working with individuals who are part of a family setup. Even those people who are no longer living with their family of origin may still have significant issues in relation to their current problem situation arising from their relationships with other family members. Equally, there may be family issues that date to a much earlier period in a person's life that are still actively influencing the situation now – for example, family habits that have played a part in shaping an individual's sense of normality and appropriate behaviour (such as manners and customs relating to meal times).

Practice focus 4.2

Mohamed was a social worker in a family placement team. When he first joined the team, he was aware that many of the children's families of origin and foster families would be very different from his own Moslem upbringing. However, what he had not realized was just how much variation there would be from one family to another.

After he had been in the team for a while he could see how significant family background issues were. In particular, he began to realize that a lot of the problems foster families had seemed to arise from a clash of family expectations. For example, a child brought up within one particular set of unwritten rules could react strongly against what he or she perceives as an acceptable way of going about things being challenged, while some foster carers – especially inexperienced ones – may feel that a child who rejects their family lifestyle, is being 'difficult' or 'defiant'.

Mohamed found this whole area fascinating and wondered about doing further training in family therapy. He could see how risky it would be for social work practice not to take account of family issues as an important underpinning of both the problems that arise and the potential solutions.

The importance of conflict management has already been mentioned. One of the significant dangers is that if we do not recognize the significance of conflict, it is very easy to misinterpret it in individualistic terms. This means that what is actually a matter *between* people comes to be seen as a problem *within* an individual. A common example of this is where two people are in conflict with one another, but each personalizes the situation by interpreting it as an example of the other person being 'awkward' or 'difficult'. Consider the following:

Person A: All I did was ask her to do me a simple favour and she makes a song and dance about it. She can be really awkward at times. I don't know what's the matter with her.

Person B: He keeps asking me to do things that are his responsibility. He must think I'm a soft touch or something. He's such a difficult person to work with. I don't know what's the matter with him.

This example illustrates the way in which *interpersonal* conflicts come to be translated into negative individual character or personality traits. This reflects a broader tendency to think in narrow, atomistic terms and to fail to appreciate the *social* nature of human experience, as the following comments about depression from Gergen illustrate:

> From the present standpoint depression is not an individual disorder; an individual 'does depression' as a culturally intelligible action within a context of relationship. Therapeutic attention thus moves outward from the individual mind ('what is wrong with him?') to the relational scenarios in which the person is engaged. In what kinds of relationship is the depression invited, with whom, and under what conditions? Are other moves in these relationships possible?

(1999, p. 137)

He goes on to add:

> Similarly, spouse abuse is not from this standpoint a natural eruption of anger, but is more likely to be embedded within subtle forms of interchange – with family members inside or outside or in the past. It has a time and a place when it 'feels natural,' but the important question is how to abort such scenarios altogether.

(1999, p. 137)

This chimes well with the point made earlier to the effect that we need to understand all action as *interaction*, and thus as part of a wider social context.

Where conflict is not recognized as a significant underlying factor, the result can be the inappropriate provision or commissioning of services, something that can lead to dependency, and thus be totally counterproductive in terms of social work's commitment to empowering forms of practice. An example of this would be where an elderly person is struggling to cope in the community and is deemed to be in need of intensive community care services, part of the situation may be a lack of support from family and it would be very easy to individualize this by simply regarding the family members as being uncaring or unsupportive. The reality, however, may be that there have been significant conflicts between the elderly person and his or her relatives and, with appropriate intervention to try and address these conflict issues, it may be possible for the family to be able to care for this relative, without the need for expensive and potentially dependency-creating community care services to be provided in what could be seen as a situation that does not require them – thus leaving services available for people who need them, but would not otherwise receive them. This is just one example of a range of situations in which a failure to recognize and address underlying conflicts can produce a disempowering reliance on services that would not be strictly necessary if an alternative problem-solving, empowering approach were adopted.

Voice of experience 4.3

Working in a multidisciplinary team of mainly health care colleagues can be quite challenging. They tend to see me as a gateway to services, so I have to keep reminding them that my job is about empowerment, and that problem solving is the main way I can do that.

Liam, a social worker in a multidisciplinary dementia care team

One implication of this is that careful consideration needs to be given to the use of mediation as a social work method. Mediation is increasingly being used in the court system to prevent the need for litigation. It is also widely used in relation to divorce issues. However, there is considerable scope for extending its usage to a wide range of situations in social work. A failure to recognize conflict, though, will therefore prevent us from taking account of the potential usefulness of this important social work tool. Consider the following examples:

> A woman with mental health problems is having a great deal of conflict with fellow residents in a 'halfway house' (a hostel for former psychiatric in-patients). As a result of this, she is experiencing high levels of stress, and may need to be hospitalized if the present levels of tension continue. If the conflicts could be solved through a process of mediation, the need for hospitalization could perhaps be avoided (and the well-being of the

woman herself and fellow residents could be boosted considerably into the bargain).

▹ A disabled man makes a complaint about a social worker who failed to do what she promised, and this leads to a lot of tension and mistrust. After this incident, the disabled man refuses services, even though this puts him at a high level of risk. A voluntary body could potentially be called upon to mediate in the conflict and find a constructive way forward.

▹ A teenager who was abused as a child is banned from a youth club after being found in possession of cannabis. The young person concerned becomes very angry, as the youth club is very important to him, and this incident results in a considerable setback in terms of the process of trauma recovery he has been going through. A social worker could potentially act as a mediator to seek to have the ban overturned (for example, in exchange for the teenager offering an apology and reassurances that the incident will not reoccur).

Finally, in relation to making partnership a reality, it is important to recognize the significance of power relations. Where there is more than one person, there is a power relation. Unfortunately, these issues have tended to be oversimplified in a number of ways over the years (see Thompson, 2007a, for a discussion of this problem). This has resulted in a polarization. On the one hand, power issues are often not addressed at all; they may be missing from many people's analysis of situations, naively failing to take account of the prevalence of power issues in the lives of the people we are seeking to help. At the other extreme, there may be an emphasis on power which fails to do justice to the complexities involved. For example, many practitioners over the years have fallen into the trap of assuming that power is necessarily a problem and that the use of power equates with oppression. Of course, the reality is that it is the *misuse* or *abuse* of power that leads to oppression, and the constructive use of power is far from being a problem.

In fact, it is a fundamental basis of empowerment. If, as practitioners, we have no power, how are we able to play a part in helping other people to increase *their* power and gain greater control over *their* lives and circumstances? Such naivety about power and empowerment is unfortunately not uncommon. It links in with the tendency to oversimplify and adopt a naive approach to partnership. This leaves the potential for discrimination as a result of power issues not being addressed. This is clearly an unfortunate and unhelpful way of addressing social work concerns. Making partnership a reality therefore has to take on board a much more sophisticated understanding of the significance of power relations and how they can be used negatively in terms of discrimination and oppression, or positively as a springboard for contributing to empowering forms of practice.

Practice focus 4.4

Mohamed's interest in family issues continued to grow and grow over time. One aspect that struck him as particularly significant was the role of power relations and how big a part these played in terms of family dynamics.

He mentioned this one day in supervision to his team manager, Val. She was pleased that he had taken an interest in this, as she saw it as very relevant to the team's work. She also suggested he should consider how his part in the situation also affected the power dynamics – how his involvement could shift the balance of power. He had never considered this before and found it quite a challenge to begin with. However, once he started to think about it, he appreciated how important an issue it was. He was able to relate it to a number of cases and situations and found it a very helpful insight. He was sad, though, that when he had undertaken his social work training, power had been presented as a negative force, a potential if not actual source of oppression. Understanding its complexities and using it positively and constructively as a basis for empowerment was something that had never been discussed. He was grateful to Val for helping him to develop his understanding of this vitally important concept.

Conclusion

This chapter has reviewed some of the complex issues relating to working in partnership. By emphasizing the significance of a phenomenological perspective with its focus on multiple perspectives, we have been able to see that a simplistic approach to partnership is a dangerous one. This chapter has alerted us to the need for adopting a more sophisticated understanding of partnership and recognizing in particular the need for conflict management skills to be a key part of working in partnership. It is not simply a rose-tinted approach that involves working hand-in-hand with others, naively disregarding the significance of conflict and the power relations on which such conflict is based.

We have also explored some of the ways in which we can seek to make partnership a reality rather than the sometimes empty rhetorical commitment that has been quite common in recent years. The discussion has been far from exhaustive, as we are addressing some substantive and complex issues here. However, it is to be hoped that the discussions presented have given sufficient food for thought to encourage you to find out more about these important concerns and have also provided a foundation for linking in these ideas with many of the topics that are to be discussed in the chapters that follow.

See page 58 | for some questions about what you have just read.

See page 224 | for some pointers to useful further reading.

Conclusion to Part 1

It is to be hoped that Part 1 has succeeded in laying down a solid foundation of understanding relating to the problem-solving basis of social work. What should be quite clear from the various topics discussed here is that practising social work is quite a complex undertaking. It therefore needs to be carried out on the basis of being able to draw upon a significant knowledge base. Parts 2 to 4 will help to contribute to that knowledge base, but you would also be well advised to consult the *Guide to further learning* at the end of the book, where you will find important suggestions about further reading.

Assessing needs and developing problem-solving strategies have been shown to be fundamental to social work. These processes can be seen to rely on a certain level of analytical skill and the ability to think clearly about the issues involved. It is for this reason that Part 2 is devoted to exploring the issues that relate to the social worker as thinker. However, before proceeding to Part 2, I suggest you make best use of the questions and exercises below to make sure you have learned as much as possible from Part 1.

Points to ponder

- What does it mean to say that needs are 'socially constructed'?
- What is meant by 'embedded' needs?
- How can unmet needs adversely affect people's lives?
- How might problem solving contribute to empowerment?

- What is meant by 'biography'?
- How can social work *cause* problems?
- How do poverty and deprivation affect people's lives?
- How might housing issues influence mental health?

- Why is grief important when dealing with change issues?
- In what circumstances might change be traumatic?

- How can force-field analysis be used as a tool for promoting positive change?
- How can it be used to prevent negative changes or deterioration?

- How is the concept of 'phenomenology' relevant to working in partnership?
- Why is conflict management relevant to working in partnership?
- What can go wrong if we do not work in partnership?
- How can partnership contribute to empowerment?

Exercises

Find someone who is willing to help you with this exercise: a friend, relative or colleague. Explain that it will involve discussing personal issues from their past. Ask them to think of a time in their life when they had some sort of problem that they were quite worried about. See if you can work out with them whether this problem arose out of a need not being met. If it did, was the problem resolved by meeting that need in some way? And, finally, consider what lessons can be learned about problem solving from this particular example.

From the example of a problem you identified in the exercise for Chapter 1, think about the *social* dimensions of that problem. What aspects of the problem situation had their roots in social attitudes, processes, interrelationships and so on? How does this compare with the problems we encounter in social work? Are there any lessons we can learn or conclusions we can draw?

Consider a major change in your life (leaving school, moving house or whatever). Think carefully about how you managed that change in terms of the feelings it created for you. Thinking back, can you identify what helped you deal with the change effectively? Was there anything that made managing the transition more difficult? What can we learn about managing change from this example?

Think about one or more projects you have been involved in with others at some time in your life (at school, college or university, at work or in your private life). Consider what made for good collaboration and teamwork. Think also about what made such partnership more difficult. Are there any patterns or themes you can identify from this, any lessons we can learn about working together?

2

The social worker as thinker

Introduction to Part 2

Social work is often characterized as a practical activity, and that is certainly an accurate representation. However, it is a very easy mistake to assume that, because it has a very practical focus, there is not much thinking involved. In reality, social work is quite an intellectual activity, in the sense that it involves being able to:

- think analytically and thus be able to make sense of complex situations;
- draw on a broad knowledge base to make sure that our practice is *informed* practice; and
- wrestle with dilemmas, contradictions and conflicting perspectives on a situation.

This is partly what makes social work such a demanding profession, requiring as it does not only skills in thinking *and* doing, but also the ability to link the thinking and doing together in meaningful and effective ways. But it is also partly what makes social work so important and so potentially rewarding.

'*What makes social work so demanding is linking thinking and doing together in meaningful and effective ways.*'

In effect, social work can be seen as a form of applied philosophy and, as Hunt noted quite some time ago: 'It is often remarked that philosophical matters are too important to be left to philosophers' (1978, p. 21). Christenson's more recent comments are also very relevant:

> can we draw any conclusions about what characteristics someone might have in order to be a philosopher? Maybe a few. A philosopher will have (1) An abiding wonder, and a desire to ask questions combined with the recognition that she doesn't know the answer and/or that he doesn't really understand the 'official answer' that has been offered. (2) A willingness to question authority not in order to be disruptive but out of a genuine attempt to understand what lies at the heart of things. (3) A willingness to ask fundamental or 'radical' questions, that is, radical in the sense of questions that probe at the roots (a radish is a root crop) of things, in the places that other people take for granted. (4) A willingness to be self critical, to subject one's own thinking to the same critical standards that one demands of others.
>
> (2001, p. 10)

All four of these fit extremely well with the thinking requirements of a social worker. If we can bear these four sets of issues in mind, they will stand us in very good stead indeed.

Social work in the UK is now a graduate profession, and this change is in large part a recognition of the important intellectual skills required for high-quality practice. Such skills are needed for dealing with complexity – something that social workers are called upon to do on a regular basis.

The four chapters

Each of the four chapters addresses a different aspect of 'the social worker as thinker', although all four are connected in various ways. Chapter 5 is concerned with critically reflective practice. This is an idea that has become increasingly important in social work in recent years, and rightly so. When I made the point above about social workers needing 'not only skills in thinking *and* doing, but also the ability to link the thinking and doing together', I could have been describing reflective practice, as that is precisely what it is about. And what makes it *critically* reflective practice is that it does not take things at face value – it looks beneath the surface as well as looking more broadly at the role of social and political factors (as discussed in Chapter 2).

Chapter 6 explores what is involved in social work as a form of educational practice. Although relatively underexplored as an aspect of social work practice, the educational potential of social work is quite significant. By seeing learning as a highly important tool for promoting change, we are able to see various ways in which the social worker as educator has a significant role to play. This chapter lays the foundations for understanding how this potential can be realized.

Chapter 7 examines the connections between thinking and feeling and, in so doing, establishes the importance of understanding the emotional issues involved in practising social work. A common misunderstanding involves conceiving of emotion as the opposite of reason, and therefore antithetical to 'thinking'. As we shall see, however, the reality is much more complex than this. An effective social worker needs to be able not only to think clearly and analytically, but also to engage effectively with the emotional demands of addressing people's needs and problems.

In the final chapter of Part 2 our concern is with the fundamental ways in which meaning and 'narrative' shape people's life experiences and are therefore very important factors to consider in relation to social work practice. As the French existentialist philosopher, Maurice Merleau-Ponty (1962) put it, we are 'condemned to meaning'. By this he was conveying the fact that human beings are meaning-making creatures: we need to make sense of our experiences, to order them in a way that allows us to construct a story (or 'narrative') that forms the basis of our identity and our relationships with the world. Chapter 8 explores some of the complexities involved in this.

Links with the other parts of the book

Part 2 shows how important thinking skills are for seeking to meet needs and address problems, as discussed in Part 1. Similarly, those thinking skills are very important when it comes to the management skills involved in social work practice (to be discussed in Part 3), as these rely heavily on being able to think clearly, to 'manage' emotions effectively and to 'tune in' to people's stories and meanings.

Part 2 is also very relevant to the discussions of professionalism in Part 4, in so far as professionalism itself is premised on being able to draw upon a professional knowledge base, engage with a professional value base and practise professionals skills – none of which is possible without effective thinking skills, especially the ability to think clearly.

Part 2 therefore covers a range of issues that are closely integrated with the other dimensions of good practice covered in the book as a whole.

Reflective practice: developing critical analysis skills

Introduction

 It is unfortunately the case that busy people can easily fall into routinized approaches based on habit that fail to do justice to the complexities of the situation they are engaged with. Reflective practice is presented as an antidote to this. It is an approach to professional practice that is premised on the idea of recognizing that our actions are based on an underlying knowledge base and that it is helpful to be clear about what that knowledge base is. In this way, we can develop our knowledge and understanding over time. We can gain confidence from understanding what is influencing our actions and we are in a stronger position to be accountable for our actions if called upon to do so.

We begin by asking the important question: why reflective practice? This involves looking at how reflective practice has come to be seen as such an important underpinning of professionalism these days. Various aspects of reflective practice are explored. This leads on to a discussion of how we can make *critically* reflective practice a reality. That is, it explores some of the important steps that can be taken to promote a more reflective approach to practice that is sufficiently critical in its outlook.

Why reflective practice?

Thompson and Thompson (2008a) make the important point that reflective practice is not a new idea. It is none the less a very important concept that has received increasing attention in recent years. A key part of it is the idea that practice should be *informed* practice and not simply based on habit, routine or the unquestioning following of 'instructions' or the uncritical copying of others.

> A career in the helping professions is likely to be a demanding one, with a great deal of pressure involved. It is understandable, then, that people will be tempted to press on with *doing* their work and devote relatively little time to *thinking* about the work. However, we have seen that this can be a dangerous temptation, as it means that we can be practising without really understanding what we are doing and why we are doing it. We can fall foul of 'mindless' practice, rather than gain the benefits of an informed and mindful approach that allows us to:

∴ Draw on our extensive professional knowledge base

◦ Be aware of potential pitfalls and dangers
◦ Develop a good understanding of the complex situations we are dealing with
◦ Be creative and do not simply rely on habit and routine
◦ Tailor solutions to the specific circumstances rather than deal with them in standardized ways
◦ Be in a position to justify our actions if called upon to do so.

(Thompson and Thompson, 2008a, p. 153)

A key part of reflective practice is the critique of positivism. This refers to approaches to science that assume that the natural science approach based on determining natural laws can be applied to the social sciences. A careful analysis of the situation shows that it is both unrealistic and dangerously misleading to attempt to apply natural science laws to situations that involve people. This is because, in the social sciences we need to be concerned with reasons and meanings, rather than hard and fast causes in the natural science sense of the term. Professional education therefore needs to be geared to recognizing that a 'scientific', technical approach is not an adequate basis for dealing with the complexities and dilemmas of practice (what Schön, 1983, referred to as 'the swampy lowlands of professional practice). Rolfe, Freshwater and Jasper take the same line of argument in exposing the inadequacies of a positivism-oriented professional education:

> Technocratic education, like technical rationality practice, involves a one-way flow of information from teacher to student and, by implication, from theory to practice. This is a top-down 'mug and jug' model of education, in which the students are the mugs who are filled from the teacher's jug of knowledge. The significance of this top-down approach for our discussion of the epistemology of practice is that it supposes that there is only one type of knowledge on which practice is to be based, that is, knowledge derived from research or other scholarly activities.

(2001, p. 8)

This is not to say that research-based knowledge does not have a part to play in influencing policy and practice, but it does mean that it is dangerous to rely solely or primarily on such knowledge. There will be professional knowledge gained through experience and exposure to the work of others as well as the knowledge to be derived from taking account of client and carer perspectives on the situations we deal with (Humphries, 2003).

Practice focus 5.1

Phil had worked in engineering before he decided to become a social worker. He was drawn to social work because his brother had received important help from a social worker after he became disabled as a result of a motor cycle accident. At first, Phil found the transition from engineering to social work quite difficult. This was because he hadn't bargained for how fluid and unpredictable human behaviour is or how significant the many variables of the social context would be.

However, he was able to make the transition in time and adopt a more flexible understanding of social work and its challenges. What stood him in good stead, though, was the way in which he was able to adapt the problem-solving skills he had developed in his earlier engineering career. He could see strong parallels between the two disciplines. Both involved drawing on an underlying knowledge base and using that as a foundation for understanding – and acting upon – the situations encountered. Both involved using that knowledge base (and the practice wisdom developed from it over time) as a means of tackling problems in a well-informed way.

Reflective practice is very important for a number of reasons. Chief amongst these is the significance of linking theory to practice – that is, making sure that our actions are drawing on a professional knowledge base and not simply on guesswork or ill-informed assumptions. This is not to say that our professional value base will provide us with certainty or anything even approaching that, nor will it provide all that we need to know about the situations we engage with as practitioners. However, given the choice between practice based on a strong professional knowledge base, and practice based on a skimpy understanding of the complex human situations we encounter, it is clear which is the stronger basis of the two. Unfortunately, there is a long tradition in social work of separating theory from practice as if practice has no connection with the world of theory and vice versa. The reality is that theory and practice are two sides of the same coin (Fook, 2002; Healy, 2005; Lovelock, Lyons and Powell, 2004; Thompson, 2000) in the sense that theory without practice is of little value and practice without theory is a very dangerous undertaking, in the sense that it can mean we are dealing with complex situations without an adequate understanding of what is involved. Theory and practice, or thinking and doing, need to be understood as closely interconnected issues if we are to be able to develop an adequate foundation of understanding for addressing the complex and subtle situations that are part and parcel of the social work world. As Butt reminds us: 'It was Kurt Lewin who was reputed to have said "there is nothing as practical as a good theory"' (2004, p. 10). Reflective practice is precisely about making sure that, on the one hand, practice is informed by knowledge and understanding (that is, by theory rather than habit or guesswork), and, on the other, theory is informed and tested by practice.

Another important part of reflective practice is clarity about values. Reflective practice encourages us to make our underlying knowledge base explicit and this can also be applied to our values. Making values explicit means that we are in a strong position to ensure that our practice is consistent with those espoused values and that there is no significant discrepancy between what we claim as our ethical basis of practice and what we actually do in reality. By being clear about our value base, we reduce the chances of engaging in unethical or oppressive practices. We are also in a stronger position in terms of accountability, that is, when called upon to justify our actions; where we are able to link these to explicit values, we are in a stronger position than we would otherwise be.

Pinkerton makes an important point in relation to values in stating that: 'values are not neat, safe, feel-good phrases but challenging guides to action within particular circumstances' (2002, p. 99). This comment encourages us to look beneath the surface of values issues so that we do not make the mistake of adopting a superficial approach to a set of issues that can be crucial in shaping practice. Critically reflective practice therefore needs to involve developing a good understanding of the values questions that are at work in the circumstances we are dealing with. This would include the following sets of values:

- **Our profession's.** Are we aware of how our professional values are shaping the way we understand the problems we are encountering and how we are dealing with them (or are planning to deal with them)? Without this awareness and understanding, we run the risk of practising dangerously, in the sense that our values may lead us down a path that is problematic in the present circumstances or not acceptable to the people concerned – for example, if we are adopting a value of empowerment, but working with a client who is very low on confidence and is frightened of taking control of his or her own circumstances. If we are not aware of this conflict, we may find that our involvement is not welcomed, and that we fail to take the opportunity to address the underlying fear.
- **Our own.** It will generally be the case that a worker's personal values will be entirely consistent with the profession's values, but there may be occasions where there is a clash between the two sets of values – for example, where a person's religious beliefs relating to same-sex relationships are not consistent with anti-discriminatory practice. Reflection on our own personal values and their relationship with professional values is therefore an important activity.
- **The client's.** There may also be significant factors stemming from the client's values that are shaping the situations we deal with – for example, there may be significant issues relating to cultural practices and beliefs.
- **Those of fellow professionals.** The point was made in Chapter 4 that there can be a clash of values across professional groups that can be a stumbling block when it comes to working in partnership.

> **Our organization's.** While the explicit or 'espoused' values of a social service organizations may well be consistent with professional values, the actual values in use can often be very different – for example, the operations of many organizations are characterized by bureaucratic values that can be at odds with professionalism.

Values, then, are complex issues that merit careful consideration, as it can be dangerously misleading not to appreciate the intricate ways in which they can influence events in practice.

Voice of experience 5.1

Working in child protection is quite demanding stuff much of the time. Some people find the responsibility quite daunting so I see it as my job to make sure that team members keep this in perspective. Accountability is important, but it is not something to be afraid of. If we are going about our business sensibly and doing everything we reasonably can to keep children safe, no one can realistically ask any more of us.

Glen, a child protection team manager

As noted earlier, reflective practice involves moving away from relying on habit, routine, copying others or uncritical following of orders or procedures. Social work is far too complex for relying on these simple factors, and we do ourselves and the people we are seeking to help a considerable disservice if we allow ourselves to fall into these forms of habit.

Reflective practice is also helpful, in so far as it provides a basis for learning. If we go about our business without really understanding what we are doing and why we are doing it and what knowledge is informing our decisions and other aspects of our practice, then there is little scope for learning. However, if we are better informed and more focused in relation to such matters, then clearly we have a much stronger foundation on which to build in terms of continuous professional development and adopting an approach to practice that allows us to continue learning, thus enhancing our practice over time.

Practice focus 5.2

Simone had worked in the initial assessment team for 18 months, but she was not happy there. She found the constant flow of new referrals quite confusing and unsettling. As a result of this she felt she had little control over her workload, and therefore tended to feel on the verge of stress most of the time. She had considered applying for another job, but her confidence was low after her negative experiences in her current post. However, what made a huge difference was the arrival of a new team manager who adopted a very helpful approach to supervision. The previous manager had simply checked that Simone was keeping her work up to date. The new manager, however, was keen to promote reflective practice and was therefore very supportive of Simone's learning. In particular, she encouraged Simone to focus on what she was doing in each case and why. This more focused approach helped her a great deal, as it gave her a lot more clarity about what she was doing. As a result of this she felt less confused and harassed – a development that made her feel much happier.

This more reflective approach also boosted her confidence and, with the support and encouragement of her manager, she started to learn and develop again – something that hadn't been happening for the last year or so.

All these benefits of reflective practice add up to a very significant further benefit – namely a significant improvement in morale. People who are practising reflectively, are likely to have a much greater sense of professional pride, a much higher level of confidence in what they are doing, a greater level of recognition from fellow professionals and greater levels of effectiveness. All these can contribute to high morale. By contrast, adopting an uncritical, routinized, mindless approach to practice gives us little foundation for confidence or for morale. There is therefore a very real danger that this will result in people feeling stuck, which in turn can lead to burnout.

As mentioned above, reflective practice is a well-established idea. It dates back to the work of Dewey in the early part of the twentieth century (Dewey, 1933, 1938), developed significantly by the work of Schön (1983, 1987, 1992) and Argyris and Schön (1974, 1978) – see Thompson and Thompson (2008a) for a summary of the main ideas. Increasingly, however, we are beginning to realize that traditional forms of reflective practice cannot be sufficient in themselves, in so far as they may not contain a critical element. That is, they may accept existing social arrangements as unproblematic and therefore fail to adopt a sociological approach. This can lead to an inadequate understanding of reflective practice based on the fallacy of atomism, as discussed earlier. Reflective approaches are therefore increasingly being referred to by the title of *critically* reflective practice. This is because the original conceptions of reflective practice did not take account of such key factors as power relations.

Murray and Kujundzic (2005), in a very thorough and detailed text, show the value of critical thinking. They make the important point that:

> Critical thinking has practical relevance; it can increase our intellectual independence, increase our tolerance for different points of view, and free us from the snares of dogmatism. We may agree with what our parents, our pastors, our friends, our teachers, our politicians and our scientists tell us, but surely not *merely* on the basis of their telling us. They may be wrong, after all, however well-

intentioned. This is the appeal of being autonomous. Critical Thinking invites us to call the bluff of accepted dogmas.

(Murray and Kujundzic, 2005, p. 4)

Challenging dogma is an important part of critical thinking in social work, as we will often encounter situations in which people have adopted a fixed idea of a particular issue or set of circumstances. For example, where somebody is very anxious, has been traumatized, or is feeling insecure for whatever reason, they may find it difficult to think flexibly and may therefore be reluctant to see the situation from a different angle. Critical thinking helps us to challenge (gently and constructively) such dogma and related problems (reliance on stereotypes, for example), and is therefore an important basis for empowering forms of practice.

Thompson and Thompson (2008a) write of the need for critical breadth and depth. By critical breadth, they refer to the need to adopt a sociological perspective which takes account of wider social issues and concerns as these are often crucial in shaping the life experiences of those who are in need of social work help (see Chapter 2). By critical depth, they mean the necessity to question things that are presented superficially. That is, they recognize the need to go beneath the surface of presenting problems. Often what seems on the surface to be a major issue may actually, on further examination, be revealed to be a relatively minor manifestation of what is a much more significant underlying problem. The discussions of conflict in Chapter 4 would be a good example of this. As we noted in that chapter, what appears to be an individual being 'awkward' or 'difficult' can, on further examination, become apparent as an indicator of a significant underlying conflict.

There is a need for critical analysis to be part of reflective practice in order to prevent such practice from being part of the problem rather than part of the solution. That is, while there are clear benefits to reflective practice, unless it also has the critical edge to which we are referring here, then there are dangers that we will make the situation worse by, for example, reinforcing existing patterns of inequality by failing to recognize them and thus failing to address them satisfactorily. Table 5.1 shows the benefits of critically reflective practice as opposed to the considerable problems associated with an approach that fails to be critically reflective.

Making critically reflective practice a reality

There are various ways in which we can make a positive contribution towards making critically reflective practice a reality. First amongst these is understanding the importance of a reflective culture and doing everything we reasonably

Table 5.1 Critically reflective practice compared with non-reflective practice

Critically reflective practice	Non-reflective practice
Based on knowledge and understanding	Based on habit and routine
Encourages creativity	Stifles creativity
In tune with professional values	Bypasses professional values
Can boost morale	Erosive of morale
Facilitates open communication	Blocks open communication
A sound foundation for accountability	A poor foundation for accountability
Produces learning	Discourages learning
Stimulating and rewarding	Mechanistic and unstimulating
Shows the client we are concerned and interested	Gives the impression that we are just going through the motions
A good basis for professionalism	A weak basis for professionalism
Potentially empowering of worker and client	Potentially disempowering of worker and client

can to promote and reinforce such a culture. Where people work in an environment where the norm is to press on regardless, in what is sometimes referred to as 'head down, get on with it culture', then it can be quite difficult to develop critically reflective practice. Where the emphasis appears to be on simply getting through the workload in terms of quantity regardless of quality and effectiveness, then a reflective approach may appear to be impossible. However, I would want to propose that, while it may be very difficult to be critically reflective in such circumstances, it is not necessarily impossible. This is because it is possible for an individual to bypass a non-reflective culture – that is, to have the self-belief to be able to continue to practise in ways that are consistent with reflective practice and the related value base. Despite pressures from others, a culture is an important influence on behaviour but it is not *all* important – it does not determine behaviour. It is possible for us to disregard the influence of a culture, although this can be difficult at times.

Practice focus 5.3

Susheela was quite disappointed when she took up her post in the mental health team after completing her social work degree. The culture there was not at all supportive of reflective practice. It was very much a 'head down, get on with it' culture, with team members not even trying to create thinking space to make sure they were doing the job as effectively as possible or to take the opportunity to learn from their experience. She found this very disheartening.

After about a month in post she plucked up the courage to raise the issue at a team meeting. Two people in the team felt it was a good point, but were pessimistic that anything could be done to improve the situation, and it was clear that other team members were not prepared to address it as an issue. She thought about applying for another job, but decided to stick with the team for a while.

Her plan was to refuse to be influenced by such a dangerous, non-reflective culture and to continue to draw on the benefits of critically reflective practice in her own work. She felt she could show at least some of her colleagues that it could be done, despite their cynicism and defeatism. She took encouragement from the fact that her practice teacher on her final placement had warned her she might encounter such a situation and had urged her not to give up on her principles if she did.

However, deciding to plough our own furrow, regardless of the culture around us, should be seen as a last resort. There are steps that can be taken to try and challenge a non-reflective culture, to attempt to influence it in a positive direction. However, this is best done collectively, rather than by an individual in isolation. One important strategy, therefore, is to seek out like-minded individuals to see whether there is scope for developing reflective approaches to practice within the existing organisational arrangements.

McDonald illustrates how dangerous it can be not to adopt a critically reflective practice in making the point that:

> Professional judgement has given way to the following of rules, and social workers currently function more as technical operators 'without any pretence of autonomous professionalism' (Lymbery, 2001, p. 131).

(2006, p. 107)

This indicates that, for many people, a professional approach to practice premised on critical reflection has been replaced by a non-reflective bureaucratic approach. As we shall see in Part 4, this is a dangerous basis for social work practice.

A key part of promoting critically reflective practice is making continuous professional development a reality rather than simply a rhetorical slogan. Many people seem to equate continuous professional development (or CPD for short) with attending training courses from time to time. However, there is much more to CPD than attendance at training workshops. There are issues to do with directly learning from practice, as it is generally the case that there is far more to be learned from actual practice than from training courses. This is not to suggest that training does not have an important part to play – it certainly does – but rather to put the situation in perspective and to recognize that there are other forms of organizational learning that are just as important, if not more so. A good example of this would be the use of supervision or mentoring to review work and draw out the key learning points from it (Clutterbuck, 1998; Thompson, 2006c). Each working day provides the raw materials for ongoing learning. Whether or not we derive learning from that will depend on the extent to which we adopt a reflective approach. The opposite also applies, in the sense that the more committed we are to continuous professional development, the easier reflective practice becomes.

Voice of experience 5.2

I struggled with reflective practice to begin with, especially the critical aspects of it, but I found it got easier over time. The more I did it, the more I learned and the more benefit I gained from it. To people coming to reflective practice for the first time, I would say: 'Don't give up. Hang on in there; it will be worth it in the end.'

Adrian, an independent practice teacher

Also important in this regard is the question of time and workload management. A common refrain from practitioners is that they are too busy to be reflective, that they do not have time to think about the work they do. This is a false economy, as to practise without any clarity about what we are doing will actually use up more time in the long run in terms of the increased likelihood of mistakes being made; higher levels of complaints; lower morale, higher levels of stress; higher levels of sickness absence and so on. A reflective approach should enable us to save time. Time and effort devoted to developing critically reflective forms of practice should therefore be regarded as an *investment* of time and effort, rather than simply a *cost*. We will get that investment back, with interest, in the medium to long term.

Critically reflective practice can also be seen as the basis of anti-discriminatory practice and, indeed, of ethical practice more broadly. This is because if we are practising in a routine, unthinking way without reference to the values that underpin our work, then there is a danger that what we actually do will fall far short of those ethical ideals. We can, in effect, have a situation whereby there is a stated commitment to, for example, equality and social justice, but actual practices fall far short of this. Empowerment would be a similar and related example. If we are practising in a non-reflective way, then we are much more likely to be producing situations of dependency, rather than making a positive contribution to enabling people to gain greater control over their lives and circumstances. It is therefore important to go beyond routine and take the opportunity to reflect on our practice: 'As David Levine writes, "if we are to learn from experience, we must not only have the experience, but also remove ourselves from it so that we can think about it" (2004: 9)' (Stein, 2007, p. xvi).

Practice focus 5.4

Sylvia was a social worker in a children with disabilities team. She was very aware of how much pressure some of the parents she worked with were under, and so she did her best to be as supportive as she could in the circumstances. This often involved arranging services, such as the assistance of a project worker or respite care.

One day she was asked to supervise a social work student for one week. The student, Nikki, was on placement at the local disability rights centre. Sylvia agreed to the request, but found the experience quite challenging. This was because Nikki's course placed great emphasis on both empowerment and reflective practice. Nikki therefore asked a lot of searching questions about how some of the services on offer made a contribution to empowerment. She saw a stark contrast between the work undertaken at the disability rights centre, which placed considerable stress on avoiding dependency, and the children with disabilities team, where the emphasis was mainly on service provision. Sylvia found it difficult to answer many of Nikki's questions and felt a little threatened by her implicit criticism of the team. This led her to think long and hard about these issues. She came to the conclusion that Nikki was basing her view on too limited an understanding of the team, but did recognize that there was perhaps a need for greater clarity about the services they offered and how they contributed to empowerment rather than dependency creation.

Conclusion

Critically reflective practice is a major topic, and one that deserves a much fuller treatment than I can afford to give it here. You are therefore strongly advised to make use of the references provided in the *Guide to further learning* at the end of the book. Reflective approaches to practice can be seen to be in stark contrast to many existing forms of practice that are characterized by routine processes that can be dehumanizing for not only the people we are trying to serve, but for ourselves. There has been a great deal of talk in recent years about the need to put the heart back into social work and to have it as a less mechanistic process geared towards ticking boxes and generating statistical information for planning purposes (Hamer, 2006; Jordan, 2007). We cannot put the heart back into social work without having a reflective approach. We shall return to these issues in later chapters, as there are connections between the fundamentals of critically reflective practice and our concerns in later sections of the book.

See page 111	for some questions about what you have just read.
See page 225	for some pointers to useful further reading.

chapter

6

Social work as education

Introduction

In thinking of the social worker as a person who is engaged in problem-solving activities, one aspect that comes to mind is the significant role of education. That is, in keeping with the theme of Part 2 of social workers as thinkers, practitioners can be seen to play a part in helping others to learn – a process that involves a great deal of thinking activity. This can apply in a number of ways, as we shall see in this chapter. This is not to suggest that social workers should be involved in giving lessons in schools, colleges or universities, although there is an argument to support that as a worthwhile use of at least some proportion of social work time. Rather, it is a matter of arguing that problems are often allowed to persist, or may actually be caused by, a lack of understanding of various aspects of the situation. Playing an educational role can therefore be an important part of being a professional problem solver and can be a significant source of empowerment by helping people gain a greater depth and breadth of understanding of the challenges they face and thereby being better equipped to tackle them.

We begin by asking the question: why education? and exploring some of the issues that are relevant to the educational role in social work. From this, we proceed to an examination of the skills and processes of an educational nature that social workers can draw upon when necessary or appropriate.

Why education?

The idea that knowledge is power is a longstanding one and one that has some considerable theoretical justification (see, for example, the work of the French social theorist, Foucault – see Faubion, 2000). This can apply at a very simple level – for example, where one person withholds important information from another, resulting in distress or suffering for the latter party. However, the relationship between knowledge and power can also be seen to apply at a much more complex level. For example, in terms of the use of professional knowledge, this can be done at a positive, constructive level where professional knowledge is used as a basis for helping others gain greater control over their lives and be able to make positive progress – in other words, it is empowering. However, professional knowledge can also be used to establish distance between us and our clientele and can be used unethically in self-serving ways rather than in ways that are supportive of genuine social work goals and our professional values. Understanding the significance of knowledge is therefore an important part of the social worker's repertoire.

Lovelock, Lyons and Powell help us move in this direction in stating that:

> Wittgenstein described our everyday ability to understand the meanings of words and to use them correctly in context as 'knowing how to go on' (1953, para 154), seeing this as involving a relational-responsive approach in which we act not only out of our own experiences and ideas but also respond in a moral way to the actions of others. In similar vein, John Shotter describes such practices as a 'social poetics', succeeding not in the sense applicable to theories worked out beforehand, but in terms of 'certain practical uses of language, at crucial points within the ongoing conduct of practice, by those involved in it' (Shotter and Katz, 1996, p. 213).
>
> (2004, p. 163)

This is an important passage that is worth examining in a little more detail:

- **Knowing how to go on.** We should not underestimate the extent to which our everyday actions are based on a significant knowledge base (for example, of social interaction 'rules' and cultural expectations).
- **Responding morally to the actions of others.** Our actions respond in large part to the actions of others, and, in order to act ethically, we need to have knowledge not only of the factors shaping the actions of others, but also the moral issues that apply.
- **Theories not worked out beforehand.** This fits with the idea of reflective practice discussed in Chapter 5, in the sense that we need to be able to reflect in action rather than come to situations with pre-formed ideas about how we are going to tackle them.
- **Practical uses of language.** Being able to influence situations is an important part of social work, and it is generally through language that such influencing takes place. Knowledge of language and its use is therefore a key part of practice (Thompson, 2003b).
- **At crucial points.** Knowledge of timing is also important. This involves having a good understanding of the subtle dynamics of the situations we are involved with.

Where people are in a disempowered situation, this is often as the result of barriers that are preventing them from making forward steps that can allow them to be more in control and be more positive about their lives. Many of these relate to a lack of knowledge or understanding. For example, many people easily get lost in a sea of bureaucracy in terms of obtaining the help they need in relation to financial benefits, health care services, housing and so on. There can therefore be a significant role for a social worker to help people learn about these issues, perhaps by pointing them in the right direction – 'signposting', as it were. This does not mean that social workers need to know all that there is to know about wider systems, but there is a need to know at least the basics and, equally importantly, to know how to find out more when required. In this way, we can help clients to move forward significantly in terms of overcoming such barriers. We can help people to gain greater control when facing the need to engage with bureaucratic systems that might otherwise be too disheartening and too discouraging for them. It is not uncommon for people who have had negative experiences in wrestling with intricate organizational systems and confusing rules and procedures to give up on such matters. When this happens, they can thereby lose out on services and other entitlements that may be significant when it comes to a greater quality of life or being able to tackle whatever problems they are experiencing. This returns us to the discussion in Chapter 1 of unmet need. Many needs may continue to go unmet because people do not have the knowledge or understanding that could, in many circumstances at least, allow them to meet those needs and the problems that have arisen in connection with them.

Practice focus 6.1

Patrick was a social worker in an older people team. One day he was allocated a referral relating to a 79-year-old man who lived in sheltered accommodation. His daughter had sorted out his finances for him, but when she died of a heart attack, he was unable to deal with his own finances – simply because he did not know how the benefits system worked and what help he had been receiving. He tried to deal with the situation as best he could, but he soon became very anxious. This, combined with his grief at losing his daughter, resulted in a deep depression and considerable self-neglect. It was at this point that Patrick was called in by the sheltered accommodation warden who had become very concerned. Patrick began his assessment and, while he could see that finances were not the only set of issues, he recognized that benefits issues clearly needed to be sorted out. He knew the basics of how the benefits system worked, but he realized that more specialist input would be required. He therefore enlisted, with permission, the support of an advisor from the local welfare rights centre. This advisor was able to do a comprehensive review of financial needs and entitlements. Getting these issues resolved was a major factor in helping to deal with the depression, as it helped to give a greater sense of control. From this case Patrick could see the value of drawing on a specialist knowledge base as and when required.

However, it is not simply in terms of dealing with bureaucratic systems that increased levels of knowledge and understanding can be of benefit to a client.

There are many other ways in which this applies. We shall return to these below under the heading of 'Using educational skills and processes'.

A good teacher is somebody who helps the student to learn. That is, it is not simply a matter of adopting a teaching role and providing information for people. Freire, the radical Brazilian educationalist, was critical of such approaches and referred disparagingly to a banking mentality (Freire, 1972a, 1972b). By this, he meant that there is little value in seeing learners as empty vessels into which we deposit knowledge. Instead, we need to see the educational role as one of *facilitating* learning. This may involve passing on information up to a point, but this needs to be done as part of a wider process of helping people to learn, rather than purely as an exercise in transferring information. A key concept here is the notion of 'empowerment through learning'. This involves not adopting a top-down approach (I have knowledge, you don't) and replacing this with an approach premised on partnership (we can work together to increase knowledge and understanding). Being an empowering facilitator of learning involves helping people to recognise their own learning capacity. This relates closely to the idea of 'power from within' (Rowlands, 1998; Thompson, 2007a), namely the ability to draw on our inner strengths. We all have experiences that we can learn from. Some of us will learn at the time, or shortly afterwards, but for others, we may not learn until significantly after the event. We should therefore see people who have had considerable life experience as having great potential for developing greater understanding if such learning is nurtured appropriately by an empowering facilitator, rather than drowned out by voices of people who are simply wishing to put themselves in a powerful position as the disseminator of information. This means that promoting learning is quite a complex process, and not simply a matter of adopting the traditional teacher role.

Voice of experience 6.1

I hadn't really thought of myself as an educator until I attended a training course on reflective practice. It made me realize how helping people learn is an important part of my job. I also realized that this was something I could do more of at times.

Lyn, a social worker in a family support team

The educational role can apply at a variety of levels. It can be done on a one-to-one basis where a social worker works directly with an individual in terms of helping to promote his or her learning and understanding about the circumstances he or she faces. For example, somebody with mental health problems may struggle to understand various aspects of social life. A skilled social worker may therefore be well placed to help promote learning in this regard. The educational role can also apply in terms of working with a few people at the same time whether a family or other small group of people geared towards developing understanding of particular issues or problems. Sometimes this can be done as part of a formal process of groupwork where there is a structured programme of meetings in which people are helped to address particular learning needs. This may be, for example, where people with learning disabilities are brought together and supported in helping each other understand about various aspects of their life experiences, their needs and their problems. While one-to-one educational work can be seen to relate well to the notion of power from within, groupwork also draws on this but, in addition, has the benefit of drawing on 'power with' (Rowlands, 1998; Thompson, 2007a) – that is, the strengths that can be gained by people working collectively towards shared aims.

Empowerment through learning therefore has much to commend it. However, there can be barriers to working in this way. One, in particular, is that difficulties can arise because practitioners may see themselves primarily as doers rather than thinkers. They may therefore not feel comfortable, to begin with at least, with the educational role of social work. Here there are links with critically reflective practice, in so far as one of the ways of promoting critically reflective practice is through the use of particular learning tools or techniques. Some practitioners need time to adjust to seeing themselves as people who can benefit from such learning exercises. Other people unfortunately never make such a transition, and therefore lose out on the benefits of both reflective practice and the educational dimension of the social work role. There are also links that can be drawn with the notion of social pedagogy, a form of social work practice in many European countries. The role involves elements of traditional social work and other elements of youth and community work, but where they focus on helping young people learn.

A further barrier to the effective use of the educational dimension of social work is that a service mentality can stand in the way of empowerment through learning. That is, as mentioned earlier, if people fall into the trap of adopting a fairly mechanistic approach that involves carrying out an assessment and then simply identifying what services can be drawn upon to address as closely as possible the needs identified, they will leave very little scope for any form of empowerment and even less for empowerment through learning. What is needed, then, is to reinforce the problem-solving dimension of social work, as this then leaves considerable scope for seeing educational practices within social work as a legitimate and very valuable contribution towards these problem-solving efforts.

Practice focus 6.2

Carla was a senior practitioner in a multidisciplinary drug and alcohol team. The team members all related well to one another at a personal level, but there were clearly significant conflicts at a professional level. Basically, this boiled down to the fact that some members of the team were quite traditional in adopting a medical model of drug and alcohol dependency, while others adopted a more critical perspective. Carla's approach was more in line with the latter view, but she was aware that a medical perspective was the dominant approach not only in her team, but also across the range of services more broadly. She could see that the team was pulling in different directions and that this was not helpful. She realized that what was needed was a linking thread – something they could all agree on that would, she hoped, pull them together.
The idea she hit on was to make problem solving a primary focus. She therefore raised the issue at a team meeting and put forward the proposal that the team should spend some time looking at how they could make the most of their problem-solving skills and experience. The less traditional team members took to the idea straight away, as they could see the links between problem solving and empowerment. The more traditionally oriented members were less enthusiastic, but Carla was confident she could win them round over time.

There are a number of factors that are important in relation to the educational role. One is the need to take seriously our own education. If we are not paying attention to our own personal and professional development, then we will be seriously undermining our capabilities as potential educational facilitators. There is considerable irony in an individual social worker trying to promote learning in others without addressing their own learning needs over time. Indeed, it could be said that it is not only an irony, but also a considerable arrogance.

Also relevant in terms of arrogance is the question of being prepared to learn from the client. It does not matter how extensive our professional knowledge base, there will still be much for us to learn and there will be various sources from which this learning can arise. This includes our direct interactions with clients. They may well have had life experiences and insights into their experiences from which we can learn a great deal. We should therefore not be arrogant enough to see the learning role as being in one direction only. The point was made earlier, and it is worth reaffirming now, that educational processes involve people working in partnership to promote learning. It may not always be an entirely equal partnership but that does not mean that learning cannot take place in both directions.

Voice of experience 6.2

Everybody has to face their own death in their own way, but even so, I have learned so much about death and dying and loss and grief from the patients here over the years. Seeing how different people face the challenges of death has been a very enriching experience for me.

Bernadette, a social worker in a hospice

We can also involve other professionals in the learning process and again make this two-way. For example, we may wish to enlist the support of a health professional to help clients understand issues relating to their health care concerns. However, again, there is learning that can be gained from the client. It may be that we are having conflicts in our partnership working (see Chapter 4) that are arising from a fellow professional not having adequate understanding of the circumstances a client faces. In this case, our role may then be one of trying to help fellow professionals learn from our clients and, indeed, there may be occasions when fellow professionals need to assist us in learning from our clients if, from time to time, we lose sight of the two-way direction of the nature of learning.

Using educational skills and processes

There are various ways in which we can help people to learn. Often this relates to helping people to develop social and life skills. These would include the following:

- **Conflict management and assertiveness.** Many people lack skills in these areas, but may have to rely on these abilities for making progress in dealing with their concerns. For example, someone with mental health problems or learning disabilities may be experiencing considerable stress and anxiety because of conflicts or other people's attempts to dominate them.
- **Communication.** So many of the situations we have to deal with have communication issues at their heart. Being able to help people improve their communication skills can therefore be a very worthwhile undertaking. For example, helping parents communicate more effectively with one another can make a significant difference in relation to parenting abilities.
- **Budgeting.** Poverty is not resolved by improving someone's budgeting skills, but assistance in this department can help people make the best of their limited resources. Interestingly, budgeting skills can also help to prevent conflicts, as it is not uncommon for conflicts in families to be in part

due to one family member's disapproval of what he or she sees as another member's overspending or unwise use of limited funds.

:: **Parenting.** One of the most difficult, demanding and responsible jobs in life is, for the vast majority of people, one that is carried out without any training or other such preparation. Parenting education can make a very positive difference in relation to coping with the pressures of bringing up children.

:: **Anger management.** Having difficulty in coping with anger can lead to relationship breakdowns, abuse and criminal charges. Helping people learn how to channel their feelings more responsibly can therefore be a very worthwhile use of social work time and effort.

Practice focus 6.3

Tim was a social worker in a secure facility for young people. He worked with adolescents with mental health problems as well as young offenders. To begin with he enjoyed the variety of the work but, over time, he found himself specializing more and more on dealing with those residents who displayed aggressive behaviour. He found that many of them (in fact, virtually all) had been abused in childhood. He could therefore understand their aggression as, in large part, an anger response to the traumas of abuse they had experienced. He recognized that it would not be enough to deal only with the aggression, but he decided to focus initially on the anger issues. He felt that, if he could make progress in dealing with the aggression issues, it would create an important foundation for addressing the other concerns in each of the resident's lives.

He therefore read up on anger management and enlisted the support of Rashmi, a psychologist at the centre who was also interested in anger as a response to trauma. Together they drew up a plan for a series of individual anger management sessions. They agreed to review the situation in three months' time and then to consider the possibility of offering group sessions once they had enough experience of the individual anger management sessions. They could both see the immense potential of anger management as a therapeutic approach.

However, this is not the only way in which we can be helpful when it comes to empowerment through learning. Another significant aspect of the educational role relates to supporting carers. This can apply in the following ways:

:: **Mental health.** It can be a very frightening experience both for the person with mental health problems and for their loved ones when mental distress occurs. Helping people to know what to expect can be significant in terms of alleviating fear and anxiety and helping people to feel more secure about dealing with the situation. For example, when someone becomes depressed, then they may have little understanding of what is happening to them and may be very appreciative of being helped to understand what is involved in processes of becoming depressed and coming out of depression when ready. In such circumstances, the educational role can also be significant in terms of counterbalancing medical perspectives that can have the effect of pathologizing and disempowering individuals. As Parton and O'Byrne point out, social workers have an important role in this regard:

> *Challenging Psychiatry.* Women of all ages frequently complain of depression. As *constructive social workers* we have a problem with this as we feel it is a story imposed on people by a discourse based on pathology being the explanation of problems and expertise being required to diagnose and treat them. Even if such treatment works the person is left in a dependent role, still unable to have control of their own life.
>
> (2000, p. 168)

‣ **Disability.** Although the social model of disability is now well established in many quarters, there are many people who still do not understand the social nature of disability (see Oliver and Sapey, 2006, for a helpful discussion of the social model of disability). Somebody becoming disabled through an accident, for example, may have little understanding of this and may benefit from being helped to understand the social significance of disability and how it is not necessary to internalize the oppressive perspectives on disability that are commonly part of dominant cultures in our society (Swain et al., 2004).

‣ **Ageing.** It is often the case that carers of older people have unrealistic expectations of their older relative or friend. For example, in relation to diet, I have come across many situations where carers have become extremely distressed when they realize how little the elderly person they care for is eating, but they may not understand that the nutritional requirements for somebody who is quite sedentary may be a lot lower than for someone who is very physically active. There can be important lessons to be learned about dietary requirements in particular circumstances – for example, when recuperating. This is just one example of the many ways in which carers can be helped to understand better what is happening in terms of ageing processes. Older people themselves can also benefit at times from seeing the broader picture that their individual circumstances reflect. This can help to alleviate anxieties and can be very helpful. There is also an important educational role in terms of challenging ageism. Helping people to learn about the processes and consequences of ageism can be a very positive contribution. For example, it may be necessary at times to help carers learn how not to make decisions *for* older people. Such matters have to be handled very sensitively, but can make an important difference when it comes to tackling ageism.

▷ **Illness.**   Although it is not a social worker's role to explain the nature, consequences or implications of illness, there is none the less a potential educational role in terms of helping people understand the social implications of particular illnesses, especially degenerative conditions or those that otherwise have a significant impact on people's interactions with other people and the social world more broadly.

▷ **Grief.**   There are many myths relating to grieving – for example, the now discredited theory that people grieve in stages (Neimeyer, 2001). Having a more thorough understanding of grief and mourning can be very useful in helping to reassure people about what is happening to them. For example, it is commonly assumed by many people who are experiencing a reaction to a major loss that they are going mad, due to the fact that the intensity of the feelings are so great and are so out of the ordinary compared with their usual understandings of the world.

▷ **Trauma.**   When people undergo a traumatic experience, the reactions can be of major proportions and can lead to the individuals concerned and those within their close social networks becoming quite frightened and disoriented about what is happening. Helping those concerned to understand the nature of trauma and how it can be dealt with can be a significant factor in promoting healing and recovery. An understanding of at least the basics of trauma is therefore essential for all social workers as we will often encounter people who have been traumatized in some way, for example, as a result of abuse, violence or being the victims of a crime.

Voice of experience 6.3

I did a postqualifying course in loss, grief and trauma, and I was so glad I did. Before that I hadn't appreciated the complexities involved. The course helped to equip me to support people who were grieving a loss or who were traumatized. I am much clearer now about helping people understand what is happening to them.

Siân, a social worker in a community care team

The educational role involves a number of key skills. These would include the following:

▷ **Thinking clearly.**   If we are muddled in our thinking we are likely to confuse people and therefore fail in our efforts to help them learn.

▷ **Communicating effectively.**   This is a further example of the fact that there is no substitute for effective communication in social work.

▷ **Getting the level at which we intervene right.**   This means making sure that how we pitch things is not too simple and not too advanced. This can take time to get right, but it is certainly worth the effort.

> **Engagement.** This is a matter of being able to form meaningful working relationships with people that allow them to trust us enough to form a sound foundation for learning.

> **The need for cultural sensitivity.** This is an important part of anti-discriminatory practice in general, but is particularly relevant to our efforts to help people learn, as a lack of such sensitivity can be a significant brake on learning.

> **Acknowledging and dealing with barriers to learning.** This would include addressing previous negative experiences in a learning environment that may have had a disempowering and discouraging effect.

> **Groupwork skills.** We need to move away from the individualism or atomism that can stand in the way of progress. Much good work can be done at an educational level on a one-to-one basis, but there are also considerable benefits to be gained from becoming involved in groupwork, even though this is an approach that is not given the attention it deserves in this day and age.

Practice focus 6.4

After the individual anger management sessions went so well, Tim and Rashmi decided that they now felt confident enough to launch a groupwork programme around the same issues.

They mapped out a structure for a six-session programme, with each session having a particular focus. However, once the group got going, they largely abandoned their detailed plans and just used the overall structure as a general guide. They found that the sessions raised so many issues and generated so much discussion that it would be necessary to extend the initial six-session run.

They were delighted with this success, as the participants were clearly benefiting from the process. Tim and Rashmi had both been involved in groupwork in a psychiatric hospital, but those sessions were fairly mundane and low key. They realized that, in having anger management as a topic, they had created a forum for so many important issues to be aired and dealt with constructively. They therefore decided that this was an approach they would use much more in future; they could both see that the learning potential offered by groupwork was well worth the time and effort invested in it.

Empowerment through learning can be seen to be closely linked to the idea of politicization, an approach to social work closely associated with the radical social work movement that was strong between the late 1960s and mid-1980s. There are strengths and limitations to this approach (see the work of Fook,

2002, for a discussion of this) and space does not allow a detailed analysis of these here. However, it is important to recognize that, by helping people to understand the political nature of many of the problems that we encounter in social work (for example, poverty and deprivation), we may be revealing avenues for progress that would otherwise remain closed to people who continue to see their circumstances in purely individualistic terms. The radical roots of politicization need to be recognized, but we also need to move away from the naivety and oversimplification that have come to be associated with a reductionist approach to politicization. For example, the marxist notion of false consciousness has been heavily criticized for assuming that there is an underlying 'true' consciousness. It has been recognized that this is an essentialist approach that is not consistent with a more sophisticated understanding of the relationship between understanding and truth. What is called for, then, is a much more sophisticated understanding of these issues. We shall therefore be revisiting them in much more detail in Chapters 14 and 15.

Conclusion

Many experienced social workers would regard an educational role as something that has never occurred to them as being an appropriate or legitimate part of their role. This is because, unfortunately, social work is practised in many settings in a fairly routine, unimaginative and uncreative way. It is very easy for highly bureaucratic organizations to reproduce patterns of practice that owe little to their professional roots and have more in common with unthinking, mechanized, routine practices. Reflective practice and the emphasis placed on it in recent years has been helpful in taking us forward in terms of recognizing that there are various creative ways of addressing unmet needs and problems above and beyond the tramlines that so much of social work practice remains firmly within. However, we still have a long way to go in terms of breaking away from the restrictions of habitualized practices that leave out the scope for approaches to our work that can be not only highly effective and empowering, but also enjoyable and a basis for considerable future development.

This chapter has therefore placed great emphasis on outlining how important and valuable an educational role can be as part of our social work repertoire and has laid some foundations in terms of giving some beginning guidance on how we can go about making an educational approach a stronger feature of contemporary social work practice.

See page 111 — for some questions about what you have just read.

See page 226 — for some pointers to useful further reading.

7 Thinking and feeling: emotional intelligence

Introduction

Social work is traditionally seen as an activity that requires a balance of head and heart. This chapter explores issues connected with the relationship between thinking and feeling. It is misleading to discuss the term 'thinking' in isolation from other aspects of human psychology. Thinking and feeling are closely intertwined, and so to explore issues of the social worker as thinker without reference to the emotional dimension would be a serious mistake. This chapter is therefore concerned with how emotions play a significant part in shaping social work practice.

The chapter begins with a discussion of the relationship between reason and emotion, drawing on a historical perspective to begin with. From this, we move on to explore the practical implications of working with emotion in the social work world.

Reason and emotion

Historically, western societies have placed great emphasis on rationality. The period in history known as the Enlightenment was regarded as a significant step forward in terms of moving away from the irrational superstition of what was assumed to have gone before. Post-enlightenment thinking therefore emphasized reason and rationality, especially scientific rationality. While there are clear benefits to this in some ways, one of the costs of this is the devaluing of the emotional dimension of social life.

Reference has already been made to the difficulties of adopting a positivistic approach to social work – that is, an approach that assumes that the 'laws' of the natural sciences can be seen to apply in parallel fashion to the social world. This is not helpful because of the people focus of social work. It also has the effect of placing undue emphasis on the rational dimension of human experience and fails to address the significant, indeed often crucial, role of feelings in the problems that social work clients encounter and the interactions between people that take place in trying to address those problems.

Practice focus 7.1

Ian was a social work student on placement at a carers project. He prided himself on how practical and helpful he could be. He was therefore very keen to be as supportive as he could. This got him off to a good start on the placement and his enthusiasm for helping was welcomed by carers and colleagues alike. However, after a few weeks, his practice teacher, Liz, was beginning to be a little concerned. This was because Ian seemed to be focusing all his efforts on being helpful in practical ways. What made Liz feel a little anxious was that Ian did not seem to be engaging with the emotional dimension of the project's work. She felt particularly concerned about the gender stereotyping that appeared to be going on. Ian, the only male among the project's staff group, was concentrating on practical issues, while leaving the emotion-focused work to his women colleagues.

She realized that she would need to raise this with Ian in supervision. She decided to link it to empowerment, as she felt a practical approach that does not address emotional issues was unlikely to be empowering. From this she felt she would be able to move on to discuss the crucial emotional issues and their central role in supporting carers.

Emotions can be seen to be to the fore in social work because of the very nature of the work. As Skidmore, Thackeray and Farley put it:

> Human relationships can bring satisfaction and joy, but also – for many people – suffering, insecurity, and other difficulties. Social work is one answer to challenges related to communication, feelings and human actions.

(1997, p. xi)

The importance of these issues can be seen in relation to a wide range of emotions such as the following:

> **Anxiety.** Clients often face situations that can generate considerable anxiety – poverty issues, relationship difficulties and so on. In turn, the situations social workers encounter can be quite anxiety provoking – for example, in managing the risk factors involved in abuse cases (see Chapter 11 for a discussion of assessing and managing risk). We would therefore be very foolish not to take the role of anxiety very seriously.

> **Grief.** The significance of loss in social work is of immense proportions (Thompson and Thompson, 2008b). So many of the situations that lead to social work involvement entail change, transition and loss, and so grief reactions are very common, even though many people fail to recognize this. Being 'tuned in' to the role of grief in people's lives is therefore an important foundation of good practice.

> **Trauma.** Experiencing a traumatic incident (as a result of being subjected to violence, for example) can also produce a grief reaction and can do long-

term psychological and social harm if not handled carefully. Practitioners who do not have a good grasp of the nature and consequences of trauma and how to promote healing and recovery are at a significant disadvantage in terms of trying to ensure effectiveness.

‣ **Conflict.** In Chapter 4 we saw the significance of conflict in social work and noted the importance of being able to manage it as constructively as we possibly can. Conflict situations can be very significant in terms of the range of emotions they can generate. Feeling confident in managing conflict therefore needs to involve being able to deal effectively with the emotional aspects of the work.

‣ **Insecurity.** This is another emotion that features quite regularly in social work. The challenges people face in their lives can lead to considerable insecurity. This can be connected with other emotions (grief and anxiety, for example) and, if we are not careful, it can appear to be infectious, in the sense that one person feeling insecure has the potential to make others feel insecure too (including the social worker). A skilled and confident social worker, by contrast, can be instrumental in reducing insecurity and thus preventing the situation from getting out of control.

However, it is important not to adopt too negative a perspective on the emotional dimension of social work. There are also various positive emotions that can be experienced as well, not least the following:

‣ **Relief.** Many of the actions we take in social work can produce an important sense of relief – for example, in helping people to exit from situations where they have been experiencing abuse and/or exploitation. Similarly, providing supportive services for people who have been struggling to cope unsupported can bring considerable relief. And, of course, there will be many developments that the social worker can find to be a source of relief.

‣ **Joy.** The occasional experience of joy can be such an important source of job satisfaction that it can make up for the many frustrating and disappointing situations we will often wrestle with. Metaphorically, they can be seen as nuggets of gold that serve as a reward that can make up to a large extent for so much of the wading through cold and muddy waters that prospecting for such gold can entail.

‣ **Compassion.** The warmth and support that can arise in many social work situations can be heart warming for all concerned. For example, at times of crisis or disaster, people will often pull together and show great concern for one another and can be quite selfless. Such compassion can be a powerful force in such situations.

‣ **Satisfaction.** Given that social work is about promoting well-being and empowerment through problem solving and addressing unmet needs, there is considerable scope for workers to achieve real satisfaction when problems are solved, needs are met, empowerment occurs and well-being is enhanced. The same, of course, applies to clients and carers who can achieve immense satisfaction from receiving the help they need.

- **Security.** As noted above, skilful social work interventions can make a very positive difference when it comes to addressing insecurity and thus promoting security as a foundation for progress. For example, in working with children, there will be many occasions where we help them arrive at a point where they have much greater security than was previously the case – for example, in the use of therapeutic techniques in working with traumatized children.

Being able to balance positive and negative emotions can often be a significant part of a social work encounter. For example, where somebody is undergoing a major change, they may see only the negative aspects of the situation and may not be tuned in to the positives. Without assistance they may therefore miss out on some very important opportunities to improve their circumstances and move forward positively.

Voice of experience 7.1

I do a lot of work with women who are depressed. As you'd expect, negative emotions feature quite a lot, but I always try to balance these out with positives. It's not always easy and it has to be done very carefully and sensitively, but it's certainly worth the effort – especially in the longer term.

Becky, a social worker at a hostel for women who have experienced domestic violence

There are two sides to emotional encounters. There is the question first of all of how the situation is having an impact on our own emotions. How do we feel about the situations we are dealing with? Do we feel confident or anxious? Do we feel positive or negative? These sorts of issues can play a significant part in shaping how things move forward. The other side of the emotional coin is the question of what impact emotional factors within the situation are having on the people we are trying to help. Are they anxious or confident, for example? How will this have an impact on the way things develop? Will emotions be holding back progress or can the emotional dimension be shaped in such a way as to be a spur to progress? These are all important questions that can prove very significant in terms of how situations develop.

These questions are very closely linked to the notion of emotional intelligence. Although the emotional dimension of human life has been a key factor in social work for decades, it is only relatively recently that other groups have begun to pay heed to emotional issues. For example, within the business world, this notion of emotional intelligence (or EI for short) has become very influential. It can be criticized in a number of ways for oversimplifying some complex issues and for 'commodifying' aspects of people's emotional life (Fineman, 2000a). However, despite these legitimate criticisms, there is still much of value in the notion of emotional intelligence. Its fundamental principle is that people can learn how to be more responsive to emotions. This is based on the idea that this is a highly effective method of managing interpersonal interactions in such ways as to make them positive and fruitful encounters for all concerned.

Emotions are commonly thought of as primarily biological matters, and there is certainly a biological component to emotion. However, it would be a mistake not to recognize that there are also wider social factors involved. As Butt helpfully explains:

> emotions do not lie there 'inside' us awaiting outward expression. Certainly we can measure physiological correlates of anger, fear and excitement, but we must not confuse these physiological states with the emotions themselves. The same physiological base can be associated with a variety of identified emotions (Schacter and Singer, 1962). The different way in which people express emotions cannot be explained in the simple release of repression.
>
> (2004, pp. 164–5)

The role of gender in society provides a helpful example of the social nature of emotions. For example, there is a great deal of research to show that emotions are experienced differently by men and women in different circumstances (Fischer, 2000). It is commonly assumed that women are 'more emotional' than men. However, this is misleading. The actual situation is that gender has a significant influence on which emotions are experienced, which emotions are shown in public and how we respond to those emotions. For example, men will often demonstrate joy and anger much more easily than women (consider a sporting occasion, for example, when such emotions can be very much to the fore, giving the lie to the idea that men do not express emotion). Emotions such as sorrow and fear, for example, tend to be more openly displayed by women. This is not to suggest that men and women are 'hard wired' differently for different emotional experiences but, rather, to show the significant role of socialization and cultural expectations in terms of the gendered nature of emotions in our societies.

Practice focus 7.2

Pam was a social worker in a disability team. She had worked with one particular family about two years previously in relation to a problem that had arisen in connection with a claim for mobility allowance. The situation was easily sorted on that occasion. However, this time, the circumstances were much more challenging. Mr Richards' wife had died and, as she was his primary carer, there were concerns about how he would cope without her.

Pam was able to commission a range of community services to support Mr Richards, but what concerned her most was that he did not appear to be grieving his wife's death. He rarely mentioned her and seemed quite calm about the whole situation. He was busy with trying to resolve the care support issues and did not appear to be upset at all. She was so concerned about this that she decided to ask her line manager for advice in supervision. It was a good job she did this, as her supervisor cautioned her against jumping to conclusions about how people grieve (or should grieve) and how they show their feelings. Pam's supervisor pointed out that it is a common mistake to assume that there is only one 'correct' way of grieving. Her advice to Pam was that she should read more about grief reactions – particularly about gender differences in grieving – before deciding whether or not Mr Richards needed any help.

There is also the significant role of culture and ethnicity in shaping emotion. There is considerable research (from anthropology, for example – see Hendry, 1999) to show that different cultures have different ways of conceptualizing emotion and of expressing it. This is shown by the fact that some emotional terms cannot be translated directly from one language to another. For example, English has the word 'pride', but French has two words for this: 'fierté' which refers to the positive notion of pride and 'orgueil', which refers to the sort of pride that goes before a fall.

Emotion, then, is a much more complex matter than our everyday understanding would have us believe. If we are to do justice to the emotional aspects of social work practice, we therefore need to develop a much more sophisticated understanding of how emotions work and the part they play in social interactions and social problems. See the *Guide to further learning* at the end of the book for some important suggestions about how you can develop your understanding of these issues further.

Working with emotion

The title of this section is deliberately ambiguous. It refers to, on the one hand, working with emotion in the sense of being aware of the ways in which we can influence the emotional tenor of an encounter and the emotional consequences. The idea of 'working with emotion', however, also means that we cannot work without emotion. This is to indicate that feelings and moods are an inevitable part of work in the helping professions, especially in social work where the problems people encounter can make emotional issues very much a salient factor in what is happening.

Voice of experience 7.2

When I started working with victims of crime I expected it to be a highly emotive area, especially when you think about how distressing it can be to be robbed or attacked. What I hadn't expected, though, was how much emotion featured in the lives of the offenders. That came as a complete surprise to me.

Angela, a social worker in a mediation and reparation scheme

Part 4 of the book addresses issues to do with professionalism. It is unfortunately the case that many people seem to associate professionalism with a lack of emotion, equating it with a dispassionate approach that does not concern itself with anything other than very rational matters. This is very misleading, because professionalism is an important part of social work, but so too is emotion. To separate the two can be very problematic. It is important to be clear, then, about the relationship between emotion and professionalism, as the two are not mutually exclusive. It would be a significant mistake to assume that professionalism means disregarding emotion.

However, what is important is that we should not allow emotional concerns of our own to compromise our professionalism – for example, by leading us into situations that are not consistent with our professional value base. This may include circumstances in which somebody is putting us under considerable emotional pressure to do something that we know is ethically unacceptable and contrary to our professional principles, but which (if we acceded to those pressures) would produce a situation that has benefits for us in terms of workload demands. This is dangerous territory – the equivalent of walking on thin ice – and we have to be very clear that professionalism and emotion can be compatible, but this does not mean that there will not be any clashes or conflicts between the two that need to be addressed from time to time.

A key theme of this book is the importance of empowerment. Empowerment is inevitably linked to notions of power. As discussed in Chapter 6, two forms of power that have received relatively little attention in the literature and the practice arena are 'power from within' and 'power with' (Rowlands, 1998; Thompson, 2007a). 'Power from within' refers to our own inner strengths and how empowering practices can help people to develop those strengths to gain in confidence, for example. It is something that can be extremely effective in terms of helping people make connections with spiritual issues, not in the religious sense, but in the sense of making their life meaningful and in terms of 'connectedness' with other people and the wider world. Helping people to deal with their emotions, particularly when such emotions may be very intense and prolonged, can be a very worthwhile social work role, in so far as it can make a very positive contribution to empowerment in relation to this specific form of power: power from within.

'Power with' refers to the beneficial effects that can be gained from people working together and supporting one another. Collective endeavours are much more powerful and effective than solitary efforts, and so the notion of power with can be a very important one in terms of developing empowering forms of practice. In relation to the emotional dimension of social work, this can be very significant, partly because there may be emotional issues that are preventing people from working together (there may be a need for some form of conflict management intervention, for example), or it may partly be to do with the highly emotionally charged nature of a particular situation making people working together quite a fraught experience. A social worker with skills in groupwork and interpersonal interactions in general can be a very useful facilitator of developments in this area; for example, within families where pressures and emotional tensions may be pushing people apart rather than bringing them together. This is closely linked with Bateson's notion of cybernetics which has, as one of its central principles, the idea that if the problem is within a family or group of people, it will have the effect of pushing them apart, whereas, if the problem is perceived as being outside the family or group, it is likely to have the effect of pulling them together (Bateson, 1973). A skilled social worker may therefore be well placed to work with a family or group to help them to reconceptualize the problems they encounter in broader social terms, so that they are perceived as being more outside the group than within, thereby facilitating a greater pulling together. If, by contrast, a family is scapegoating a particular individual and seeing him or her as 'the' problem, then they are likely to be pushed apart by this dynamic. If they can be helped to see the situation in more holistic terms, then that can have the effect of bringing them together and thereby being in a much stronger, more empowered position to address whatever is causing them difficulties within their family without personalizing this in terms of pathologizing an individual (the scapegoat). This is the basis of much family therapy work and can also be a useful aspect of working with groups and communities in a broader sense.

Practice focus 7.3

Chris was a social worker in a children and families team. The job was quite varied, including a mixture of child protection work and family support. What she particularly enjoyed were the cases where she could work with the whole family and help them deal with their difficulties as a unit – healing any rifts and conflicts where possible. The case of the Warburton family was exactly where she felt most comfortable and effective. Danny Warburton was eight years old when Chris became involved with the family. His behaviour at home and at school was becoming increasingly disruptive. The school was threatening to exclude him and his parents were saying they could not cope with him at home if his behaviour continued to be so challenging.

Chris was careful not to fall into the trap of scapegoating by pathologizing him as a 'bad lad'. Instead, she focused her assessment more broadly on the family as a whole. Very soon she could see that there were a number of tensions and difficulties. In particular she noticed that there were no clear channels of communication. From this, she was able to work out that Danny's behaviour was understandably a response to the insecurities at home. The family responded to his behaviour by labelling him as a 'problem child', but still did not communicate effectively with one another. Chris therefore decided to focus her energies on helping the family to communicate better, in the hope that this would reduce the insecurities.

Emotions and empowerment are therefore closely related although many people do not recognize this. They conceive of empowerment as being a hard-edged political concept geared towards making significant structural changes in society and would not necessarily associate it with the softer issues of emotional dynamics. However, I would see that as an oversimplified and unduly narrow conception of empowerment. Without people being able to feel reasonably comfortable and in control of their emotions, then it is unlikely that they will find the energy and commitment to be part of a broader movement of positive change.

Voice of experience 7.3

I have an interest in eastern philosophies, and that has helped me to understand that there has to be an element of personal transformation involved in empowerment. It's what Taoism calls 'spiritual alchemy'.

Sharon, deputy manager of a mental health resource centre

There are various skills involved in handling emotion. It is worth exploring each of these in a little more detail:

> **'Tuning in'.**   This refers to the ability to be sensitive to what is happening in a situation, to pick up on the emotional vibes, as it were, and therefore be in a much stronger position to be able to respond appropriately to what is happening. The social worker who fails to 'tune in' in this way is not only going to be in a much weakened position, but may actually

do a lot of harm. The importance of this emotional sensitivity cannot be overemphasized.

> **Holding.**   This is a concept that has its roots in psychodynamics, but is also more broadly applicable to other theoretical perspectives that recognize the central role of emotions. It refers to the ability to provide a degree of security for one or more people so that, when they are experiencing intense and potentially damaging emotions (as a result of a traumatic experience, for example), the person doing the 'holding' is charged with the task of helping the people concerned to feel at least a degree of security, to feel that there is somebody who understands their situation and is willing to be supportive. In many situations, this can make a crucial difference to the outcome of the social worker's efforts. Being able to contain the emotion in this way gives people the scope to work through some of the emotional processes that are necessary to gain a balanced perspective and be in a better position to judge how to deal with the circumstances they face. Holding, in this sense, is something that can be done by individuals, groups of people or even whole organizations. Some organizations provide a very secure and supportive environment for their staff and other stakeholders, while others do very little in terms of this. This can be a very significant issue in terms of staff care and whether or not the emotional needs of the worker are recognized and appropriately addressed.

> **Influencing.**   Being able to influence the emotional aspects of a situation can be very valuable in terms of moving the situation in a positive direction. This can be highly skilled work, but it is premised on a set of skills that can be developed over time and with sensitivity to the emotional aspects. However, there is an ethical dimension to consider here, in so far as influencing should not be equated with manipulating. I am using influence in a positive sense to refer to trying to help people move in a direction which is beneficial to them. Manipulation, by contrast, means manoeuvring people into a position that is beneficial to the person who is doing the manipulating (but not necessarily the person who is being manipulated) and is therefore neither a positive move in terms of social work, nor is it an ethically acceptable way of behaving. Influencing and manipulating should therefore not be confused, as they are significantly different, both pragmatically and ethically.

> **Anchoring.**   This is similar to holding. It means when people are going through a crisis or other distressing situation, then being able to provide a firm base for them in an emotional sense is something that can be very useful. This is because it helps to maintain a degree of stability in a rapidly changing situation, and can therefore be a very positive thing to do, and

so the term 'anchoring' is very appropriate in this sense, as it is based on the metaphor of an anchor keeping a ship firmly in place, even in stormy seas – just as social workers are often involved in helping people keep calm and focused in very turbulent circumstances.

> **Communication.** This is a topic we keep returning to, such is its central role in social work. If we are going to be able to respond appropriately to emotional issues, then we need to be very skilled in communication, both in terms of being able to put forward our messages clearly and unambiguously without risking escalating any conflicts or tensions that may be about, and being responsive in terms of being a good listener: someone who shows that he or she understands to a certain extent and is keen to understand further. This is a very positive message to give to people.

Practice focus 7.4

Liz had been anxious about raising the issue of Ian's tendency to focus on practical help and neglect the emotional dimension of the project's work. However, she was very pleasantly surprised by how positively he responded to this. He was very keen to learn how he could be better equipped to respond to the emotional challenges of supporting carers. Liz tackled this by helping Ian to think more about the 'why' of the situations he was involved in: why did people need help? Why did they see the project as a potential source of help? Why did he think in predominantly practical terms when he could see his colleagues tackling their work at a deeper, more emotion-focused level? These questions (and others like them) helped Ian to look beneath the surface of the presenting problems. This then gave him an excellent platform for gaining a much better understanding of the emotional issues that were shaping the situations encountered and people's responses to them. Liz was delighted with his response and felt that he now had the basis for the balance of heart and head that is so characteristic of good practice in social work.

Conclusion

Emotions are clearly a fundamental part of social work practice. Engaging in social work without a reasonably sophisticated understanding of the emotional component of our work is potentially a recipe for disaster. It could do a lot of harm for the people that we are seeking to help and it can also lead to significant emotional difficulties for ourselves as we are not robots who are able to be totally impervious to the emotional dynamics that are going on around us. We therefore have to have the emotional intelligence that helps us to not only appreciate and tune in to other people's emotions, but also to be sensitive to our own and to seek help and support where we need it. We should not fall into the trap of adopting a macho approach that sees emotional responses as a sign of weakness or inadequacy. Emotions are a sign of being a human being and we should not forget that social work is about person-to-person encounters – that is, it is very much a human experience.

We also need to bear in mind that addressing our own emotional needs is a key part of self-care, and so these issues will also feature again to a certain extent in Chapter 9 when we explore the vitally important topic of self-management.

Perhaps the most important emotional issue of all is hope. Social work can be seen to be premised on hope. So much of what we do in terms of addressing unmet needs and related problems is about helping people to establish some degree of hope where they do not have any and building as much as we can on whatever degrees of hope are already present in the situation.

See page 111   for some questions about what you have just read.

See page 226   for some pointers to useful further reading.

8   Narratives and meaning making

Introduction

We have seen that thinking is not simply a matter of rationality and logical analysis. There are other dimensions to what is generally regarded as thought. One aspect of this is the question of meaning making. How do we make sense of our lives? How does social work play a part in shaping the meanings of people's lives? To what extent can social work itself be seen as a process of meaning making? These are all important questions, and so this chapter is concerned with the processes involved in thinking about what our lives and circumstances mean to us and the narratives or stories that we use to give a coherent thread of understanding of how our lives are unfolding.

The chapter is divided into two main sections. In the first one we look at making sense of experience. This explores some important issues about narratives and their role in shaping our life experience. The second part is entitled 'Focusing on meaning', and this latter section allows us to explore the implications of meaning making for social work practice.

Making sense of experience

Thinking is often presented as if it were a relatively linear matter – that is, as if we simply think in straight lines. Rationality is often presented in such terms, and these are, of course, misleading, as they oversimplify some very complex issues. If we think of mind maps, for example, we can see how they represent the ways in which lines of thought diverge and often go off in different directions at the same time (Buzan and Buzan, 2000). This is not the sign of an illogical or irrational mind but, rather, a more accurate reflection of what actually happens in thought processes. In order to have a better understanding of the idea of the social worker as thinker, we therefore need to move beyond simple logic (as a set of linear processes) and look at how thoughts are connected together into the meaningful whole. Such thoughts will also be connected with, as we saw in Chapter 7, emotional aspects of the situation. The thinking and feeling therefore become united in a structure of meaning. The term generally used to refer to this is 'narrative' which literally means 'story'. It refers to the sort of structures of meaning that we use to make sense of our experience and give a coherence and focus to our lives and what is happening to us on a day-to-day basis. Narratives are also an important part of our identity. Indeed, we can see identity as being largely a narrative that provides a unified structure to the complex and diverse range of experiences we encounter as we go through life.

Narratives can be linked to wider 'discourses' (frameworks of meaning and action that can be very influential in determining social behaviour). That is, meanings are not just shaped by particular individuals, but are also heavily influenced by wider culture and structural factors. For example, someone who has a commitment to a particular value or set of values as part of his or her identity narrative will, in large part, have derived those values from the wider social sphere. While the particular individual may have tailored them to suit his or her personal views, they will not have arisen in a social vacuum. It is inevitable that we will be influenced, one way or another, by the cultural formations around us. The phrase, 'one way or another', is a particularly important one, as this shows that we can be influenced by culture in one of two main ways.

2

First, there can be a direct influence whereby we accept certain cultural assumptions as the norm. Indeed, this is a key part of what sociologists refer to as socialization. It is a process by which we become part of our culture and our culture becomes part of us. However, it is not simply a matter of taking on board cultural assumptions in this way. That would leave individuals as puppets who are shaped by their culture in a unilinear way, with no opportunity for rejecting aspects of that culture. McDonald explains this as follows:

> Standing in contrast is what has been described as an over-socialized conception of agency in which individuals routinely and unquestioningly accept, follow and reproduce social norms (for example, social workers uncritically accepting work-fare rationalities, processes and practices). Within the genre, both the rational actor and its alternatives are rejected in favor of a conception of agency operating within a model of *bounded rationality* (Perrow, 2000), in which agents deliberately work out how to 'go on' on a moment-by-moment, day-by-day basis. In other words, social workers are *knowing actors* – but their awareness and the span of action is bounded, limited, and circumscribed to the context and time frame in which they are located.

> (2006, pp. 136–7)

The second way, therefore, in which a person can be influenced by a culture is by rejecting it, or at least aspects of it. For example, in a consumerist culture there may be influences in the direction of consumerism, but there will also, for many people, be influences against consumerism. That is, for many people, a key part of their value base, and thus their identity, will be a rejection of consumerism or at least certain consumerist ideas.

Practice focus 8.1

Liam was a social worker in an emergency duty team. One night he received a referral from an on-call GP who had been called out to a house to attend to a child who had severe stomach pains. He had managed to deal with the stomach problem, but was concerned that the family were living in what he described as 'appalling squalor' and certainly no fit place to bring up children. He insisted that Liam make an urgent visit to see to the children's welfare (there were three children under the age of ten in the family). Liam explained that he could not do this as the circumstances he described did not warrant an emergency intervention and, besides, it could be quite distressing for the family, including the children, to receive an unannounced visit late at night from a social worker. The GP was not entirely happy with this, but accepted Liam's explanation.

Liam referred the matter to the local child protection team so that they could deal with it as they saw fit. A few days later he received an email to say that a social worker had visited the family, but had found no concerns. The social worker described them as a 'new age' family, with a very untidy house and unconventional furniture and clothing. The house was clean and the children were clearly loved and well-looked after, so there were no concerns. The GP, Liam mused, had clearly disapproved of the family's Bohemian lifestyle and values and equated all this with 'squalor'.

This is not to underestimate how powerful cultures can be in shaping discourses and therefore narratives that, in turn, influence our sense of who we are and how we fit into the world. We have to remember that narratives as stories are, in fact, more often than not the stories of the powerful. Inherent within discourses will be sets of power relations. That is, the stories that we are exposed to in terms of the various frameworks of meaning that are part of our culture and broader society are not free from power relations. There will be assumptions made within narratives about relative merits in terms of prestige, status and such matters. Social hierarchies and associated assumptions are therefore significant parts of the meaning making that we are all part of. Power relations and the attendant inequalities will therefore also be very relevant to this. In a sense, a discourse is a set of institutionalized meanings or narrative and this shows that there is a sociological dimension to meaning making as well as a personal or psychological one. This can be seen to apply in a number of ways:

> **Race and ethnicity.** How we see the world will owe much to whether we are located in a dominant or subordinate racial group as well as to the cultural assumptions that are very much part of an individual's ethnicity.
> **Gender.** This is clearly a dimension of social life that is very significant in shaping how we perceive our life experiences.

⊳ **Age.** What our lives mean to us will, of course, change over time, and so age will be a significant factor in shaping life meanings.

⊳ **Disability.** The social model of disability has shown that disability is rooted in social attitudes and formations, and this will have far-reaching implications for how people with disabilities experience the world, and thus for the meaning they attach to their experiences.

⊳ **Sexuality.** The stigma commonly attached to minority sexual orientations is likely to be a key factor for many people in terms of the narratives they construct.

⊳ **Client dependency.** It is also important to recognize that simply being a client has implications for meaning making. Where clients become dependent on services, then the implications are even more profound.

Voice of experience 8.1

I find the whole issue of class and culture quite fascinating. I was brought up in a strongly working-class environment but now live in a middle-class area and do what tends to be seen as a middle-class job. And yet most of the clients I work with are working class. What all this has taught me is that class is very important in shaping how we see the world.

Jen, a social worker in an adult learning disabilities team

In an earlier discussion, we encountered the term 'phenomenology', which emphasizes the importance of perception and interpretation. This is clearly an important underpinning when it comes to making sense of experience in terms of structures of meaning or narratives. Phenomenology helps us to understand the idea that we should not judge a person until we have walked in his or her moccasins, as the saying has it. Phenomenology helps us to understand that it is not simply a matter of uncovering the absolute or objective reality but, rather, that, through complex processes of perception and interaction with other people's perceptions, we develop socially and personally constructed universes of meaning. This is the basis of how we make sense of our lives. It is closely linked to ideas of spirituality, a point to which we shall return below.

Focusing on meaning

As indicated earlier, discourses are linked to power and therefore have the potential for (i) oppression, or (ii) empowerment. Which direction things take – the negative direction of oppression or the positive direction of empowerment – will depend to a large extent on the quality and direction of practice of the individual social worker at the time. This places a considerable emphasis on the impact of social work practice. What we have to recognize is that, given the significance of meaning and the power of interpersonal and social interactions to shape and redefine meanings, how we practise can be crucial in terms of influencing a person's processes of meaning making. For example, if our interactions have the effect of pointing out quite strongly a person's difficulties and problems without any counterbalancing discussion of their strengths and opportunities, then we may unwittingly increase a possible tendency towards low self-esteem, in the sense that we may be reinforcing any negative views an individual may have had, leaving little room or encouragement for more positive aspects of the situation to emerge. This relates to what has come to be known as the strengths perspective in social work (Nash, Munford and O'Donoghue, 2005; Saleebey, 2005).

Practice focus 8.2

Diane had taken to heart the lesson she learned on her social work degree that it is necessary to take account of people's strengths as well as any problems or difficulties they may be having, when she qualified and took up post in a children and families team, she was looking forward to putting these ideas into practice, as she had done during the practice learning opportunities that formed part of her degree. However, she was quite surprised to note that a strengths perspective was not part of the team's culture.

She noticed that her colleagues were very committed to doing a good job, but, for the most part, they seemed oblivious to the fact that they seemed to be discounting the idea that people with problems also had strengths (and, indeed, it was often their problems that were somehow preventing them from using their strengths – as a result of a crisis of confidence, for example). She was reluctant to discuss the matter with the team manager in case he interpreted it as a criticism and became defensive. Fortunately, she had a friend who was a very experienced practice teacher, so she asked her advice. She was pleased with the response she got, which was the suggestion that, when she felt well established enough in the team to do so, she should offer to do a presentation about the strengths perspective at one of the team's quarterly lunchtime staff development sessions.

In the strengths perspective there is a lot of emphasis placed on identifying and reinforcing the skills insights and other strengths individuals and families may have so that we do not adopt a purely negative or unbalanced approach to the circumstances we are seeking to ameliorate. By contrast, a social worker who is able to help individuals adopt a more balanced view of their situation, through realizing what strengths and opportunities they have to capitalize on, can play a significant role in terms of empowerment.

Yet again, we encounter the importance of communication. Listening to what is really being said and going beyond stereotypes and preconceived notions is a key part of practice in this area. If we are to recognize the great significance of meaning in people's lives, then we have to be able to tune in to what it is they are saying, what is really important to them, and what type of message they are trying to convey to us. It is very easy for stereotypical assumptions or other distortions to get in the way of that process happening smoothly and effectively. If we are not careful, we can discourage people from communicating with us and therefore disadvantage them and, in effect, disadvantage ourselves in the process, in so far as we then make our job a lot harder than it needs to be. Skills of communication are therefore very important in this area (Moss, 2008). It involves being able to develop a picture of what the situation means to the individual and then to identify how that fits with our own perspective. Where there is a significant consensus or overlap that gives us strong foundations on which to build; where there are conflicts or tensions, it provides us with an opportunity to use our conflict management skills to take matters forward constructively.

Also of major importance in relation to meaning making is the notion of crisis. As we noted in Chapter 3, a crisis is a turning point in somebody's life which means that they cannot continue as before. Things will either get better or they will get worse. If things do continue as they are then, by definition, it is not a crisis situation. Where a crisis does occur – for example, when somebody experiences a major loss or undergoes a traumatic experience – then our sense of normality (what the textbooks refer to as 'homeostasis') can be shattered, leaving us confused, insecure and unsure of how to proceed. It is at times like this that people will be looking for help and will be more interested in hearing what suggestions we may have about how to resolve the situation.

Crises, therefore, have to be handled very carefully because, on the one hand, there is excellent potential for making progress – crises will often free people up from whatever factors have been holding them back up to now. However, on the other hand, there is also great potential for a situation to be abused, in the sense that a crisis situation can be used to manipulate a person who is in a vulnerable place in a direction that may suit the worker, but will not necessarily suit the individual (see the discussion of the differences between influencing and manipulating in Chapter 7). Crisis, loss and trauma can therefore be seen as key factors in affecting our frameworks of meaning. Indeed, it is likely that even where a person is not in crisis at the moment, their current set of meanings or narrative will owe much to crises, losses and perhaps also traumas they will have encountered in their life to date, as such events can be very significant in a formative sense. This can be positive or negative. That is, from such occurrences we can take great strength and move forward (transformational grief or post-traumatic growth), but also we can be left weakened and in a less well-prepared frame of mind for dealing with the pressures and challenges we face. In order to appreciate more fully the significance of meaning and narrative, we therefore have to have a very good understanding of such issues as crisis, loss and trauma. See the *Guide to further learning* at the end of the book for guidance on developing your knowledge and understanding in this very important area.

Voice of experience 8.2

The thing I like most about working in this team is that we are called in to deal with people who are in crisis. It brings a lot of responsibility that we have to take seriously, but it also brings great potential for helping people to bring about real change in their lives. Until I came to work here, I didn't appreciate how significant crises are in people's lives, and how they really can change the way we see our lives.

Annette, a social worker in a crisis team

In relation to loss, grief and trauma, one important theory that has developed in recent years is what is known as meaning reconstruction theory (Neimeyer, 2001; Neimeyer and Anderson, 2002). The main idea behind it is that, when a person experiences a major loss (and that need not be through death, it can be any major transition in life), then he or she loses not only the person or thing that is important but also what that person or thing means to them. Grieving can therefore be seen as a process of meaning reconstruction, of going through the very painful steps of constructing a new framework of meaning because the old one, the one with which we are so familiar and secure, has been shattered by the loss experience. In most situations, people will be able to go through this, albeit painful and difficult, process unaided, or at least without the need for professional assistance. However, in some situations, people will experience difficulties to the extent that they need professional help. Where such help is based on meaning reconstruction theory, it involves helping the individual concerned to 'co-construct a more empowering narrative'. This is a term used to refer to the process by which an individual helper, whether social worker, psychologist, counsellor, nurse or other such professional helper, works closely with the grieving individual (or individuals) to move away from a painful dis-empowering narrative towards one that is about growth and moving forward as constructively as possible. Clearly, such activities are highly skilled and should not be entered into lightly, but they have excellent potential for making a positive difference to people's lives at a time when they need it very badly.

What this discussion should help us to realize is that there is a major danger in underestimating the significance of loss and trauma in people's lives. In social work, we encounter these very often although it is not always the case that people recognise what is happening as being connected with some sort of loss or trauma. Grief is often unrecognised in many social work situations. This is something that can lead to not only a failure to help but also making the situation significantly worse.

Practice focus 8.3

Jan was a social worker in a special care baby unit at a general hospital. She often dealt with grief issues as a result of a baby dying. She did not find the work easy, but she found it very rewarding and worthwhile, as her input often made a very positive difference. However, one day she realized there were aspects of grieving she had not been considering, In particular, in working with the Johnson family, she could see similarities between their reactions and the reactions of parents whose child had died – even though their daughter, Dawn, had survived. She was quite puzzled by this to begin with, but over time it became clear to her that Mr and Mrs Johnson were grieving for the non-disabled child they had been expecting. Dawn had spina bifida and therefore possibly a lower level of life expectancy, as well as other restrictions associated with the condition.

Jan found this quite a helpful insight and could appreciate the complexities involved. She realized that she would need to strike an important balance between acknowledging, and working with, their loss, on the one hand, and not falling into disablist assumptions about Dawn being in some way a disappointment, on the other.

Reflecting on the importance of these issues, Jan realized how dangerous and potentially destructive it could have been not to have recognized the significant role of grief in this family's circumstances.

Our stories can also be seen to be linked to self-image. How we see ourselves will depend in large part on the messages that we receive from others and how we interpret them. This will apply at both the micro and the macro level. That is, each individual will be influenced to a certain extent by how other people they know (on a one-to-one or small-group basis) seem to perceive them and relate to them (for example, with what degree of warmth). However, there is also the macro dimension to consider in terms of the fact that how people see us will be related to such wider structural factors as class, race, gender and so on. Our personal self-image, then, has to be seen to have a broader sociological dimension to it. If we ignore this, we fall into the trap of atomism mentioned earlier, and fail to do justice to the complexities of the situations in which we are involved. In terms of thinking about meanings, we therefore disadvantage ourselves by omitting a significant dimension of what makes people's lives meaningful. This has to be linked to power relations as well, because being assigned to a particular class or racial group, for example, is not a power-neutral activity. It will be seen as an advantage or a step up for some people, or a disadvantage or step down for others. Society is not a level playing field, and so where we are located within that society will have significant implications in terms of our power and life chances. It would be naive and, indeed, dangerous to fail to recognize this. Meaning, then, is highly personal in the sense that how I perceive my world and my part in it will have very strong personal and intimate implications for me, but individuals do not exist independently of the wider world, and so we have to recognize that self-image and other aspects of meaning are sociological as well as psychological – that is, they are psychosocial.

Reference was made earlier to the notion of spirituality. This is something that is often closely associated with religion, but the two terms are not necessarily connected. This is because it is possible to be religious without being spiritual and to be spiritual without being religious (Thompson, 2007b). Kellehear reinforces this point:

> there is no reason why spirituality need be necessarily and automatically connected to religion (Kellehear, 2000b), if by that term we speak about the meanings people construct to transcend their everyday sufferings. If humanist existentialism is not written off as a 'religion' there is no reason to expect that intellectual debates and research, or community or professional discussion of spiritual matters cannot be culturally inclusive of the religious and non-religious members of any community.

(2005, p. 113)

Spirituality is about finding meaning in our lives, developing a sense of connectedness to other people and to the wider world and understanding our place within it so that we can have a degree of security and a sense of being 'at home' in this world. Religion is also about meaning but, when it comes to religion, we are talking about structured and institutionalized systems of meaning, whereas spirituality implies that this is something that relates to each individual in his or her own way. This is not to say that spirituality is an atomistic issue that is not connected to the wider social sphere, but there is a focus on the spiritual needs and issues of individuals, whereas religion is at a much more macro level of understanding (large-scale national and international frameworks of meaning that have generally been codified in centuries of discourse – ancient scriptures as well as ongoing contemporary writings and other social practices that reinforce frameworks of meaning). Religion is very much about meaning but is closely tied to wider, cultural and political factors. Spirituality is not disconnected from these concerns, but it has a much stronger emphasis on biography – that is, those factors that while shaped by the social sphere are none the less unique to the individual concerned. A good social worker needs to be able to understand both sides of this coin, to be able to tune in to the wider social factors (the sociological domain) as well as what makes the experience unique to *this* particular individual, in *these* circumstances, at *this* point in time (the psychological dimension or 'biography').

What this means is that, for many people, their sense of spirituality will derive primarily, if not exclusively, from a formal religious institution. For others, their spirituality will be partly influenced by a religion, but they will perhaps have adapted aspects of this to suit themselves, rejecting some aspects of a religion's core beliefs while accepting others. A third group of people will have developed coherent value-based systems of meaning that have little or no connection with religion and are none the worse for this. A fourth group of people will be struggling with spirituality; they will be struggling to find any coherent thread of meaning in their lives and will perhaps have significant problems in terms of their well-being as a result of this. Social work can involve working with people from any of these four groups but, in my experience, it is often the fourth group that is quite significant. This may be because personal and social circumstances have conspired to produce a situation where the individual concerned has struggled to sustain any coherent sense of identity and a meaningful narrative. This could be as a result of such factors as social stigma and other aspects of people's circumstances that can be disempowering. These are important issues that, as social workers, we need to give careful consideration.

Voice of experience 8.3

I had never given much thought to meaning in people's lives and spirituality always seemed a very airy-fairy term to me. But I must admit that the narrative therapy course I went on changed all that. It made me realize that you are not going to get positive change in people's lives without considering what the issues *mean* to the individual concerned.

Mel, a social worker in a mental health team

Spirituality is also about 'connectedness'. This involves relationships, respect, power and, on a negative note, the potential for abuse. How we relate to other people can be positive, enhancing, enriching and, indeed, empowering, or it can be demeaning, degrading and oppressive – in effect, abusive. These are not just factors that are relevant to the individual circumstances in a direct and straightforward way, but may also have more indirect and subtle implications in terms of how they have shaped a person's understanding of the world and their attitudes towards it. This will include both their identity or biography and the narrative that connects them to wider social narratives or discourses. As Healy puts it: 'one's subjectivity is produced through discourses' (2000, p. 45).

A further aspect of spirituality that is important is having a sense of purpose or direction. Many people can find themselves temporarily, or on a longer-term basis in a situation where they feel that their lives have no sense of direction or focus. This can be very disconcerting and can lead to depression and other difficulties. Sometimes social workers can play an important role in helping people to address these issues. For example, the education role, discussed earlier, can be significant in helping people to get a sense of direction focus, purpose and meaning in their lives. Also of significance is Seligman's (1975) concept of 'learned helplessness'. This refers to the process by which an individual can internalize negative messages from social experiences which lead to a sense of hopelessness. The individual concerned, in effect, becomes conditioned to see life as hopeless and therefore learns how to feel helpless. This can be a significant barrier to working in partnership, as a client in a state of learned helplessness may be very reluctant to work in partnership and may simply want things done for them. That, then, also presents barriers in terms of empowerment. People cannot be empowered against their will, and so the challenge of learned helplessness is quite a significant one. It is therefore important for social workers to be aware of this aspect of the spiritual dimension of people's lives. If they have what could be seen as a spiritually empty life, then learned helplessness can be both a partial cause and effect of that. If we are not aware of the significance of learned helplessness, we can therefore miss important opportunities to move forward or waste a great deal of time trying to move forward in a way that is simply not going to be acceptable to the client and is therefore wasteful of time and resources, and an unnecessary intrusion into the life of the client concerned.

These comments show the significance of spirituality as not simply an individual dimension of the wider social phenomenon of religion. As we have seen, the intertwining of religion and spirituality is more complex than this. It is important to have an understanding of how religion has an impact on people's lives that may be an important part of our assessment in many cases. However, there is more to it than this, because even people who have no attachment or affiliation with a religion will none the less have spiritual issues to be considered. We run the risk of significant failure if we do not take account of such factors. When it comes to meaning making and narrative, then we are never far away from the subject of spirituality.

Practice focus 8.4

Donna had always associated spirituality with religion and had used the terms more or less interchangeably. Not being a religious person herself, she had not attached much significance to these issues. She could appreciate the need to take account of a person's religious beliefs and customs in carrying out an assessment and providing or commissioning services, but she had never given any consideration to the wider issues of a person's spiritual needs.

This came to the fore when her service area was subject to a quality assurance inspection. Overall, the inspection report was very positive. However, there were some criticisms made by the inspectors. One particularly important one was the relative neglect of spiritual aspects of service users' lives. It was felt that not enough attention was being given to how people's belief systems (whether religious or not) were of significance. It was clear from the report that it wasn't simply a matter of taking account of religious issues in general. This gave Donna considerable food for thought and, the more she thought about it, the more she realized that spirituality was a much broader concept than religion and was a very significant factor in people's lives. She decided that this was a topic she needed to read up on.

Conclusion

This chapter has explored a number of important issues relating to narrative and meaning making. It has not offered any simple solutions because that approach would fail to do justice to the complexities involved. What I have tried to do here is to paint a picture of the significant role of narrative and meaning making in people's lives in general and in social work practice in particular. It is to be hoped that this will have helped to provide a bedrock of understanding that future practice and learning will be able to build on.

See page 111	for some questions about what you have just read.
See page 227	for some pointers to useful further reading.

Conclusion to Part 2

Kellehear makes the important point that: 'There are few recipes for a good community development worker other than being a lateral thinker, problem-solver and communicator' (2005, p. 124). Much the same can be said of social workers in general, although I would want to emphasize the role of thinking skills in general, as well as the creativity of lateral thinking in particular.

It is to be hoped that Part 2 has shown just how important thinking skills, broadly defined, are in the day-to-day practice of social work. We have seen how practice needs to be:

- **Critically reflective** – successful in linking theory and practice and based on critical analysis.
- **Aware of its educational potential** – making full use of promoting learning as an important social work tool.
- **Emotionally tuned in** – sensitive to the feelings issues in the situations we deal with.
- **Sensitive to meaning and narrative** – able to take account of what situations mean to the individuals concerned and to be appropriately empathetic.

This sounds quite a tall order, but we have a strong tradition of good practice in this area and every opportunity to build on that tradition in the future.

Points to ponder

- Why is positivism not a sound basis for practising social work?
- What do you understand by the term 'mindful practice'?
- What is meant by the 'breadth and depth' of criticality?
- In what way does the comment, 'I'm too busy to do reflective practice' show a lack of understanding of reflective practice?

- What is meant by the idea of 'empowerment through learning'?
- Why is a 'banking mentality' to learning not helpful?

- How can the idea of 'power with' be used in social work practice?
- In what ways can conflict management skills be useful in social work?

- What do you understand by the term, 'emotional intelligence'?
- In what ways are emotions social?
- Name three skills involved in managing emotions.
- What part do emotions play in empowerment?

- What role do narratives play in people's lives?
- Why is it important to consider the role of meaning in social work?
- What do you understand by the term 'spirituality'?
- How is it relevant to social work?

Exercises

Think carefully about your approach to practice and ask yourself the following questions: How can you create opportunities for reflective practice? What obstacles might you encounter? What can you do to remove or circumvent them or to minimize their impact?

   Then, after you have done this, think carefully about what this tells you about possible ways of improving your practice.

Make a list of the ways you believe social work can be an educational process. For each of these, consider whether you have the knowledge and skills necessary to make best use of these opportunities. For any gaps you are able to identify in your knowledge and skills, think about what you need to do to fill those gaps as far as you reasonably can.

Make a list of as many emotions as you can. For each of these, ask yourself the following two questions:

- How might this emotion manifest itself in a social work context?
- How might you need to deal with this emotion as and when it arises (either in you or in other people)?

Having reflected on your answers to these two questions, think carefully about what lessons you might learn about emotional intelligence.

Consider the term, 'spirituality'. Do you think of yourself as a spiritual person? If so, in what way(s)? If not, why not? How might your ideas about spirituality affect your practice, especially when dealing with people who have a strong sense of spirituality (whether through religion or some other way)? Think carefully about what implications these issues may have for your practice.

3

The social worker as manager

3

Introduction to Part 3

Note that the title of this part of the book is 'The social worker *as* manager', and not 'Management skills for when you become a manager later in your career'. In other words, our focus here is on the management skills *practitioners* need. This is an important point to emphasize, as some practitioners have been known to make the mistake of trying to carry out their duties without developing the managerial skills needed – predictably with very disappointing results.

As with each of the other three parts of the book, Part 3 contains four chapters. Each of these focuses on a particular aspect of the repertoire of managements skills that practitioners need. The overall message is that good practice depends on being at least proficient in managing various things, including ourselves. Indeed, it could be argued that self-management is probably the most important aspect of management for the simple reason that if we do not get that right, we will be seriously undermining our efforts to get the other aspects of management right, and indeed our practice as a whole.

'Managing means taking responsibility.'

Managers need to be able to coordinate and plan, to make the best use of scarce resources, weigh up risk factors, motivate and influence people, negotiate effectively, deal with conflicts, use authority ethically and responsibly, and, of course to manage *themselves*: their time, their pressures and their feelings. But these are not limited to people who hold management positions in their organizations. If we think carefully about this, we should be able to recognize that every single one of these also applies to social work practitioners. Part 3, then, is not about preparing for a career in management. Rather, it is concerned with identifying those aspects of practising social work that have a managerial component to them and exploring what is involved in using these as a foundation for high-quality professional practice.

The four chapters

Chapter 9 lays the foundations for the other three chapters by discussing the importance of self-management, with a strong emphasis on self-care. This is because if we do not look after ourselves, we leave ourselves in a very weak position to look after the concerns and interests of others. We also put our own health and well-being at risk. This is therefore a very important chapter, with some important messages to take on board.

Chapter 10 is concerned with managing processes, tasks and outcomes. Processes are of central importance, as there are so many of these that go on in the complex dynamics of social work practice. If we are oblivious to these, we will miss out on what can be some crucial issues. Similarly, identifying what tasks need to be achieved and doing what we reasonably can to achieve them can be of significant benefit, while losing sight of these can be highly problematic. Finally, the question of outcomes is discussed. Having clarity about what we are trying to achieve (what agreed outcomes we are working towards) has long been established as an important part of good practice. However, there has been a recent surge of interest in this topic and it is now getting renewed emphasis.

Chapter 11 combines two important topics, risk and resources. Like outcomes, risk is a topic that has a long history of importance, but has received even more attention in recent years. Unfortunately, though, this additional emphasis has, to a large extent, produced a heightened level of anxiety that has proven counterproductive in some situations. What has also not helped has been a strong tendency to oversimplify risk issues (this is no doubt partly as a result of the increased levels of anxiety). This chapter therefore looks at why it is necessary to adopt a more balanced and sophisticated approach to risk.

Resources are also an important issue and closely related to the topic of risk, as it is often decisions about risk that influence how resources are deployed. Another important issue in relation to resource management is that we cannot realistically expect to have enough resources to meet everybody's needs. The challenge of dealing with a relative scarcity of resources is therefore an important part of social work. Risk and resources are therefore both significant issues that need to be managed wisely and carefully.

Chapter 12 also covers an important set of issues that need to be handled carefully, namely the management of expectations. Where people have unrealistic expectations the result can be considerable stress and strain. It is therefore essential that social workers are able to negotiate expectations effectively – that is, to give clear messages about what people can and cannot expect from them. Internalizing other people's unrealistic expectations can amount to setting ourselves up to fail. Learning how to manage expectations is therefore a topic worthy of close attention and careful consideration.

Links with the other parts of the book

Part 3 should cast a great deal of light on the issues discussed in Part 1. Being able to identify needs and associated problems and putting ourselves in a position to deal with them appropriately touches on many of the management issues to be discussed in this part of the book.

Part 2 was concerned with the thinking skills involved in high-quality social work. As we explore the management aspects of practice, we will be able to see that these too rely on using our intellectual capacities to understand the complexities involved. We would really struggle with the management challenges involved in practice if we did not have a basis of clear thinking, a grasp of emotional intelligence and an understanding of meaning and narrative to depend on.

Part 3 sets the scene for Part 4, where issues of professionalism are our concern. What management issues and professionalism have in common is a concern with *ownership* – recognizing that we are responsible for our actions and therefore making sure that they are based on sound understanding of the situations we are called upon to deal with.

Managing self

This is the first of four chapters that explore the significance of aspects of management in the repertoire of skills needed by social workers if we are to be successful in our efforts to promote well-being and social justice through problem solving and empowerment. In particular, we focus on what I shall be referring to as self-management – that is, those ways in which it is important that we are tuned in to how we are influencing situations and how those situations are influencing us. This is an important part of self-awareness, as we shall see below. A basic argument underpinning the chapter is that we will struggle to manage the complex, difficult and demanding situations we encounter if we are not doing a good job of managing ourselves.

We begin by looking at the importance of self-management and explore some key issues around why such factors are so critical in effective social work practice. This leads on to a discussion of the various ways in which we can rise to the challenge of self-management. This is intended to be a practical guide to the issues involved, but based on sound theoretical understanding.

The importance of self-management

The *Palgrave Companion to Social Work* (Thompson and Thompson, 2008b) is based on seven underlying principles, one of which is the importance of self-management. Self-management can be closely connected with the idea of self-awareness. As I have pointed out in one of my earlier works (Thompson, 2002a), there are two sides to self-awareness. There is that aspect which involves looking at what impact on the situation the individual is having. Am I aware, for example, of how other people are perceiving me and responding to me? The second side of self-awareness is to look at what impact the situation is having on me. We will not all feel comfortable in equal measure in all circumstances, and so we need to understand what circumstances will make us more or less comfortable so that we are better able to deal with them. Without this, we may find that we are in situations that make us feel very uncomfortable, and for which we are not prepared, or, at other times, we may become too comfortable and risk becoming complacent, with all the dangers that are associated with that.

Practice focus 9.1

Michelle was a social worker in a child protection team. She found the work demanding, but she could see how important it was, so she was highly committed to doing the best job she could. While this commitment was admirable, it also brought problems, in so far as it created a danger of Michelle overstretching herself by taking too much on, and thereby creating unrealistic expectations for herself. Unfortunately, this is precisely what happened. As time went on, she became increasingly stressed, but without realizing what was happening. She had become so engrossed in what she was doing, that she lost sight of her own needs and what was realistic for her. That is, her level of self-awareness had dropped to a dangerous level, and this was putting her health and well-being at risk.

Fortunately, her line manager was sufficiently tuned in to the risks of child protection work that he was able to recognize what was happening and to intervene positively. He did this by raising the subject in supervision and making Michelle aware of what was happening. This came as a complete surprise, but on reflection, she could see what had been happening. This process had helped her to understand the importance of self-awareness and the dangers of losing sight of this.

This can also be linked with emotional intelligence, as discussed in Chapter 7. A skilled worker with a good degree of emotional intelligence will be able to tune in to emotions in both directions – that is, will be able to answer the questions: What are my emotions in this situation? What are the emotions of the other significant people and how are they interacting? This is all part of self-management because if we are not able to recognize and deal with our own emotions and how these are interacting with other people's, then we will be ill-equipped to deal with the situation and may find that we are functioning at a far from optimal level in our professional role. We have to remember that we are part of the dynamic of the situations that we work in. We are not just neutral disengaged technicians, operating on people's problems; we become part of those problem scenarios in various ways and this will have an impact on the people we are trying to help and that, in turn, will have an impact on us. It is both naive and dangerous to fail to see the significance of this.

An important part of self-management is being able to identify our own vulnerability factors. What might trigger a particular problem for us? Are there any particular anxieties or concerns that we may struggle to deal with if they arise? Do we have any situations that have occurred in our lives before that have proven painful, that might open up old wounds in certain circumstances? These are the sort of questions we need to ask ourselves if we are going to be able to make best use of ourselves as a tool. Indeed traditionally, 'use of self' in social work has been recognized as a vitally important tool. As the passage from Hamer (2006) quoted in Chapter 3 makes clear, we neglect the role of self at our peril. Jordan (2007) also supports the importance of self as a social work tool.

Voice of experience 9.1

Social work used to be very individualistic in its focus, and got rightly criticized for not taking enough account of the social context. Then the tide changed and there was a major emphasis on the social issues, but somehow in all that we lost sight of this crucial idea of 'use of self'. I am so glad to see it making a comeback now.

Elaine, a social work tutor at a university

Another important part of self-management is making sure that, in recognizing that we are an important tool in our own right, we do not waste those valuable resources. This means that we need to look carefully at how we make the best use of our time and energy levels. This involves elements of self-care in the sense that, if we do not look after ourselves, we may become so worn down that we are of little value to other people. This is a point to which we shall return below.

It should be clear from this brief discussion that self-management is an important role for the social worker. We do not have to have the title of manager to be somebody concerned with managerial issues, and this is especially the case when it comes to managing ourselves. Social work, as we shall see in Part 4, is a professional undertaking. As such, it is not simply a matter of following orders from above. So, much of the time, we have to weigh up the situation and decide how best to proceed, based on a careful analysis of the circumstances that draws on our professional knowledge and listening carefully to the people we are serving. This same logic applies to use of self and therefore to self-management. We will not, in the majority of cases, receive instructions about how to conduct ourselves in various situations or how to manage our workloads. That is a challenge that we face with support from others (supervisors and colleagues, for example), but the ultimate responsibility for which lies with each of us individually. Such is the nature of a professional endeavour. Hamer captures this point well:

> You can survive as a front line professional in this demanding work. You can keep your spirit intact and function holistically and authentically, but the responsibility for that is yours. You need to look after your spirit and your emotions. Nobody will do it for you, nobody will even notice or care that you are not coping until it is too late. You have to take responsibility for these things yourself.

(2006, p. 52)

Rising to the challenge

There are various ways in which we can improve our skills and enhance our capabilities in terms of managing self. The following issues are by no means an exhaustive list but they should be sufficient to give plenty of food for thought and guidance on how to develop our self-management skills and the knowledge base on which such skills are premised.

The point we made earlier that self-care is a key part of effective social work; what it boils down to is that, if we do not look after ourselves, we are in no position to look after or support other people. We therefore need to be clear about our own needs and make sure that we do not allow ourselves to become overloaded with work. Assertiveness skills can be very valuable in this regard to prevent overload situations. Many managers are very supportive about such issues and fully appreciate that giving people more work than they can cope with is counterproductive. However, there may be times when this does not happen as it should and people find themselves in the situation where they are feeling strained. When such stress occurs, it can be very harmful, even in the short term, but where it persists over a long period, it can do considerable damage to our health and well-being. We therefore need to be clear about our own needs in this regard. We also have to understand that, as we saw in Chapter 6, social work is an emotional activity. We therefore have to be careful to ensure that we do not allow the highly charged emotional aspects of some parts of social work to lead us into a position where we are emotionally overloaded.

An important part of this is being able to maintain the distinction between empathy and sympathy. The latter refers to sharing feelings with people: feeling sad when they are feeling sad, and this is something that we cannot really afford in social work, as we would very quickly become overloaded. We have to be able to be sensitive to other people's feelings and suitably responsive and caring, but without actually taking those feelings on board ourselves, and this is what is meant by empathy – tuning in to other people's feelings and responding appropriately, but without necessarily sharing those feelings in any direct way.

Practice focus 9.2

Megan was a social worker in a children's hospice. She had previously worked in a family centre but wanted a new challenge. However, she hadn't realized how much of a challenge the job was going to be. This was because she found herself absorbing much of the grief she encountered on a daily basis – it was as if her work experiences were opening up old wounds from her own experiences of loss.

In her previous post she had encountered a great deal of upset and distress in the lives of the people she was supporting. However, she had managed to keep a certain distance between herself and these feelings because she had never experienced grinding poverty, stigma and social exclusion, abuse or domestic violence or the other factors that lay behind the situations she had been dealing with. But, when it came to grief, it was a different story, as she had experienced a number of significant losses in her life. In her previous job she had been able to work on the basis of empathy – to recognize people's feelings and deal with them sensitively and appropriately, but without being overwhelmed by them. In her current post, however, she was struggling to do this, and was therefore finding the emotional dimension of her work increasingly difficult to deal with. Fortunately, she had an experienced and supportive supervisor who recognized what was happening and was able and willing to help her deal with the emotional challenges she faced.

Part of this is making sure that we continue to gain job satisfaction from our work, that we do not allow the pressures to overwhelm us (hence the importance of being able to use the support available to us, as discussed above). This involves getting stuck in unthinking routines or 'tramlines' that do not involve creativity. As the discussion of reflective practice in Chapter 5 made clear, we need to stay alive to the complex issues and dynamics going on around us and not switch off. As Hamer argues: 'If our own creativity is stifled, then it becomes difficult to foster the creativity in others that encourages them to pursue the kinds of lives they hope to have' (2006, p. ix). That is, allowing ourselves to slip into non-creative, routinized approaches is disempowering both for ourselves and for the people we are seeking to help.

In addition, people often now have unrealistic expectations of social workers, partly because, as we shall see in more detail in Chapter 12, the general public and many professional colleagues tend to have little understanding of what social work is all about and where the social work role begins and ends. This can mean that we often find ourselves in situations where people have unrealistic and inappropriate expectations of us. If we are not well-equipped to deal with managing such expectations, we can find ourselves suffering a great deal as a result of the overload that comes from trying to fulfil the impossible. It is for this reason that we have a whole chapter dedicated to the idea of managing expectations (Chapter 12).

It has long been recognized that people who are under considerable pressure can become very hard on themselves. They often adopt a very harsh attitude towards their own situation and their part within it. If they were as hard on other people as they are on themselves, they would probably get quite a strong reaction. Where this occurs, it is important that we try and put a stop to it, as it can lead to a vicious circle in which being harsh in this way can undermine our confidence, increase feelings of negativity and then lead to feelings of demoralization that can in turn, in many situations, lead to burnout. Burnout is a situation where we have become emotionally exhausted and are functioning largely on automatic pilot. It is very dangerous, both for the person concerned and for the people he or she is trying to help.

Linked to this is the challenge of self-doubt. In situations where people are pressurized and often dealing with tensions and conflicts, sometimes with few, if any, examples of encouragement and reassurance to draw upon, they can begin to doubt themselves. Good supervision should challenge this and should help the worker to establish a more realistic and more positive self-image. However, it is unfortunately the case that not everybody in social work receives good-quality supervision. We should therefore be aware of this ourselves and try to fend off any temptation to slide into self-doubt, as this too can become a vicious circle in which the more we doubt ourselves, the less confident we become, leading in turn to actually achieving less – which can then have the effect of reinforcing the sense of self-doubt. We can then go on into a vicious circle of doubt and low confidence that, in effect, creates a tailspin, and we can become out of control in a spiral of negativity.

Voice of experience 9.2

There have been times when I have started to let self-doubt creep in, especially at times when things have been bothering me for some reason. But what always helps is when I think back to what my first practice teacher said to me: 'You can't expect other people to have confidence in you, if you don't have confidence in yourself.'

Dave, a social worker in a large voluntary organization

Social work is not for the fainthearted. There will be many challenges and many pressures, but this is not to say that the work is necessarily stressful. Stress occurs when people are overwhelmed by pressure, when the pressures have become so great or so intense that they do harm to health, well-being, social relations, quality of work and other important aspects of our lives. Social work, then, is not inevitably a stressful profession, but we have to be realistic and recognize that the potential for stress is ever present. A good social worker will therefore be tuned in to the self-management issues involved in managing pressure and thus preventing stress. See the *Guide to further learning* at the end of the book for guidance on the literature available to help in this regard.

For me, an important word in the social work vocabulary is that of humility. This means recognizing our limitations and not expecting too much of ourselves, and (in line with the discussions to come in Chapter 12) not allowing other people to have unrealistic expectations of us. Being humble about what social work can achieve is not about being negative, cynical or defeatist; it is about being realistic, recognizing that we can make a hugely positive difference to people's lives in many situations but, however positive and successful we can be, there will always be limitations to what we can do. It is surprising how many people fail to recognize this and become quite stressed and demoralized when they are not able to achieve everything they would like to. An important part of this is, as mentioned briefly above, assertiveness skills. These will help us to prevent work overload in two ways. First, if clients or carers are expecting too much of us or trying to pressurize us into doing inappropriate things, then our assertiveness skills can be an excellent way of preventing that from turning into a highly problematic situation. However, assertiveness can also be important when it comes to workload allocation, as some managers may be less sensitive than others when it comes to picking up on the problems associated with work overload. This is also closely linked with the question of workplace culture. Some cultures are fortunate enough to have a positive, supportive environment for people so that, if they are going through a period where, for whatever reason, they are finding life difficult and potentially stressful, they will gain the backing of their colleagues. However, in some workplace cultures, there is quite a macho attitude which can be summed up by the idea: if you don't like the heat, get out of the kitchen. I prefer to see situations in terms of: if we can't stand the heat, let's open a window (in other words, let's do something about it). It is still unfortunately the case that some managers fail to appreciate the significance of stress and work overload and become insensitive in giving too much work to their staff and thus adding to the problems, rather than playing a positive role in terms of dealing with them.

All this has much to do with time and workload management skills, involving such challenges as being able to manage priorities, remaining focused on task and not allowing ourselves to be distracted by red herrings, and so on. Part of this is not setting ourselves up to fail. It is not only others that can give us unrealistic expectations; sometimes we can give ourselves unrealistic goals to aim for, and thus set ourselves up to fail. A key part of time and workload management is therefore being able and willing to seek out and use support where necessary. It is dangerous to adopt a macho approach which is based on the misguided notion that we should be tough enough to cope with whatever comes our way. Anyone who adopts such an approach in social work is: (i) naive about just how powerful and potentially destructive some of the social work situations we encounter can be (in situations of abuse, for example); and (ii) is uninformed about how unhelpful such a 'tough guy' attitude is in dealing with complex and highly sensitive issues, as we so often do in social work.

Practice focus 9.3

Terry had been a social work assistant for several years before starting his social work degree. During this time he had carried a high caseload of relatively straightforward cases (the qualified social workers in the team dealt with the more complex cases). When he qualified he wanted to make a good impression on his team manager by making it clear to her that he was able to and willing to carry a high caseload. Unfortunately, his team manager took this at face value and, when he asked for more cases, she gave them to him. This had the effect of reinforcing his desire to impress, to show how he could cope with a high volume of work. However, Terry soon found himself in considerable difficulty, as he was finding his caseload as a qualified worker much more demanding than what he had been used to as a social work assistant. He was struggling to cope, but a combination of his pride and his continuing desire to impress meant that he did not feel able to ask for help from his manager, or indeed from anyone. He therefore found that he had to cut corners with his work, just to get through the demands being made on him. This was a dangerous strategy and put him in a very invidious position. But this was the only way he could think of to deal with the otherwise unmanageable situation he had created for himself.

While some people are not fortunate enough to have good supervision, many are. Where we are fortunate in this regard, we should seek to maximize the potential of supervision, to use it very constructively for help with workload management, for planning and guidance, and for drawing out the learning from our experience. It is also an important source of support about whatever issues may be affecting the quality of our work. For those who do not routinely receive good-quality supervision, then there is a challenge here in terms of trying to find that elsewhere, or at least, trying to influence one's supervisor in a positive direction – for example, by specifically asking for support and help with learning in relation to specific issues.

Underpinning the effective use of supervision is an openness to learning. This in itself is a central part of self-management because, if we adopt a closed mind, an approach based on the idea that 'there is little or nothing I can learn now', then we are heading for a fall. Such arrogance has no place in social work, although, unfortunately, there are still some people who continue to have the naive notion that, after a few years of practice, there is nothing further they can learn. If no learning takes place, it is not because of the lack of opportunities, but because of the failure to capitalize on those opportunities. That is a central part of managing self, making sure that the self is one that is constantly growing and learning all the time and has not become stuck in a rut.

It is interesting to see the different responses I get on the training courses I run. Some people take every opportunity to learn – they get fully engaged in discussions, they make the links with practice and identify how they will put the learning into practice. Other people seem to think that they will learn simply by being in the room and don't make much effort. They don't see learning as an active process that they are responsible for – despite what I might say at various points during the day!

Sanjay, a training and development officer in a local authority

An important part of this is being prepared to listen to self-care feedback. What this means basically is being able to tune in to what is happening in our lives. For example, what is our current bodily state? Is our body telling us that we are pushing it too far? Are we constantly tired? Are we worn out by nervous exhaustion because we are not relaxing enough? Are other people expressing concern about how we are looking or how we are coming across to them through our behaviour? These telltale signs can be very important and need to be taken seriously. Self-management involves being able to identify such key messages and being prepared to respond to them as and when required, rather than naively pushing on in the hope that things will resolve themselves in due course. That can do a lot of harm, in so far as it can leave us ill-equipped when it comes to dealing with the challenges we are likely to face.

One particular tool or technique that can be very useful in terms of many of the issues described here is what is known as compartmentalization. This means being able to draw a line between pressures at work and pressures outside of our work domain. The worst-case scenario is when somebody is at work and worrying about home-based concerns, but not able to do anything about them (precisely because he or she is at work), while, at another time, being at home and worrying about work issues. Compartmentalization involves being able to identify clear boundaries between home life and working life and not allowing the two to intrude upon one another. If we do have concerns both at home and at work, these are much better managed by being kept separate so that, when we are at home and in the best position to deal with home-related concerns, then home-based problems should be our primary focus. By the same token, when we are at work, we should be focusing on work concerns and, as far as we reasonably can, leaving our home concerns for later. It has to be recognized that this is more easily said than done, but the effort that needs to be put into developing work habits that allow this clear separation between the two domains of home and work is very positive in terms of the potentially excellent results that can arise. This is all an important part of what is known these days as work-life balance – that is, the ability to be able to balance work pressures and other life

3

pressures without feeling that we are between a rock and a hard place. It can be difficult to engage with this to begin with, but the efforts are well worth it in terms of the very positive results that can arise. This is a central part of that crucial process of self-management.

Practice focus 9.4

Sue was a social worker in a child and adolescent mental health team. The work could be quite challenging at times, but nothing she couldn't normally cope with. However, the situation changed drastically when, at around about the same time, her father died, leaving her 77-year-old mother struggling to cope, and her very supportive line manager left to take up another post, leaving the team leaderless until a new manager could be appointed – a process that was likely to take months.

Either of these significant changes would have been difficult enough to deal with on its own, but in combination they presented an enormous challenge. Sue was really feeling the pressure both at home in her private life and at work. She worried that the situation would be too much for her to cope with and knew that she would need to be on her mettle if she was to get through this difficult time unscathed. She realized that the only way she was going to be able to do this would be to 'compartmentalize' her pressures – that is, to focus on work issues while at work, and focus on home and family issues while at home. She knew this wouldn't be easy, but she couldn't think of a better way of handling the immense pressures she felt.

Conclusion

There can be no social work without social workers, and no social worker can be effective without making sure that we are in tune with our own needs, our own circumstances and how these are playing a part in the situation. This chapter has explored some of the complexities involved in this and has shown that there is much more for us to learn. There are no simple answers to the challenges of self-management, but it is to be hoped that the discussions in this chapter will have laid a foundation on which we can build. Some of the discussions of management issues in the remaining chapters of Part 3 may cast some light on some aspects of this but, overall, what it comes down to is that, while social work is in so many ways a collective endeavour, each of us as an individual has responsibilities to make sure that we are not overstretching ourselves. This involves ensuring that we are managing ourselves in ways that are not wasteful of energy and precious resources, nor dangerous to ourselves or others. If we can keep in mind this important principle of self-management, we will be in a much stronger position than those who occasionally allow themselves to lose sight of the significance of managing oneself.

Self-management can be quite a daunting challenge, especially in the early stages of a social work career, where we are still finding our feet and building up our confidence, as well as our knowledge base and skills. However, we should not allow the challenges involved to overwhelm us. Taking the time and investing the energy and commitment needed to develop our self-management skills is certainly a positive step that should pay dividends in the short term and especially in the longer term, as you will be developing ways of working that are important foundations of effective practice and you will be avoiding some of the many problems that arise when people lack self-management skills or neglect to put them into practice. In the next chapter we shall explore some of the key issues relating to managing processes, tasks and outcomes – fundamental parts of the social work role. Without the benefits of confident and effective self-management we will make the effective handling of processes, tasks and outcomes much more difficult, if not impossible. It is therefore to be hoped that the guidance offered in this chapter will stand you in good stead in tackling the issues we shall be discussing next.

See page 166   for some questions about what you have just read.

See page 227   for some pointers to useful further reading.

3

10

Managing processes, tasks and outcomes

Introduction

Being an effective social worker involves having an overview of the various processes and tasks that are needed and linking these to clear outcomes. This chapter is therefore concerned with what is involved in this aspect of the social work role. The chapter is divided into three main sections. In the first, we explore what is involved in managing processes, and there is a discussion within this of the various types of processes and how they interrelate. The second section relates to managing tasks, and here there is a discussion of the significance of having a clear focus on what tasks are needed in a given set of circumstances, how these relate to the overall process and the desired outcomes we are working towards. The third section relates to managing outcomes. This is a discussion of how to keep a clear focus on what goals we are aiming for.

It is important to stress from the beginning that we need to have a clear picture of these three elements: processes, tasks and outcomes, as there has been over the years, considerable confusion about each of these and how they relate to one another. For example, some people create a false dichotomy between processes and tasks, as if it were a case of process versus task. This dichotomy is unhelpful, as the reality is that it is not a case of *either* process *or* task, but rather of *both*, and how each of these is related to the desired outcomes that we are working towards. Therefore, when people say things like: 'I'm not a task person, I'm a process person' (or vice versa) they are sadly missing the point.

Managing processes

The point was made in Chapter 6 that being professional does not mean being unfeeling, but it does involve a degree of keeping our feelings under control. It is about being both compassionate and dispassionate. The two are not mutually exclusive, except at a very superficial level. One of the important processes involved in social work, therefore, is keeping a balance between head and heart, thoughts and feelings (as discussed in Chapter 7).

Social work is premised on person-to-person encounters, and so the interpersonal processes involved are highly significant. In particular, interaction skills are very important. Being able to relate to other people, put them at their ease, treat them with respect, manage conflict constructively, and so on, are all essential parts of managing interpersonal processes in an ethical and constructive way. There has been much written and talked about in relation to skills in social work, but the fact remains that being able to manage the processes involved in dealing with other people is at the heart of what we do. In some circumstances, social workers can become so overburdened with work and under so much pressure that they can sink into a mechanistic form of working and forget about the basics of social work as a human endeavour. It is therefore worthwhile for even very experienced social workers to revisit their core skills from time-to-time and remind themselves about how much of a role effective interpersonal skills play in determining the success or otherwise of our efforts to help.

Such efforts need to be part of what is known as 'the helping process'. This is described quite fully in Thompson and Thompson (2008b), and so I shall not go into great detail here. I shall simply emphasize that our work needs to be structured in a way that has clear beginnings, middles and endings, and that we should seek to learn from these processes at all times. Adopting a very unstructured approach without any clarity about where we are up to in our role is not likely to be helpful. See the discussion below on systematic practice, the benefits of being clear and focused, as opposed to the significant difficulties associated with being unfocused and lacking clarity.

There are also processes of learning that need to be managed. This includes learning from mistakes, so that we are wise enough not to repeat them in future. We have to be open enough to recognize that we will make mistakes from time to time – they are inevitable – but the important point is that we need to learn from these, while also trying to keep such mistakes to a minimum. But, of course, learning from them will help to make sure that there are fewer mistakes in future.

Practice focus 10.1

Terry tried valiantly to conceal the fact that he had taken on too many cases. He did not want to lose face in having to admit that he had mishandled the situation, nor did he want to be seen to be 'not coping'. However, as time went on, it became increasingly apparent to Vicky, his line manager, that he was struggling with the number and complexity of cases. She therefore decided to raise this in supervision with Terry.

To begin with he denied that there was a problem, but Vicky had done her homework and had enough examples to hand of situations that were not working out. She handled the situation very well, achieving the right balance of firmness and support. Terry was embarrassed to have to admit that she was right, but he was very pleasantly surprised at how helpful Vicky was in trying to draw out the lessons that could be learned from what had happened. He was expecting to be ridiculed and made to feel small, which had been his experience of being criticized in the past.

After the supervision session, Terry felt so much better. He could see the mistakes he had made and how much more positive it was to try and learn from them, rather than try and cover them up. The fact that Vicky had admitted she made a mistake in allowing him to take on so many cases in the first place also helped – a case of leading by example.

But, getting it wrong is not the only source of learning opportunities; getting it right can also be a very rich source of learning. What was it we did well? What strengths can we build on in future? Even though we did well, is there any way in which we could have done better so that we can improve our performance even more? These are all important questions. Supervision can be very helpful in this regard, but that does not alter the fact that the responsibility for learning rests primarily with each of us individually. We should therefore be keen to make sure that we learn as much from our experience as we can. This links in with the discussion of reflective practice in Chapter 5.

But there is not only our own learning to consider. We have seen in Chapter 6 how social workers have an important role to play as educational facilitators in terms of trying to benefit from the principle of empowerment through learning. Many people that we encounter in a social work context will have had many negative strokes – that is, they will have had lots of negative messages (as opposed to the positive strokes of encouragement, support and nurturance). Where people have had a history of predominantly negative strokes (in other words they have been put down, demeaned and/or demoralized), then there may be a strong element of 'unlearning' that they need to do if they are to be able to maximize the potential of their lives. That is, part of our role will often be to make efforts to help people move away from negative self-defeating ideas about themselves, to learn a more balanced approach which takes account of strengths as well as any weaknesses or areas for development. This can be tough work, as so many people (for example, as a result of abuse and similar difficulties) will have internalized very negative images of themselves. These took a long time to build up and they can take a long time to break down. In many cases we will not have the time or resources to be able to carry through the long-term work needed to do this but, in some cases – many in fact – we will have the opportunity to make at least a significant positive inroad in terms of trying to promote a more balanced understanding of self that contains a significant positive element.

There are also processes relating to ourselves as workers that we need to take into consideration. One in particular is that of self-disempowerment. What can easily occur, if we are not careful, is that a vicious circle develops in which being dissatisfied with the circumstances we face, perhaps because our expectations are unrealistic (see the discussion of humility in Chapter 9), can lead to a lowering of morale, in some circumstances going so far as to create a mindset of defeatism and cynicism. If enough people in a team or work group have this negative mindset, it can become a culture of defeatism and cynicism, leading to burnout for many members of that team, if not all of them. This can lead to further feelings of dissatisfaction and thus even lower morale, resulting in a significant degree of self-disempowerment. Instead of workers being able to pull together to try and tackle whatever problems and dissatisfactions they have, they allow themselves to fall into such a vicious circle of negativity that is of no help to anybody. Although managers have an important part to play in terms of preventing and dealing with such circumstances when they arise, there is also an element of individual responsibility here in terms of self-management. There is a great irony that, although social workers are in many ways professional problem solvers, it is often the case that, when we have problems to face of our own, we do not practise what we teach, and that we do not always develop problem-solving strategies but, rather, slide into unhelpful processes of moaning and complaining that do not take us forward in a positive direction. Instead, such negative processes hold us back and often have the effect of making situations worse.

Voice of experience 10.1

I've always thought it's amazing that social workers can be so good at addressing other people's problems, and yet they so often don't apply the same logic to themselves or their own problems. They would be keen to prevent families from simply giving up on their problems and becoming defeatist, and yet when it comes to dealing with organizational problems, that's exactly what so many people do. It's like a form of learned helplessness.

Brid, a team manager in a local authority

Managing tasks

An important part of the assessment role in social work is establishing what needs to be done. Some people unfortunately have a simplistic understanding of assessment as being primarily a process of gathering information and little else. The information that someone obtains is, of course, of great importance in terms of forming a picture, but what is also an essential part of that picture is working out in partnership what steps need to be taken, what needs to be done, to address the unmet needs identified and to address the associated problems (see Chapter 1). A good assessment should therefore identify tasks that need to be achieved in order to ensure progress is made.

One approach that places such tasks at the heart of the endeavour is what is referred to as task-centred practice (Marsh and Doel, 2005). This is a specific approach that involves identifying the current situation and what is problematic about it; next identifying what situation we would like to be in; and then developing an understanding of the tasks that need to be achieved to move from the unsatisfactory present situation to the desired future situation. For example, if we are talking about an abuse situation, then we would perhaps want to move from a situation in which there is an unacceptably high risk of abuse at the moment to a future situation where the level of risk has either been removed substantially or at least reduced to a level that is acceptable (as we shall see in Chapter 12, there is no such thing as a risk-free situation). The tasks that will achieve this are then identified as part of a protection plan. Focusing on these tasks is very important in terms of: (i) establishing a clear plan that will be a source of motivation for both worker and client; and (ii) providing a relatively easy means of monitoring progress and deciding whether or not the assessment needs to change as new information comes to light and the situation unfolds further. However, even if workers do not explicitly adopt this as a practice modality, all social work intervention involves tasks of some description, in the sense that demands are being made on us and, in turn, we may be making demands on clients in terms of what we are asking them to do in order to help resolve their problems. There may be tasks that clients need to accomplish in order to progress. For example, a person with mental health problems who has become socially isolated may need to take steps that involve making connections with other people. The worker may be very helpful in supporting this person in doing so, but it is a task that cannot be done *for* the person concerned.

A common misunderstanding of task aspects of social work is that the term 'tasks' refers specifically to so-called 'practical' tasks. However, it is not as simple as that, as the tasks that are involved may include, for example, addressing emotional issues. It is therefore a significant mistake to assume that tasks in a social work context mean basic, straightforward practicalities. That is a gross distortion of a much more complex reality.

Practice focus 10.2

Fiona was a hard-working social work student who was keen to learn, both at the university and while out on placement. On her first placement she was lucky enough to have a very experienced and helpful practice teacher. One day she was allocated the case of a family who were experiencing a number of conflicts and tensions. Her practice teacher asked her if she was familiar with task-centred practice and when she said yes, it was suggested that it might be a good approach to adopt in this case.

Fiona took up this suggestion and set about working with the family in a task-centred way. However, she adopted a very superficial approach to this and concentrated only on practical tasks. This had the effect of confusing the family up to a point, as they weren't sure what she was doing and why she was doing it. But they went along with her suggestions, even though they couldn't see what the point was.

Fiona recognized that things were not working out, and so she raised the issue with her practice teacher. What quickly became apparent was that Fiona hadn't fully grasped what is involved in task-centred practice and had been using a very watered-down version of the method. On her practice teacher's advice she read up on this approach and realized that there was much more to it than simply sorting out practical problems.

In Chapter 9, we discussed the importance of workload management and making sure that we do not allow ourselves to become overloaded and therefore become counterproductive in our efforts to make positive changes. Part of this can be identifying the tasks that we need to do within our workload, prioritizing them and making sure, as far as we reasonably can, that we are not taking on too many tasks or tasks that are too difficult for us at our current stage of development, or which may require support or resources that we do not currently have access to. Managing tasks therefore involves understanding priorities and taking the necessary steps to keep our morale and energy levels as high as we reasonably can, in the sense that it has been established that workload pressures can sap people's morale and energy, thereby leaving them less well equipped to deal with those pressures (in turn leading to a vicious circle). Everybody has the same amount of time, 24 hours in a day, 7 days a week, but how much we achieve within that time will be partly down to our skills in managing our tasks and also just as importantly, our skills in managing our energy levels to make sure that we do not allow ourselves to become burnt out. This again links back to the discussion of self-management in Chapter 9.

Whether we are talking about tasks in relation to working directly with clients or other tasks that we face as social workers (in terms of recording and administration, for example) one thing that can be extremely helpful is being well organized. This will include, for example, having systems for information management. It is amazing how much time (and energy and therefore morale) can be wasted by spending ages looking for an important piece of information that could have been accessed much more quickly if we had set up a proper system of information management in the first place.

Voice of experience 10.2

At the beginning of my degree course one of the tutors emphasized the importance of having a good filing system. I took that to heart and it has stood me in good stead. I've seen other people, though, who are all over the place and totally chaotic, drowning in bits of paper and wasting a lot of time and effort trying to cope with the mess. I'm so glad I learned that lesson at an early stage in my career.

Danielle, a social worker in an initial assessment team

Priorities are an important part of workload management tasks, but how do we decide on priorities? How do we review them in a shifting landscape of problems and issues? This is something that develops with experience, a sensitivity to working out what is important enough that it has to take precedence over other things, and what is relatively less important and can therefore take its place in the queue. A common mistake in this regard is for people to confuse urgency and importance. What can easily happen is that important tasks actually fall to a lower level in the priority order because something urgent, but less important, takes over. This can become such an issue for some people that the term 'urgency addiction' has been coined. This refers to people who are always keen to rush about and do things that need doing sooner rather than later, but these are not necessarily the most important things. We then get another vicious circle which develops, in the sense that, if people do not prioritize the important things and leave those till later, they then become urgent, and so the whole situation becomes much more difficult to manage. Part 2 of the book was devoted to exploring issues about the social worker as thinker. This is another example of how significant being a thinker is in social work practice. We need to have a clear understanding of these complex issues and not allow ourselves to slip into bad habits whereby we end up running around in a very unfocused way because we have failed to manage our priorities and tasks effectively at an earlier stage.

The other side of the coin to managing tasks is the challenge of maintaining the energy and morale we need to keep us going through. This raises the question of job satisfaction. What is it that gives us job satisfaction? What are the factors that make us pleased, satisfied and relatively happy with our work? There must be some, otherwise we would not continue to do them, and it is to be hoped that we are able to focus clearly enough and be realistic and appreciative enough to recognize the very many positives of the work we do. Social work is not an easy option; it is an undertaking characterized by challenge. We therefore have to be realistic and not expect to have major success in everything we do. By definition, we are doing difficult things in difficult circumstances. If the circumstances were not difficult, people would not need a social worker.

We therefore have to hold on to a clear view of the fact that our job is about making the best of bad situations. Even though we may not be able to achieve all that we want to, there is still much satisfaction to be gained from making a positive difference, however small that may be, compared with the overall scheme of things. This is another aspect of humility.

Beckett uses the term 'realism' in a similar sense to how I am using humility. He comments that:

> Part of the duty of realism is recognising the constraints that social workers operate under in terms of time, material resources, knowledge, skills, training and support. If you are provided with inadequate resources to do your job you can and should challenge this – realism is *not* about accepting things as they are without complaint: it is about refusing to pretend that things are better (or worse) than they actually are – but the fact remains that it is irresponsible to go ahead with a plan of action if the resources at your disposal mean that it will be impossible to carry the plan through, just as it would be irresponsible (for instance) for a doctor to carry out a surgical procedure if she lacked the appropriate equipment or expertise.
>
> (2006, p. 27)

Another important set of factors to consider in relation to morale and motivation are the 'drag' factors, as they are sometimes called – that is, those aspects of our working lives that may de-motivate us and hold us back. There are clear links here with self-awareness in terms of understanding what the aspects of our job are that have a positive effect and what the aspects are that have a negative and potentially demoralizing effect. We can ask ourselves the important question: how can we maximize the positives and minimize the negatives? Keeping a clear focus on this and helping one another to do so can be an important part of laying the foundations for high-quality social work practice.

The need for clarity about the tasks we are engaged in or charged with brings us to the important question of systematic practice. This is an approach that is closely linked with the idea of managing outcomes, and so it is to that topic that we now turn.

Managing outcomes

Systematic practice is a long-established practice modality. However, what is relatively new in social work is the terminology of 'outcome-focused practice'. There is a great irony here, in so far as outcome-focused practice can in some ways be seen as old wine in new bottles. However, the terminology is not the real issue. What is of particular significance in reality is that there are clear dangers in adopting an unsystematic, unfocused approach, as opposed to the benefits of systematic practice. These issues are discussed in some detail in

Thompson and Thompson (20008b), and so I am not going to repeat them here. However, it is worth identifying the strengths of the systematic approach as opposed to the clear problems identified with an unsystematic, vague or unfocused approach – see Table 10.1.

Table 10.1 Systematic versus unsystematic practice	
Systematic	**Unsystematic**
Focused	Unfocused, vague
Clear	Unclear, confusing
Avoids drift	Encourages drift
Helpful in terms of accountability	Unhelpful in terms of accountability
Motivating	Demotivating, demoralizing
Promotes confidence	Undermines confidence
Aids recording	Provides no sound basis for recording
Aids reflective practice	Inhibits reflective practice
Aids empowering and anti-discriminatory practice	Blocks empowerment and anti-discriminatory practice
Discourages dependency	Promotes dependency
Promotes learning	Blocks learning
Gives clarity about when to end our intervention	Provides no guidance about ending our intervention
Gives opportunities for celebrating success	Denies opportunities for celebrating success
Transparent	Lacking in transparency
People know where they stand = less anxiety	People don't know where they stand = source of anxiety
Provides a sound basis for confidence and empowerment	Does not provide a basis for confidence and empowerment – can be disempowering and erosive of confidence

Practice focus 10.3

Al first came across systematic practice on a training course he attended. Straight away it struck him as a potentially very useful way of making sure his work was clear and focused. He could see how it would help to prevent him drifting away from what he was supposed to be doing – something he was prone to do, especially when he was busy or tired. He gave it a try with a few of his cases and found it very helpful. This prompted him to raise it as an issue in supervision. His line manager was also quite impressed with the approach and suggested that Al do a short presentation on it at the next team meeting. He wasn't keen on this, as he wasn't very confident in doing public speaking. However, he decided it would be worth it to get the message across.

On the day of the team meeting, Al was nervous, but none the less, did a very good job of it. One member of the team made an interesting comment when she said that she too had come across the idea on a training course and had thought it would be useful – but it was only now that she realized that she had never actually put it into practice. Al responded that perhaps team members should support each other in using the approach – a suggestion the team manager fully welcomed.

Focusing on outcomes in a systematic way includes a range of important skills. These include the following:

> **Keeping a clear focus.** This charges us with the responsibility of thinking clearly and not allowing the complexities to confuse or distract us. A central part of social work is wrestling with complex and difficult situations; that is the nature of the work. It is understandable, then, that some people may lose the plot, become unfocused and cease thinking clearly. However, this is a temptation that we should strongly resist, as the value of thinking clearly is immense.

> **Effective communication.** It seems that in social work we are never far away from the importance of effective communication. What is particularly important in relation to managing outcomes is the significance of what we earlier referred to as 'tuning in'. This means being able to listen carefully enough in a focused way to become sensitive to what the key issues are for the person or persons we are trying to help and for other stakeholders in the situation. If we are not sensitive enough to pick up on these issues, then we will struggle to work in a way that is based on clear outcomes.

> **Negotiation skills.** Being able to work in an assertive (rather than aggressive or submissive) way is an important part of social work. There may be conflicts involved in identifying what outcomes are necessary, because what one person regards as a desirable outcome, another person may not. We therefore have to use our skills to be able to negotiate a clear way forward that all parties are reasonably happy with. This may not be an easy or quick process, but it is a vitally important one as, without this, it is unlikely that partnership will work and, without partnership, the chances of success are generally very limited.

> **Setting out our stall.** We shall revisit this theme in more detail in Chapter 12, but for now it is important to note that we need to be clear

in communicating what we can and cannot do, what is and what is not our role. Without this, we can be dragged in all directions and open to all sorts of pressures to do things that are not appropriate and not the best use of our limited time and resources.

This is quite a significant range of skills but, with practice over time and with further study and learning, we can become quite expert in using these skills very effectively, with the result that we are able to help our clients much more than we would do if we did not have the ability to work in such a clear and focused way.

Voice of experience 10.3

I don't take any pride in saying that, when I first qualified as a social worker, I was very unfocused in my work. What shook me out of it was my first appraisal which identified a need for clarity and focus in how I went about my business. It was even suggested that I might fail my probationary period if I remained so slack. I can tell you that that made a big impact – it really made me sit up and take notice.

Kim, a social worker in a looked-after children team

The question of outcomes is one that many people associate with evidence-based practice. This is a term that has grown in popularity over the years. The basic idea behind it is that we should base our practice on the best available evidence. There have been two main schools of thought or two approaches in relation to evidence-based practice. The first, what I refer to as the strong version, placed very great emphasis on the use of scientific research as an underpinning for practice and raised all sorts of complex issues about the appropriateness of a positivistic approach to social work. Space does not allow for a detailed exploration of this, but it is possible to state that there are concerns about what can be called 'scientism' creeping into social work. McDonald uses the related term of 'positivism':

> Essentially, evidence-based practice proposes that social work intervention knowledge should be developed through the application of (for the most part) positivist research methods and that social work practice, particularly the decisions that social workers make in the conduct of case intervention, should be based on the best available evidence.

(2006, p. 156)

However, a less extreme version of evidence-based practice, what I shall refer to as the weak version, has since emerged. This does not seek to put all the eggs in the positivistic research basket, but does recognize the importance of having evidence to underpin our work as far as reasonably possible. However, it is not only research evidence that is included under this heading. There is also evidence from the wealth of practice experience that has grown up over decades and, just as importantly, there is the evidence that comes from taking on board the perspectives of clients and carers (Shaping Our Lives National User Network, 2003). What is now beginning to emerge, then, is an approach that seeks to find a balance between an unrealistic, distorting positivism at one extreme, which is clearly not applicable to social work and, at the other equally unhelpful extreme, work based on pure guesswork or random activities that have no basis in any sort of professional rationale or justification based on a clear knowledge base. In between those two, we have what we described in Chapter 5 as reflective practice, or more specifically, critically reflective practice. This helps us to understand that it is important to be clear about what informs our practice. If we are not, then we are much less likely to achieve the outcomes that we are working towards.

Social work can be seen as a craft, in the sense that it is a balance of science and artistry. Science is characterized by logical, structured approaches that have some benefit, but should not be applied rigidly or dogmatically, or in ways that fail to take account of the wider picture. Art, by contrast, can be characterized by free expression, a lack of rules and boundaries and this is what can make art both exciting and emotionally satisfying, being able to transcend boundaries and creatively explore new understandings of our reality. Social work cannot afford to be purely artistic in this sense, as we are dealing with very serious issues that relate to people's well-being. However, a craft can be understood as a balance between the benefits of the scientific understanding plus a degree of the artistry involved in what a craftsperson does to produce a satisfying product. A craftsperson has to follow some rules and direction about what they are trying to produce. For example, if somebody places an order for a particular form of pottery, then there will be a degree of science that goes into the production of the finished product, and there will be a degree of artistic creativity, but the potter will not be allowed free rein in their artistry if they want to be paid by the person who commissioned their endeavours. Nor would they be successful if they tried to stick purely to the science without bringing in any element of creativity to what they do. For me, social work is therefore a craft, a blend of so-called science and art but, what makes it a craft, rather than a pure art, is that there is a focus on clear outcomes that we are working towards, rather than a purely creative artistic movement that could take us in a direction that is out of touch with where the person we are trying to help needs to get to.

 Practice focus 10.4

Curtis was a social worker in a team for children with learning disabilities. He had no major difficulties with the work, but he was not the most confident of people. He was therefore reluctant to try out new ideas or approaches, and so he tended to be quite unimaginative in how he tackled the situations he came across in his work. What he also tended to do quite a lot was to go to his line manager and say: 'What do you think I should do now?' His line manager was not very helpful in this, as he would give Curtis a lot of specific guidance about what he should do, rather than encourage him to be more imaginative and reflective in his approach. However, the situation was to change quite drastically when his team manager left and was replaced by a woman who adopted a different approach to supervision. She was much more challenging. When Curtis asked for specific advice on what to do, she turned it back on him by asking: 'What do you think you should do?' She encouraged him to weigh up the options and to take more responsibility for his own work. She emphasized that social work is a craft and that he needed to develop his skills more, rather than expect someone else to provide the 'answers'. He wasn't comfortable with this at first, but after a while, he could see that his previous supervisor had not been doing him any favours and had actually held back his development.

At root, systematic, outcome-focused approaches are about making sure we are clear about the *purpose* of our actions and plans. Hamer makes apt comment when he elegantly points out that:

> When you visit a client's home you need to be clear about your reason for being there. If you have no clear purpose in that client's home then you are just more mud on their carpet.

(2006, p. 13)

He also offers interesting food for thought when he argues that:

> On every visit you need to have a clear sense of purpose and direction.

> > Many people complain that they have broken down through overwork. In the majority of such cases the breakdown is more frequently the result of foolishly wasted energy. If you would secure health you must learn to work without friction.

> > James Allen

> Friction comes from fear borne of unnecessary pressure and lack of clarity. When you can work without applying pressure, when you can remain calm and clear about your tasks, then the whole job becomes much easier for you and for them.

(Hamer, 2006, p. 11)

This is a helpful passage, in so far as it links in with other important themes discussed in this book, namely:

> ▷ **The importance of self-management.** To prevent the detrimental effects of work overload we need to have well-developed self-manage-ment skills, including assertiveness.

◦ **The value of conflict management skills.** Clarity and focus can help: (i) to prevent conflicts; and (ii) deal with them when they do arise.
◦ **The need for effective time and workload management.** We have to be careful that we do not allow our energies to be wasted by practising in unfocused ways.

Conclusion   Managing means taking responsibility. To manage processes, tasks and outcomes therefore involves taking responsibility for a proactive approach to these issues; not sitting back and waiting for things to happen, but trying to shape what happens. As the established wisdom in the world of management puts it, a good manager is somebody who *anticipates* the future; an excellent manager is somebody who *shapes* the future. As a manager of outcomes, tasks and processes, the same can be said of the social worker.

Managing these various aspects of practice must be based on partnership. It must involve the people we are trying to help. It is not about doing things *to* them. Without that element of partnership, our efforts to be a creative and constructive manager in often difficult circumstances will be severely hampered.

This discussion of these important issues lays the foundation for Part 4 of the book. This is because the major theme there is professionalism, and a key part of professionalism is informed decision making, rather than simply following instructions blindly. To be able to have informed decision making, we need to be able to do the important things this chapter has discussed. Being a manager, in the sense used here, and being a professional are therefore entirely compatible, and should not be seen as competing perspectives.

See page 166 | for some questions about what you have just read.

See page 228 | for some pointers to useful further reading.

3

11 Managing risk and resources

The subject of risk is one that has taken up a lot of people's time and energy in recent years. Risk factors have always been a significant issue in social work, but there has been increasing emphasis on this aspect of practice since the 1980s when a number of incidents occurred that led to children being killed. Unfortunately, in many ways this has produced a defensive reaction to risk and, as we shall see below, this has caused a number of problems. Managing risk is therefore a key part of social work. Alongside risk come resources. Resources are not unlimited, and so a key part of what we do in social work practice addresses the issue of resources. The two sets of issues – risk and resources – are closely interconnected, because risk management has resource implications, and the use of, or shortage of, resources has implications for how risk is managed. This chapter is therefore concerned with some of the various issues that relate to both risk and resources.

The chapter begins with a discussion of assessing and managing risk. Some important questions are asked about what is involved in undertaking an assessment of risk factors and how we can then subsequently manage any risk situations that are identified in such an assessment. This is followed by a discussion of managing resources and the significant issues and dangers that are involved in this. A key message of this part of the chapter is that social work has to be resource sensitive, as budgets are not unlimited, but it should not be resource led, in the sense that resources become the primary concern. If the latter arises, social work can become reduced to a mechanistic process of rationing resources.

Assessing and managing risk

Sociologists for some years now have written about the 'risk society' (Beck, 1992; Webb, 2006). This is a concept that refers to how risk has become seen as an increasingly important factor in people's lives and this has especially been the case in public service in general and social work in particular. Denney's work on risk reflects these wider sociological concerns and how they have changed aspects of the nature of professional practice:

> Giddens (1990, 1998) has suggested that in the transformation from modernity to late modernity the judgements made by professionals are being constantly exposed to scrutiny. Any claim made by a professional to know what is best

can be called into question as a result of clients' greater awareness of what can constitute risk. Professionals are more open to questioning from clients, can be exposed to charges of incompetence, and are required to justify their actions and present the service user with possible alternatives for action. Users of professional services are now faced with a proliferation of knowledge from various sources, which can conflict with what they are being told by professionals.

(2005, p. 73)

This increasing emphasis on risk is largely, but not exclusively, a result of a number of high-profile child protection cases where children were either killed or seriously abused, even though there was social work input into the case. We have learned a lot from these tragedies but, unfortunately, there has also been a price to pay, in so far as many people have become 'risk averse'. That is, they have chosen to focus on minimizing risk, rather than managing it. Parton and O'Byrne echo similar concerns when they make the point that:

> we have become concerned that social work both in the way we think about it and practise it has become very defensive, overly proceduralised and narrowly concerned with assessing, managing and insuring against risk.

(2000, p. 1)

This can be a very stifling approach and, in some circumstances, can be quite oppressive. This is because risk taking is often a key part of people's identity, their sense of who they are and how they fit into the wider world. To seek to minimize risk can therefore have significant implications in terms of life chances for the people we are seeking to serve. Such an approach also encourages defensiveness which has long been recognized as a very poor form of practice (see, for example, Thompson, 2005). A defensive approach is one in which the primary concern is 'not getting into trouble', and this takes away attention from what should be our priorities in terms of making our practice as effective as possible in our efforts to help to meet people's needs, address the related problems and, in doing so, promote social justice and well-being.

Practice focus 11.1

Marie was delighted to be appointed as team manager of the older people team. She was very committed to anti-ageist practice and saw this job as an ideal opportunity to promote these principles. However, she was very surprised at what she found in the team. What had developed was a very defensive culture, with a major focus on risk issues, and little attention paid to wider concerns relating to challenging discrimination or promoting empowerment.

She raised this as an issue at a team meeting, and was not surprised, considering the defensiveness around, to receive a cynical and defeatist response. The team seemed convinced that they could not focus on the wider issues, as they were so concerned with making sure the risky situations they were dealing with did not blow up in their faces. Marie was dismayed that such a short-sighted approach to issues of risk had developed. She emphasized that things would need to change, as the current approach made no contribution to empowerment or social justice and was therefore potentially oppressive. She realized that she had a tough job ahead of her, but she was determined to clear up the dangerous misconceptions about risk that had become part of the team's culture.

This risk averse approach is also inaccurate, in so far as it is based on an oversimplified understanding of how risk works in human experience. Risk is a fundamental part of life. There are so many situations in which risk is a central factor, but even in those situations where it does not occupy a central role, it is never far away. Taking on a particular activity or task involves risks, but then not taking it on also involves risks. What is called for, then, is an approach based on risk *management*, rather than risk *avoidance*. We therefore need to develop a much more sophisticated understanding of risk. Simply trying to keep risk to a minimum is both oppressive and doomed to failure. Despite this, however, many people continue to focus their efforts on risk avoidance and minimization. Denney comments on the futility of an approach geared towards creating a risk-free situation by describing it as illusory:

> Contemporary notions of risk appear to contain an illusory searching to conquer uncertainty itself. The certainty of security in all aspects of experience appears now to be a desirable and marketable commodity.

> (2005, p. 12).

He goes on to discuss how perceptions of risk can be misleading. Referring to the work of Ferguson (2001), he argues that:

> the relationship between knowledge and risk perception is complex. There are two forms of knowledge used by individuals when they assess risk: there is raw knowledge, which is what people know; and there is 'calibrated knowledge', which refers to what people think they know about a risk (Ferguson, 2001). It is the latter that will tend to guide individual action.

> (pp. 20–1)

What this tells us is that a degree of caution is called for when weighing up risk, as there is considerable potential for misreading situations.

A further effect of this narrow conception of risk is that it encourages atomism. As Denney notes: 'the management of risk has become more individualised, privatised and pragmatic' (2005, p. 43). Risk management, like all other aspects of social work, needs to be psychosocial, blending individual and social factors into a meaningful whole, rather than remaining purely at an individual level.

The great irony of such a narrow focus that fails to see the 'big picture' of risk is that a risk aversion approach is actually more dangerous than a risk management one, in so far as the former leads to poor practice. The former involves not connecting with people on an I-Thou level, but rather relating to them at only an I-it level. In such situations the primary concern is with defensiveness, and this amounts to putting the worker's needs before the needs of the client. That is clearly not a satisfactory position either ethically or pragmatically.

Voice of experience 11.1

When I took up post I was concerned about the team's approach to risk. It was very mechanistic and defensive and not exactly empowering. I had to work quite hard to get people thinking in broader and more flexible ways about risk, but it was worth the effort, as the team was a lot less tense once we clarified our thinking about how best to deal with risk management issues.

Jill, a team manager in a children's services department

One approach to risk that has been very influential is the risk assessment scheme developed by Paul Brearley over 25 years ago now (Brearley, 1982). Despite it not being a new idea, it remains an important approach. Brearley's model is based on the following factors:

1 *Identify the cultural, racial and religious context of the situation.*
    It is important to begin with an understanding of the context in which we are working, as this is likely to have a crucial bearing on how we deal with the situation. A false assumption at this stage (about someone's religious beliefs, for example) could have major implications in so far as it could totally invalidate later aspects of the situation.

2 *List the dangers involved.*
    A danger is something we are trying to avoid, or fear might happen (perhaps a fall or a non-accidental injury). It is suggested that we prioritise these concerns at this point, identifying which ones we are particularly concerned about.

3 *List the hazards in the case.*
    In this context a hazard is defined as something which might lead to the danger you have identified becoming a reality (perhaps an ill-maintained staircase, or the presence of a violent adult in a household with young children).

4 *Identify the hazards as either:*
    (a) *predisposing* – something that creates vulnerability on an ongoing basis, such as dementia or a learning disability. It may not place the person in a particular danger at a specific time but may be thrown into significance by a situational hazard.
    (b) *situational* – defined as something specific which happens and has an

immediate effect on the danger identified earlier, perhaps a kitchen fire or a child accidentally damaging some property during play.

5 *Identify and list the strengths in this situation.*

Strengths can be defined as factors which could serve to make the danger less likely to occur. Regular visits from a supportive family member might be an example of this.

6 *Identify what other information you believe to be necessary.*

Based on the other information you have analysed this far, you should be able to work out what else you need to know in order to be able to do your risk assessment. For example, you may need to establish whether someone you think poses a threat to a service user's safety is permanently resident with him or her, or visits only occasionally. You might also need the opinion of a colleague about, for example, a service user's intellectual capacity to make their own judgements. It might be as simple as finding out when the staircase is to be fixed.

7 *Indicate the decisions you feel should be taken.*

In addition to helping you through the assessment process and giving you confidence in your own judgement, the ability to be able to demonstrate that process to others in written form is likely to do wonders for your professional credibility.

(Thompson and Thompson, 2007, p. 79)

Risk assessment, then, is clearly an important foundation of good practice. However, we also need to go beyond the risk *assessment* to consider issues of risk *management* – that is, to identify what needs to be done to make sure that we have an appropriate balance of risks where we avoid an unnecessary level of danger, but without an unnecessary stifling of people's activities. This means that a risk assessment needs to be more holistic than many often are. Some forms of risk assessment are very simplistic and involve identifying some sort of risk score. This attempt to quantify risk may appear to be scientific but, in reality, has little basis in hard science. A more realistic approach to risk assessment involves identifying key factors underpinning what is contributing to the risk situation and developing a plan for what steps need to be taken to make changes if the level of risk is for some reason unacceptable. A risk assessment also needs to make clear: at risk of what? Some risk assessments are very vague on this. They talk in general terms about 'at risk' situations or in an unspecified way, such as 'Mr Davis is at significant risk' without going into any detail of specifying at risk of what and why, and what needs to be done as a result of this situation. Webb discusses how an oversimplified approach to risk assessment and management can fall back on an essentialist conception of what is involved in risk: 'As Furedi (1997) points out, "being at risk" becomes a fixed attribute of the individual, like the size of the person's feet or hands' (2006, p. 71). This is a good example of how not to manage risk.

In a similar vein, we can note that it has unfortunately become the case that risk issues have created a considerable level of anxiety on the part of many people, with the result that complex issues are often oversimplified and dealt with in a relatively mechanistic way. It is also unfortunately the case that risk has been given a primary focus in so many assessments, without taking account of other aspects of the assessment process. Watson and West discuss this very point:

> The changing nature of assessment in recent years away from need to risk is a cause for concern as it moves the aim of assessment away from a more holistic stance of the person and their situation to one particular aspect – risk (Parton 1996). Risk is important, but overemphasis on this one area means that workers are liable to fail to understand the service users' situation and may inappropriately target resources. It also has the potential to shift the focus of assessment away from what can be done – building on the positive – to what should be avoided – emphasising the negative. What is required is a balance between these activities, reflecting who the service users really are and what they are capable of doing to their lives.
>
> (2006, pp. 36–7)

There is another irony here, in so far as falling into this trap can lead to a very ineffective level of practice (because of the lack of an adequate assessment on which to base our actions), and the net result can therefore be greater dangers for the people we are trying to help (and greater dangers for ourselves in terms of being open to criticism for poor practice).

Practice focus 11.2

Margaret was the manager of a community care team. She was a little taken aback one day when she received a phone call from the Department's legal team to say that a claim had been made against the Department by the relatives of an elderly woman who had been denied services by the Department.

Margaret and the social worker concerned, Janet, attended a meeting with the legal adviser to discuss how they would respond to the claim in court. The case papers were sent to the legal adviser in advance so that he could read them before the meeting. At the meeting it was explained that the family were claiming compensation for their relative being denied community care support. Janet was quite anxious about the situation, and so Margaret tried to reassure her by saying she had nothing to worry about, as she had done a good assessment. However, the legal adviser had a different view. He said that the only assessment he could find on file was a risk assessment, and there was little or no information that could be seen to constitute an assessment of 'needs and circumstances'. He went on to say that he felt a barrister in court would have a field day in pointing out the lack of an assessment. It was only at this point that Margaret realized just how focused on risk the team's work had become and how much they had lost sight of other issues that needed to be part of the assessment.

We have to recognize that risk is an important part of people's enjoyment, of feeling alive. To restrict risk unnecessarily in a defensive way can therefore have a very detrimental impact on such important factors as self-esteem and confidence. If we have too simplistic an understanding of risk issues, we can therefore be acting in a way that is oppressive and thus counterproductive when it comes to trying to be helpful. In a similar vein, risk aversion can lead to depression, in the sense that if people are denied activities that involve risk, they can feel that there is little that their life offers them. Risk aversion can also lead to other risks. For example, if foster carers were to be too restrictive in terms of children's activities, the result may be that the child absconds and, in running away like this, puts him- or herself at a much greater risk of harm.

Voice of experience 11.2

In recent years we have seen a significant shift towards an emphasis on risk. There is a very real danger that risk issues get dealt with in a very simplistic superficial way. Some people don't seem to realize that reducing one set of risks may actually increase another set of risks.

Lou, a children's guardian

Risk factors bring to the fore one of our recurring themes, namely the significance of communication. In situations of high risk, it is important that communication channels are kept open and in all the necessary directions. Are we keeping the necessary people informed of the developments they need to know about? These and other relevant questions need to be addressed if we are to do justice to the complexity of risk management.

It can be helpful to understand risk issues by reference to the wider social policy context and the development of what has come to be known as 'managerialism'. Denney gives us important insights into this when he argues that:

> The ascendancy of the concept of risk can be associated with systematic de-professionalisation. In the public sector, managers set targets for professionals which are prescribed by central government. Such managerial imperatives now appear to dominate professional considerations. Professional pre-eminence has given way to a more managed form of professionalism. Professionals are now accountable to audit appraisal and inspection, while service users have emerged from the margins to a position where they have gained a voice (Foster and Wilding, 2000).

(2005, pp 73–4)

As we shall see in Part 4 of the book, there is now a strong movement in the direction of reaffirming professionalism and thus to a certain extent countering the managerialist agenda that has developed. However, it is likely that managerialism will continue to hold sway for some time to come yet, and with it a defensive emphasis on risk. Part of this perspective on public service is the development of a blame culture as a result of the defensiveness generated by the tendency to adopt a rigid approach to risk and related matters. Webb helps to explain this in stating that:

> Within blame culture, risk avoidance becomes a key priority for care managers and front-line practitioners. Ever tighter mechanisms of accountability and transparency are introduced. This in turn hardens the defensive tactics of front-line workers, resulting in secrecy and mistrust. People become scared. In local authority social services departments elaborate complaint systems are put in place the purpose of which is to make definitions of responsibility specific, narrow, and precise, rather than to nourish a sense of shared responsibility. In line with neo-liberal practice they put the question of responsibility into the context of a contest, not the context of common values. Cynics argue that rather than making professionals more accountable these blame systems put a very high premium on avoiding responsibility and deflecting possible blame or legal liability onto someone else.
>
> (2006, p. 70)

This passage raises important issues that are worth exploring in a little more depth:

> ▷ **Mechanisms of accountability.** In a professional context accountability is an important safeguard to protect the public, the individual professional and the profession as a whole. It is therefore a positive thing to be valued and defended. However, in a rigid managerialist context characterized by bureaucracy that encourages a defensive overemphasis on risk, accountability becomes something to be afraid of or an obstacle to be avoided.
>
> ▷ **Defensiveness, secrecy and mistrust.** These factors are clearly not conducive to effective social work, but they are unfortunately characteristic of approaches to risk that are overly bureaucratic and lack a sophisticated understanding of the complexities involved.
>
> ▷ **Complaints systems.** These can and should be an important part of working in partnership, giving clients the opportunity to have their voices heard if they have any concerns that have not been addressed. They have the potential to be used very constructively. However, rigid and oversimplified approaches to risk management can again make them something to be feared and potentially a stick to beat people with.
>
> ▷ **Legal liability.** Fear of being sued can 'up the stakes' when it comes to assessing and managing risk. Ironically, handling risk issues in a simplistic and overly defensive way makes it more likely that there will be a reason for people to seek legal redress, rather than less, due to the failure to address the real issues involved.

3

We shall return to a discussion of these issues in Part 4. But, for present purposes, we should note that there are very real dangers in assessing and managing risk in ways that do not do justice to the complexities involved (see the *Guide to further learning* for suggestions about relevant reading on this important subject).

Managing resources

The first point we need to recognize in relation to resources is that we are necessarily dealing with a situation of scarcity. This is because the provision of resources will always be finite, but the potential demand is infinite. Even if budgets were to be doubled overnight, there would still be people whose needs would go unmet. The aim of social work, then, cannot realistically be to try and meet all people's needs at all times. We have to be much more modest and realistic in our aims – that is, to try and meet as many needs as we reasonably can in the circumstances, while always recognizing that they will not be the total amount. Some people adopt a very cynical approach to resource issues and take the view that it is all a matter of budgets, and nothing else is important these days. However, while there is an element of truth in this, it is not the whole story. Given that budgets will always be limited, it is important that we aim for a situation in which those scarce resources are not wasted. Issues of *effectiveness* (that is, making sure that what we do does what we want it to do – that it works) and *efficiency* (making sure that goals are achieved without unnecessary expenditure of resources) become key issues.

Practice focus 11.3

Colin had been a social worker in a child protection team for almost four years when he was promoted to the position of team manager for the looked-after children team. As a social worker he had always been quite cynical about managers and management, being quite critical of what he saw as their fixation with budgets and lack of focus on 'the real issues'. He was ready for a new challenge and felt he could make a better job of management than the people he referred to as 'bean counters'. That is why he applied for the promotion.

However, he soon found himself reconsidering his earlier attitudes. He soon had various social workers making requests for significant sums of money to support children in their placements. He realized that, if he agreed to all these requests, his budget would run out halfway through the financial year. And, when he attended a managers' meeting and mention was made of possible budget cuts, he realized that there was a lot more to management than he originally thought. He was determined not to lose sight of the professional issues and values he was committed to, but realized he would also have to make sure the limited funds available were spent wisely, with no waste or inefficiencies.

An important part of this is making sure that resources are not wasted, and this can be seen to apply in at least two main ways. First of all, there is the significance of assessment. If we are successful in carrying out a holistic assessment that is of a high standard, then we will be in a much stronger position to make sure that any resources used are appropriately targeted and are likely to be as effective as they can be in the circumstances. Second, what is also of importance is the need to review situations regularly. Unfortunately, there are many cases on record of where services have been provided for somebody and have not subsequently been reviewed (or not reviewed frequently enough), with the result that a change in a person's circumstances produces a situation in which the resources are no longer needed, but are none the less being provided unnecessarily.

Managing resources involves adopting a balanced approach. On the one hand, we need to make sure that limited resources are used as effectively and efficiently as possible, but, on the other, we need to make sure that we do not become overly concerned with resource issues. The following passage from Lloyd illustrates this well:

> Overconsciousness of limited resources leads to a tendency to make a service-led assessment, not necessarily with any cost saving. Research into informal caring has long demonstrated that what carers actually want is often more low-key, cheaper alternatives than the sometimes underused schemes developed by service providers (for example, Haffenden, 1991).

(2002, p. 163)

As with risk issues, there are dangers in adopting too narrow and simplistic a perspective on what are actually quite complex issues.

A further significant aspect of resource management is ensuring that: (i) decision-making processes are as transparent as possible – that is, that everybody is clear about what needs and problems are being addressed; and (ii) how the use of resources is appropriately geared towards that. Where there is any sort of secrecy about such processes, it can lead to confusion and suspicion that can result in a lot of time, effort and energy (and these are important resources too, of course) being wasted.

What is perhaps the most important aspect of resource management is making sure that the processes that take place are geared towards our primary role of addressing needs and problems and, in doing so, promoting social justice and well-being. It is very easy for the resource issues to become the primary concerns, thereby displacing an I-Thou approach with an I-it. People come to be seen as nuisances because they have needs that draw on scarce resources, rather than, as it should be, people being seen as our primary concern. Where social work has been reduced to a simple rationing of resources, something has gone significantly wrong and the situation needs to be reviewed urgently by all involved within it. It is not acceptable, ethically or pragmatically, for people to take a defeatist approach to this and simply accept that social work these days is primarily a process of rationing resources.

Voice of experience 11.3

Social work has always involved working with scarce resources, and no doubt always will, but it worries me that some people seem to think that social work is nothing but a process of rationing resources. That sort of cynicism can be a dangerous attitude to adopt.

Keith, a social worker in an adult services team

Central to this is recognizing that a major feature of social work is the pursuit of empowerment. It is very easy for the focus on empowerment to be lost if the major emphasis is on resources being rationed. There is a considerable irony, in so far as what can easily happen is that efforts become centred on service provision rather than empowerment. This, of course, is an expensive option in terms of resources, as empowering people to address their own needs and problems as far as possible is by far the best use of the limited resources available to us. Having a service-led mentality that leads to dependency is extremely expensive in terms of resource usage, and means that those resources are being used in a counterproductive way, in so far as they are being used in ways that undermine the underlying ethos of social work. An example of how empowerment can be developed is the increasing use of re-ablement schemes in working with older people. Traditional approaches to working with older people have often been dogged by a major focus on the provision of supportive services, such as home care, day care and so on. Increasingly now we are seeing an emphasis on intensive efforts being made to change the situations that lead to older people having the need for those services. This is a significant step forward and an important example of how resources can be used creatively in a focused and meaningful way, not simply rationed in a mechanistic way that can do more harm than good.

Practice focus 11.4

Bet, a second-year social work student, was delighted to learn that she had been allocated a placement fairly close to home. However, she was puzzled to learn that it was to be in a re-ablement team, as this was something she had never come across before. She was therefore looking forward to the pre-placement planning meeting to find out what was involved, as she really didn't know what to expect.

At the meeting it was explained to her that the team is part of a multidisciplinary project to try and reduce dependency for older and disabled people. The placement would involve working with people who received services on a long-term basis to see what changes could be made to reduce or even remove the need for services. It would also involve working with new cases to try to prevent the need for longer-term services. There would be a major focus on rehabilitation. Bet was really pleased with this and couldn't wait for the placement to start. Her tutor was also very pleased, as she felt this would be an excellent opportunity to explore issues of empowerment through avoiding dependency creation. This was clearly a placement with a lot of potential.

Conclusion

Risk and resources are both central features of social work. Without an understanding of each of these, we will at best struggle to get through our workload and, at worst, we will be a significant factor in making situations more pressurized and demanding for people.

It is to be hoped, then, that this chapter has played an important role in laying foundations for developing a much fuller and clearer understanding of risk. There is a growing literature on both risk and resources and you are strongly advised to consult the *Guide to further learning* at the end of the book to see the guidance there on how to take your learning forward.

See page 166 for some questions about what you have just read.

See page 228 for some pointers to useful further reading.

3

12 Managing expectations

Introduction

The general public tend to have relatively little understanding of what social work is all about and, unfortunately, members of other professions often share this lack of awareness to a certain extent. It is therefore vitally important that we are able to clarify expectations to make sure that there is not a mismatch that can lead to a wide range of problems, as we shall see below. This chapter is therefore concerned with what is involved in this important process of being able to manage or negotiate expectations.

The chapter is in two main sections. In the first one, we look at why expectations are so important and consider what a difference they can make in positive terms, or how problematic it can be if they are not clarified at an early stage. From this we move on to look at what is involved in negotiating expectations, what can be done to make sure that there is no mismatch that can be harmful to working relationships and can stand in the way of producing positive outcomes from social work involvement.

Why are expectations important?

The primary reason that expectations are important is that they shape, to a large extent, what is likely to happen further down the road. That is, they can put great pressure on people to conform to those expectations and, as such, they are a major influence on behaviour. They are also a significant source of conflict, in so far as unclear expectations can leave people with conflicting views about what should be done and how it should be carried out. It should be borne in mind that roles are sets of expectations, and so unclear expectations mean that people's roles can become confused.

Without clarity about expectations, there is therefore scope for considerable negative conflict. By contrast, where efforts are made to clarify expectations and the related roles, then any underlying conflict can be identified and dealt with positively and constructively so that we are then on a much firmer footing when it comes to relating to other people, whether these are clients and carers or members of other professions – or indeed colleagues within our own agency. Such clarity is therefore needed as a basis for partnership working, as discussed in Chapter 4.

A lack of clarity about expectations will tend to create considerable confusion and uncertainty. This can lead to an unnecessarily high level of anxiety, both for ourselves and for those we are working with. This in turn can lead to a degree of insecurity, and this can produce unwelcome negative consequences in terms of contributing to reduced levels of confidence and thereby preventing progress towards desired outcomes. One significant consequence of this is a possible lack of trust. Where there is confusion over what is happening (who is doing what and why), then there is unlikely to be a strong basis of trust. It has been established that mistrust is stable while trust is unstable (Slovic, 1999). What this means is that it can be difficult to shake off mistrust once it is established, but trust can easily be lost if we fail to live up to people's expectations in relation to that trust. Losing trust, or failing to establish it in the first place, is therefore an extremely costly thing for a social worker to do. Where we are trying to be helpful, we need to be clear about what we can do and what we cannot do, about what is our role and what is not our role.

Practice focus 12.1

Roy and Lucy were foster carers in a respite care scheme for children with learning disabilities. They looked after an autistic ten-year-old boy one weekend a month, partly to give his worn-out parents a break, and partly to give the boy a wider social network and opportunities for development. They found their caring role quite demanding at times, but it was very rewarding. They had their own 'link' social worker who was very supportive and admirably clear and focused in her role. They found her a pleasure to work with.

Rick, the boy they looked after, had his own social worker normally, but had not had one for some months since his previous worker had left and there had been a delay in filling the post. One day Roy and Lucy received a phone call from someone called Janet who announced herself as Rick's new social worker. She arranged to visit the following Friday, early evening, when Rick would be there. When she arrived there she spent about 15 minutes making small talk with Roy and Lucy, while Rick watched a dvd in his room. Lucy then asked Janet whether she would like to see Rick and then took her up to his room. Janet said a quick hello to him and then said she had better go as she did not want to 'get in the way', and she left. Roy and Lucy were totally baffled by her visit – it seemed to have no purpose and she had made no effort to explain why she was there and what her role was. What a contrast this was with their link worker who was very skilled in 'setting out her stall'. They felt they could trust her, but would find it very difficult to trust Janet.

Without this clarity, we will be open to pressures from others to work in ways that may suit their concerns, but which are not consistent with social work values or roles. For example, I have encountered many situations where fellow professionals without a genuine understanding of the social work role have tried to pressurize social workers into doing things that would be helpful for the professional concerned, but which are not really consistent with what social work is all about. The following instances of this are instructive:

- A police officer asks a social worker to make childcare arrangements for a woman who has been arrested. The police officer does not understand that this is not part of a social worker's duties, and so the social worker asks the police officer to suggest to the arrested woman that she contacts a relative to make the necessary arrangements. This is an example of where a relatively straightforward informal matter is brought to the attention of the social services as a formal childcare concern when this is neither necessary nor appropriate. In this instance, the police officer was not acting out of malice, but simply did not have a good enough understanding of what is and what is not a social work role. He was acting in good faith, but without the necessary knowledge of other people's roles to make multidisciplinary partnership a success.

- A housing officer makes a referral to social services because a man is in arrears with his rent. The tenant concerned does not have a disability, does not have mental health problems, nor is he vulnerable in any other way. He has simply not paid his rent. There is clearly not a social work role in this case and, again, the housing officer was not acting out of malice, but just out of a lack of understanding of where a social worker should or should not be involved. Dealing with such matters can be very time consuming and can also sap morale as a result of the frustration involved.

- A psychiatrist asks a social worker to arrange a holiday for a family in which both parents have mental health problems, but where there are no specific concerns about the welfare of the children. It is just seen as simply something that would be a pleasant experience for the family, but the parents, due to their mental health problems, have had difficulties in making the necessary arrangements. The social worker suggests that the psychiatrist contacts a voluntary organization that may be able to provide a volunteer to assist in this matter, but points out that such issues are not really part of the social worker's duties. The field of mental health seems to be particularly prone to misunderstandings about the role of social work in general and thus of individual social workers.

- A nurse is denied access by a family who are clearly at home, but who are refusing to answer the door. She requests that a social worker visit the house, but is unable to identify any particular concerns other than the refusal to allow entry. The social worker points out to the nurse that if the family will not let a nurse in, then they are almost certain not to allow a social worker in, and social workers do not have any right of entry to a person's property without their permission. This type of misconception probably stems from a common false assumption that social workers have the statutory powers to enter people's homes where there are concerns about somebody's welfare.

➢ A GP makes a referral to her local social services department, asking for someone to pick up a prescription for a patient who is housebound. The social worker points out to the GP that several local chemists have home delivery schemes for housebound patients and that collecting prescriptions is not a social work role.

Voice of experience 12.1

When I took over as team manager, it was clear to me that the team were under immense pressure, so one of the first things I did was an analysis of the workload. It soon dawned on me that we were wasting a lot of time on inappropriate referrals, so we agreed to set aside half a day for an extended team meeting to see what we could do to sort this problem out. We came up with quite a few useful ideas.

Lyn, team manager of a children and families team

These are just some of many examples of how other people can try to create situations whereby the social worker is acting in a way that would be very helpful for the professional concerned, but which are not part of the social worker's role. We therefore have to have clarity about where our role does begin. We need to be able to avoid what can be referred to as a 'sedimentation' model. This refers to the idea that social workers can be expected to pick up all the work that other public services are not able to deal with. In fact, it is a very common event for people making referrals to say things like, 'But, if you don't do something about this, nothing will be done', as if to try and pressurize the social worker into taking on tasks that are not actually a social work responsibility. It would be wholly unreasonable and unrealistic to expect social work services to be able to plug all the gaps that exist in the health, education, housing and criminal justice systems. We therefore have to make sure that we do not allow ourselves to be pulled into this sedimentation trap by trying to cover all the ground that other major services cannot cover.

Instead of this, we need to be able to have a clear idea about what precisely we are doing. This will, of course, vary from situation to situation, depending on the legal and policy context relating to that particular area of work. It will also vary in terms of the level of concern. Realistically, we cannot respond to all concerns about people within communities, and there has to be some sort of cut-off point at which we have to allow situations to continue as they are and perhaps redirect people to voluntary services where they may possibly be able to get some assistance. Of course, what we must not do is create or reinforce an expectation that a social worker is there to plug all the gaps and meet all the needs that are not met elsewhere. Pragmatically, this would amount to setting ourselves up to fail and leaving us less well equipped to deal with those matters that are genuinely our concern. From a social policy perspective, it involves trying to address political issues relating to the allocation of resources to welfare concerns by means of technical solutions, thereby distracting attention from the important matter of adequate funding for public services.

Earlier chapters in this book should be helpful when it comes to being clearer about what is realistic for social work. For example Chapter 1, with its discussion of needs and problems, should give some clarity about where we have a role and where we do not. However, what is also important is the significance of experience. Students and inexperienced practitioners may need a lot of guidance to begin with from more experienced colleagues about where the line tends to be drawn between what can be seen as a realistic task and role for a social worker and what is outside of our ambit.

It is important to recognize that, in terms of the clientele we serve, they will often be under considerable pressures, and people under pressure will understandably often want to push boundaries to try and get help from wherever they can, even if they realize that this is not actually the role of the individual concerned. We will therefore, on a fairly regular basis, come under pressure, not only from fellow professionals, but also from clients and carers to go beyond our role. A simple example of this would be where, following a discussion at a home visit, the client says to the social worker: 'If you're going back to your office now, would you mind giving me a lift into town?' If the social worker is indeed returning to their office at that point, then this is of course a reasonable request. However, when on a subsequent occasion the client telephones and says that he or she needs a lift into town and asks the social worker to pick them up, then that is clearly not a legitimate social work role to provide that sort of transportation service. What it all boils down to is having clarity about why we are involved in a particular situation and what steps we are supposed to be taking to remedy the unmet needs and the problems identified. We are not there as general helpers to be supportive in any way possible. That would make our job unmanageable and would also exacerbate the difficulties mentioned above that come with a lack of clarity about what can be expected. Furthermore, trying to be a general helper in this way is likely to encourage dependency, rather than be a sound foundation for empowerment.

Kelly was a social worker in a family support team. The primary goal of the team was to work closely with families where one or more children were in danger of being received into care, with a view to keeping the family together as far as reasonably possible. She found the work interesting and rewarding, although it could be highly pressurized at times.

When the local authority she worked for introduced an appraisal scheme, she hoped it would not be too time consuming. Her first appraisal meeting involved her line manager and the service manager. The meeting was a very positive one overall, but there was one notable criticism of Kelly's work. The service manager commented that the team as a whole, and Kelly in particular, had a poor record when it came to closing cases, often keeping them open long after the threat of family breakdown had been dealt with. We are not there to be general family helpers, encouraging dependency in the process, the service manager said. Kelly felt this was more a criticism of her team manager than of her personally, and therefore not appropriate for her appraisal. However, it did make her realize that the team did have a tendency to stay involved longer than was necessary, and so the risk of creating dependency was a very real issue.

One further aspect of expectations to consider is that they can be a significant source of stress. This can be in two ways. First, where expectations are unclear, that can prove to be an additional pressure on top of existing demands, and this can, in certain circumstances, be enough to overspill into harmful stress. Clarity about expectations is therefore important to prevent such situations from arising. Expectations can also be stressful where they are unrealistic. When people expect too much of us, and we do not negotiate those expectations downwards, then we leave ourselves open to a potentially very dangerous situation in terms of our own self-care. Linked to this, it is essential that we do not allow ourselves to set our own unrealistic expectations – for example, by being too ambitious about what we can achieve in any given set of circumstances. This brings us back to the important topic of humility.

It should be clear, then, that expectations are a significant factor, and our ability to be able to manage those expectations is an important part of effective practice in a social work role.

If you were to ask me what is the greatest weakness in modern-day social work, I would have to say that it is our tendency to take on too much and spread ourselves too thinly. I think that, as a profession, we need to learn to be more selective and more realistic about who we can help and who we can't.

Tom, a project manager in a voluntary organization

Negotiating expectations

The point was made earlier that there is often a lack of awareness of what social workers do. While the general public will have at least a basic understanding of what nurses do and what other professionals, such as police officers do, most will have little real understanding of social work. More often than not, any understanding of social work within the general public is likely to be distorted and inaccurate, mainly as a result of media representations that rarely do justice to what social work is actually all about. Fantasies about social workers being primarily concerned with taking children into care create tensions and false expectations that can do a lot of harm. We are, then, starting from a position of a general lack of awareness of what social workers do. This is reinforced by the fact that the vast majority of the public will tend to have no dealings with social workers during their lifetime. Virtually everybody will come into contact at some point with people like doctors, nurses, police officers, and so on, but the same is not the case in relation to social workers. It is therefore not surprising that most people have little understanding of what social work is and what to expect from a social worker. What adds to the complexity is that social work is such a diverse set of activities. The range of social work tasks is very broad indeed. What we do will vary from situation to situation (see Thompson and Thompson, 2008b, for a discussion of this). Therefore, the vast majority of people, even if they do have dealings with social workers, will have an understanding of only that aspect of social work they have encountered, and where they come into contact with a social worker working in a different role, they may still not have an understanding of what they can realistically expect. For example, we may have a situation whereby parents do not send their children to school and therefore come into contact with an education social worker in relation to poor school attendance. At a later date, those same parents may come into contact with a different social worker from a different team, or even a different department, in relation to, say, an elderly relative who is in need of community care support. They may find it difficult to see any common links across the two social work roles that they have encountered and so, again, it is not surprising that there is a lack of understanding.

Practice focus 12.3

Rachel was very pleased when she was invited to give a talk about careers in social work at the local sixth-form college. She had been involved in social work for over six years and had never had the opportunity to do anything like this before.

She prepared a short presentation that gave an outline of her own career development and widened out to include a picture of social work in general. She decided to leave plenty of time for questions and discussions. On the day she was pleased that her presentation went well and that she had not let her nerves get the better of her. However, what she hadn't anticipated was how many questions she would be asked and how indicative the questions would be of the lack of understanding of social work among the group. She therefore found herself spending a lot of time clearing up a lot of misapprehensions about what social work is all about. She had not expected a great deal of awareness of social work, but was surprised to realize how many false perceptions of social work there were.

It is therefore to be anticipated that there will be conflicts of expectation, that what we expect to offer and what others expect of us may not necessarily dovetail together nicely. This raises the crucial question of how can such conflicts of expectation be managed? The following pointers are intended, not as a definitive guide, but as a general help to how we can go about wrestling with these complex issues:

> **Setting out your stall.** This is an important idea that we have already encountered earlier in this book. It means, at an early stage in our involvement with an individual or family, spelling out how we see our role in that particular situation. This involves being clear about what processes we are likely to go through and what resources or services we may possibly be able to offer or commission. It can be helpful to be clear about our role in relation to identifying needs and associated problems. It is, of course, important to avoid jargon, but we can still get the message across clearly that our focus is on helping individuals and families to be able to move forward in terms of addressing any such unmet needs or associated problems. We have to make it crystal clear what the limits of our role are, that we will not, for example, be a general helper around any concerns they may have, but will want to focus specifically on whatever the key issues are in that situation.

> **Clear and effective communication.** Clarity of expectations has to come from clarity of communication. This involves making sure that we are communicating with others effectively in terms of:

(i) the messages we are seeking to put forward – for example, in avoiding inappropriate terminology. Consider, for example, the use of the term 'assessment'. This is widely used in social work, but often to the general public the term assessment means a test that they will either pass or fail. Therefore, using a term like assessment without explaining what it means may create undue anxiety, as well as creating confusion and therefore being the exact opposite of clarifying expectations.

(ii) The importance of listening carefully, to hear where people are coming from, to understand the situation from their point of view, not just our own (another example of an I-Thou relationship).

▷ **Boundary setting.** People who have little understanding of social work may have inappropriate expectations and this is not necessarily a problem as long as we tackle the issue carefully, sensitively and constructively at an early stage in the process. This is likely to involve establishing boundaries, and what this means is being clear about what we can and cannot do, what is our role and what is not our role, what services we may have access to and what we cannot have access to, and so on. Many people have an expectation that we are able to access any sort of 'welfare' services, even those provided by other agencies, such as the health service or voluntary bodies. We may therefore have to clarify the limitations of what we can offer – that is, establish boundaries around what is realistic to expect from us.

▷ **Conflict management skills.** Where there are conflicts of expectation, this need not lead to an escalation and any unpleasantness. A skilled social worker should have a good repertoire of conflict management methods that he or she can draw upon to deal with any tensions or misunderstandings that can occur in relation to expectations. The sooner we can deal with these, the better, as this means there is less chance of the situation escalating.

Voice of experience 12.3

I did a conflict management course recently and it made me realize just how important conflict management skills are in social work. Conflict isn't just about out-and-out fighting; it's also all the subtle tensions, disagreements and conflicting values and perspectives.

Sam, a social worker in a mental health team

▷ **Systematic practice.** We have noted that it is important to be clear about goals that can be realistically achieved, how we are going to achieve them and how we will know when we have achieved them. This approach can be an excellent basis for managing expectations. It is also important to remember that revisiting those goals from time-to-time will help to keep people on track in terms of making it clear about what the nature of our involvement is in the situation. If they waver from this and start to expect something that has not been part of the negotiated process of work, we can then consider whether this is an appropriate social work goal to be incorporated into a revised plan, or we can point out that this is not part of our agreed plan and that this is something we therefore cannot help with. If we are skilful and sensitive in handling these matters, they need not be a problem.

⋗ **Acknowledging people's feelings.** As we noted in Chapter 6, we are often dealing with people's emotions and, if we are not tuned in to these and do not make it clear that we are tuned in by acknowledging those feelings, then the situation can get out of hand. People will have both hopes and anxieties in their dealings with social workers and, if we are not aware of these, or lose sight of them at any point in the process, then we can do people a considerable disservice. We can end up being unhelpful, rather than a positive source of assistance.

⋗ **Developing a team philosophy.** It can be a very useful exercise for a team to develop its own carefully considered and well-crafted philosophy document, in which not only are the team's values made explicit, but also there is a clear statement about what the team does and does not do. Circulating such a document to partner agencies and making it available to clients and carers can be very helpful in establishing clarity.

This is not an exhaustive list of how expectations can be negotiated but should be enough to be a clear starting point for developing our knowledge and skills in this area.

Practice focus 12.4

Barry was very pleased to be involved in a brand new community outreach programme for people with mental health problems. He was working alongside a psychologist, community psychiatric nurses and an occupational therapist. He was enthusiastic about bringing a social perspective to mental health, as he was very critical of the limitations of a medical model approach. At first things went well and he developed good working relationships with his colleagues. However, over time he started to realize that the other team members seemed to be making assumptions about his role that were not consistent with how he saw it or how he wanted to develop it. He found that he was getting very little opportunity to do any therapeutic work, even though he was very experienced and talented in that area. Increasingly, he found that he was being expected to deal primarily with such issues as housing and financial benefits. He realized that he was going to have to 'educate' the team about social work in general and his role in particular, It became very apparent that he would have to do a very convincing job of renegotiating people's expectations of him. He saw this as a significant challenge, but not one that was beyond him.

Conclusion

When people come together, it is inevitable that they will have expectations of each other. We do not start with a blank sheet of paper, as it were. We enter a situation with some degree of expectation even if there may be a great deal of confusion associated with this. If we are not skilled and committed enough to make sure that we manage these expectations, then we can encounter considerable difficulties, because such expectations may be inappropriate or may continue to be unclear and confused, thereby undermining our efforts to establish a relationship based on confidence and trust. So, either way, there is a strong message that we need to take seriously the challenge of managing expectations.

All this needs to be done in a spirit of partnership. We are not there to dictate to people what should happen in a top-down way, nor are we there simply as servants to them to do their bidding. Experience has taught us that neither of these approaches is helpful and our value base also tells us that neither of these approaches is ethical. A top-down approach can be seen as coercive and oppressive. Any use of formal powers should be a last resort and not a basic foundation of our work. Similarly, working in a way that does not bring into play our knowledge, skills and values in a helpful way for people, will contribute to situations of drift and confusion, and will then lead to higher levels of insecurity than is necessary. This is clearly not an acceptable approach to practice.

What is called for, then, as I hope this chapter has made very clear, is a firm commitment to managing expectations as effectively and skilfully as we can. This is something that we may find difficult at first but, with continued experience and learning, we can become quite expert in lubricating the wheels of social interactions by making sure that neither party has unrealistic, unhelpful or unclear expectations of the other.

See page 166 for some questions about what you have just read.

See page 229 for some pointers to useful further reading.

Conclusion to Part 3

Social workers undertake an important role in our society, and it is often a demanding role due to the nature of the work. Social workers would therefore be very unwise to try and tackle their day-to-day tasks without having a solid foundation of knowledge and skills to rely on. Part 3 has shown that many of these skills are, in effect, management skills – even though social workers may not be regarded as managers in terms of their job descriptions (although many social workers will have the title of 'care manager').

By exploring four different aspects of these management skills in four different chapters, we have seen just how relevant and significant they are for good practice and how ill equipped we would be if we did not have at least a basic level of skill in these areas. It is to be hoped that this part of the book has provided a sound foundation for taking forward your learning in these areas so that, over time, you can develop your management skills as fully as possible. If, at some point in the future, your career takes you in the direction of a management post of some description, then your social work experience based on sound managerial understanding and skills will stand you in very good stead. If, however, you remain in practice throughout your career, then the full development of your management knowledge and skills will continue to be a great asset to you in terms of maximizing your potential as a practitioner. Either way, time and effort devoted to developing the management knowledge and skills associated with social work will be a worthwhile investment.

Points to ponder

- What are the dangers associated with neglecting self-care?
- What is meant by the term, 'use of self'?
- Why is it important to distinguish between empathy and sympathy?
- What is 'compartmentalization' and how might it be useful?

- What is meant by being both compassionate and dispassionate?
- What are 'negative strokes' and why should they be avoided?

- What is 'task-centred practice'?
- Why is systematic practice important in managing outcomes?

- What is meant by the term, 'acting in a risk averse way', and why might this be a problem?
- According to the Brearley risk assessment model, what is the difference between a danger and a hazard?
- What is the difference between effectiveness and efficiency?
- How does re-ablement contribute to empowerment?

- Why is trust so important?
- What is meant by 'setting out our stall'?
- How might unrealistic expectations be stressful?
- Name three ways in which we can negotiate expectations.

Exercises

This is an exercise in self-awareness. It involves thinking about how you show signs that you are under too much pressure (or are close to that point). How would someone who knows you well become aware that pressure was causing you problems? What 'signals' would you be giving off? How would *you* know that you were in this position? How would you be able to identify the potential danger of stress? Finally, can you identify any ways in which this awareness can help you to avoid becoming stressed?

Consider a task or project that you are involved with or have been involved with recently. Use the three key questions of systematic practice to analyse this piece of work:

- What are you trying to achieve?
- How are you going to achieve it?
- How will you know when you have achieved it?

Carefully consider what help and insights this approach gives when it comes to establishing clarity about desired outcomes.

Reread the section on the Brearley risk assessment model in this chapter. Then, when you have done that, take a project or piece of work that you are involved with or have been involved with lately. Use the Brearley model as a framework to assess the risks involved, then consider carefully what light this process has cast on understanding the risk factors involved in the situation.

Think about the concept of 'setting out our stall'. Consider carefully how you might do that. What would you want to say or do to get your message across about what you are able to offer and what you are not? What steps would be helpful in this regard? Having explored these issues, think about what lessons you can learn from this about negotiating expectations.

4

The social worker as professional

4

Introduction to Part 4

In the tribute to Milton G. Thackeray at the beginning of Skidmore, Thackeray and Farley, a very important point is made: 'The very heart of social work is the need to dignify the human process' (1997, p. iii). What this shows is that social work is premised on a set of values. Values, in turn, are a key part of what makes social work a profession, alongside other professions – a commitment to a professional value base. These values mean that the professionals concerned are committed to particular ethical principles, such as equality, dignity, empowerment, social justice and so on (Moss, 2007). This, in turn, means that it is not simply a job, not just a means of putting food on the table, as it were. Professionalism involves a commitment to the well-being of our clientele that may at times bring us into conflict with our employing agencies. Our conditions of professional registration make it clear that we must not act in ways that are detrimental to the people we serve, and so we have a duty to uphold our professionalism in that way.

> 'A key part of what makes social work a profession is its commitment to a professional value base.'

As we shall see in the pages that follow, professionalism also involves a professional knowledge base and a professional skills base, as well as a significant degree of accountability. Professionalism is therefore very much part of the contemporary social work scene. However, this has not always been the case, or at least not in the UK anyway. We have had the rejection of traditional professionalism, followed by a period of 'anti-professionalism', and then a significant period of confusion about whether or not we are professionals. It is only in recent years that a new form of professionalism has begun to reassert itself. This final part of the book explores some of the most significant issues relating to this complex story of professionalism. Its basic message is that professionalism is vitally important, but this must be a partnership-based, empowering form of professionalism (what I shall be referring to as the 'new' professionalism), and not a return to the elitist days of traditional professionalism.

The four chapters

Chapter 13 has a mainly historical flavour and outlines how earlier ideas about professionalism in social work were quite elitist and exclusionary. It goes on to show how such ideas are no longer applicable in contemporary social work, as they are inconsistent with principles of social justice and empowerment. It also shows how these ideas have none the less left a legacy that can still be seen in today's social work world. For example, traditional professionalism adopted a medical model and, despite some quite significant progress in some respects, there remain some clear signs of medicalization to this day. As Rogers and Pilgrim helpfully observe: 'Objective forces of oppression generate concurrent subjective consequences of demoralisation and despair which are readily and misleadingly susceptible to medicalisation' (2003, p. 4).

Chapter 14 also has a strong historical flavour. It traces the rise of 'anti-professionalism' as a result of the critique of social work that emanated from a movement that came to be known as radical social work. While I would be the first to recognize the important positive contribution of radical social work, I would also have to acknowledge that it came at a price, and a big part of that price was the tendency to reject professionalism, to see it as part of the problem, rather than as part of the solution. This chapter therefore discusses some of the significance of this shift in thinking about professionalism and its implications for the present day.

The next chapter explores how we can and should return to a stronger notion of professionalism, but with a clear and firm emphasis on empowerment and partnership. This refers to forms of professionalism that eschew traditional patterns of dominance that involve adopting a top-down approach and telling people what is best for them (because the professional 'knows best'). This 'new' professionalism offers the advantages of traditional professionalism without the elitism that ran counter to social work values. Chapter 15 is therefore concerned with mapping out a route for pursuing more appropriate forms of professionalism that are consistent with the social work values of partnership and empowerment.

Chapter 16, the final chapter of the book, presents an overview of professionalism and summarizes the key messages of the book as they relate to the professionalism debate. In doing so, it presents a useful overview of the challenges we face in trying to make the new professionalism a reality, rather than just an aspiration.

Links to the other parts of the book

When people's needs are going unmet and they are encountering problems because of this, they will be able to benefit from what professionals can offer. However, if those professionals operate on an elitist, top-down basis, then the result can be oppression and disempowerment, rather than partnership-based assistance and support that can make a positive contribution to empowerment. How we construe (and practise) professionalism is therefore very significant in relation to the issues we discussed in Part 1.

Similarly, Part 2 issues also connect with professionalism, in so far as being a professional involves an element of theorizing (that is, weighing up situations, making sense of them and developing a plan of action for dealing with them based on that analysis). There is also the important point to recognize that partnership-based empowering forms of professionalism need to be based on critically reflective practice, this latter notion being a key concept discussed at length in Part 2.

The emphasis in Part 3 on managements skills dovetails well with the issues discussed here in Part 4. As I noted at the end of Part 3, what management issues and professionalism have in common is a concern with *ownership* – taking cognizance of the fact that we are responsible for our actions and therefore making sure that they are based on sound understanding of the situations we encounter in our work.

13

Traditional professionalism

Introduction

The term 'professionalism' is one that has created a lot of confusion in the social work world in the last two decades or so. At one time, professionalism was seen as a key factor in social work, but there came a time when this was rejected and a period of what could be called 'anti-professionalism' came to the fore. That change will be the subject matter of Chapter 14 but, before we look at the changes that have developed, I want to take the opportunity in this chapter to explore the significance of traditional approaches to professionalism and what these have meant for social work over the years, to identify and consider the implications for present day practices.

The chapter is divided into two main parts. The first section examines problems with professionalism. It looks at how unsuitable a traditional top-down approach to professionalism is for modern-day social work (and, indeed, was for previous generations of social workers). The second part focuses, in particular, on the problem of 'medicalization', of how social work at one time adopted an openly medical model of practice. This has been heavily criticized over the years and largely replaced by a more psychosocial approach. However, as we shall see, there is still a significant legacy of medicalization that has a continuing detrimental impact on social work.

Problems with professionalism

We have a notion in our society of the 'true' professions, such as medicine, law and architecture. Other professional groups, such as nurses, teachers, town planners and so on, are often referred to as semi-professionals, as if they are not worthy of the official status of a professional. This is a distinction that we shall not be following here. Professionalism, as it is understood in this part of the book, is about the knowledge, skills, values and accountability that form the bedrock of social work practice. As McDonald recognizes: 'Social work, as well as being an entity which works towards the promotion of individual and collective wellbeing, is a *professional project*' (2006, p. 18).

Within traditional models of professionalism, there is an inherent elitism characterized by the idea that 'we know best'. Traditional approaches are closely associated with the view that the professional is the person with the knowledge

4

and is there to help the unknowing client. However, this is misleading and potentially oppressive. Kellehear is right to identify some of the problems associated with traditional forms of professionalism:

> But there are disadvantages to professionalism and these have been well documented in histories and sociologies of the rise of the professions (see Friedson 1971, North 1972, Willis 1989). 'Paternalism, self-interest, reluctance to share knowledge and inability to work *with* rather than *on* people' are key observations made by Baum (1993: 37). In matters to do with death and dying, professionalization has led to viewing end-of-life care as a series of discreet problems (as opposed to experiences) that can, or even should be dealt with by professionals rather than families, friends and co-workers. The professionalization of death has led to a gradual deskilling of modern populations from care of the dying, to preparation of the dead body, to burial, and even to moral and social prescriptions for grieving.

(2005, p. 99)

However, professionalism does not have to be like this. There are alternative models of professionalism, as we shall see in outline in this chapter and in more detail in Chapter 15.

In this book, my focus is on professionalism, not as a form of elitism, but as a commitment to high standards of practice. This is captured in the idea of the following four key elements:

- **A professional knowledge base.** As we have noticed in earlier chapters, there are significant dangers of an uninformed approach to social work. Reflective practice has helped us to understand the need for significant links between our professional theory base and actual practice (see Chapter 5). To practise without reference to a knowledge base that provides an understanding of the complex situations we are dealing with is clearly to enter very dangerous territory. Knowledge is a defining feature of a profession. For example, medicine as a profession relies on a significant knowledge base of the human body, disease processes and so on. Similarly, the legal profession relies on an extensive knowledge of the law and legal processes. Social work is no exception, as our knowledge base is quite vast: psychology, sociology, social policy, the law, ethics, social work theories, methods and processes, knowledge of specific client groups and so on.
- **A professional value base.** Here there are dangers of unethical practice and the potential abuse or misuse of power. If we are not clear about what our values are, then we may easily find ourselves in situations where we are acting in ways that are contrary to those values. An explicit understanding of the values informing our work is therefore a key feature of professionalism. All professions are characterized by a set of values, but the value base is particularly significant in social work, partly because we

work with some of the most vulnerable and disadvantaged members of society, and partly because social work is explicitly premised on a commitment to promoting social justice. Values are therefore not only a key dimension or aspect of social work, they are also a fundamental underpinning or rationale.

▷ **Skills.** With the knowledge base comes a skills base. Being able to put that knowledge into practice is not always a simple, straightforward matter. A set of skills are required to be able to translate theoretical and research-based knowledge into the wisdom of practice. Such skills are therefore another important aspect of being a professional. Just as social work has an extensive knowledge base, it also has a very broad range of skills (see, for example, Trevithick, 2005, and/or Thompson, 2002d).

▷ **Accountability.** Professionals need to take ownership of their actions. We need to be able to justify decisions made, and by justify I do not mean adopt a defensive position. We need to be able to show that our actions were legitimate in the circumstances. This is, in effect, an exercise of power and to make sure that such power is not used inappropriately, we need the safeguard of accountability. There are various systems in place whereby an individual professional can be called to account for their actions. This includes the process of supervision, as well as situations in which a client may make a complaint, where there may be an investigation as a result of alleged misdeeds or, in some circumstances, there may be a tribunal or court case relating to particular practice issues that require us to provide a rationale for our actions.

Practice focus 13.1

Shafiq was a student on placement in a children and families team. His practice teacher, Les, could see that he had a lot of potential. However, she recognized that he needed help with his record keeping which was very descriptive and provided little by way of helpful information. She showed him examples of good practice in record keeping – analytical accounts that showed clearly the processes involved in decision making. He told her that he found these helpful and said he would try to make sure that his records were more like this in future.

However, while there was some improvement in the quality, his records continued to be largely descriptive, with no clear lines of professional accountability in terms of the decision-making processes underpinning his work. She was surprised by this, as he was an intelligent young man and very articulate. She raised the issue with him again and once again emphasized the importance of professional accountability. At this point Shafiq became clearly very anxious and fell silent for a moment. 'Is there a problem about this?', Les asked, and the fact that he continued to look down and say nothing indicated that there was. After a lot of very skilful reassurance from Les, Shafiq felt able to say that he worried that he might be criticized for 'getting it wrong' if he spelled out what he had done and why he had done it. This gave Les the opportunity to explain that the opposite was the case, and that he would be criticized for not making his reasoning clear. If he ever did get it wrong, he would then have the opportunity to learn from the experience.

This fourth element, that of accountability, should not be confused with blame. Parton and O'Byrne explain this as follows:

> O'Hanlon distinguishes blame from *accountability*. Accountability empowers and promotes self-agency; blaming alienates – it does not invite people to responsibility. Accountability attributes responsibility, where blame attributes bad intentions and bad personal characteristics such as selfishness – it does not invite cooperation, rather it tends to close down possibilities.
>
> (2000, p. 88)

Accountability, then, is not something to be afraid of or a problem to be solved. It is an important part of professionalism and is therefore something that we should welcome. It is also something we should encourage in our clientele. If we are to take empowerment seriously, then we need to do whatever we reasonably can to encourage people to take ownership of their situations and support them in doing so. Beginning with a point I referred to in Chapter 1, Milner and O'Byrne offer an important perspective on this situation:

> The person is not the problem, the problem is the problem, and the problem is spoken of as having a detrimental effect on the person. This may sound as if there is a let-off for the person and that only the problem is taken to task. But in these approaches there is no let-off from accountability. However, blame is avoided. *Blaming* alienates and does not invite people to take responsibility. It attributes bad intentions. On the other hand, *accountability* promotes self-agency and responsibility for what is to be done next, and responsibility for the consequences of doing nothing.
>
> (2002, p. 267)

We need to bear in mind, then, that accountability is certainly not the same thing as blame. This is an important point in relation to managerialism, a topic we shall discuss in more detail in Chapter 15.

These four elements show how important the notion of professionalism is. However, in the late 1960s and on into the 1970s the professionalism of social work came under severe attack from a movement that came to be known as 'radical social work' (see Chapter 14 for a more detailed discussion of this). The result was that it was not the elitism of traditional professionalism that was rejected, but professionalism itself, and we shall see later why that was very problematic.

Traditional professionalism, with its emphasis on a top-down approach left little room for conflict management skills. This was because it was expected that people would do what was asked of them. However, this was a significant flaw in adopting this type of approach to social work because, while the so-called true professions have a lot of status to back up their top-down approach, social workers do not have, and never have had, that degree of status and therefore sway. What is needed, then, is a movement away from the traditional idea of a top-down approach to one based on working in partnership, and this is where our conflict management skills come to the fore because, without the ability to negotiate effectively with the people we are trying to help, we are going to struggle to be able to pursue high-quality social work practice. This is an important topic to which we shall return in Chapter 15.

Voice of experience 13.1

Social work has changed an awful lot since I came into this work 19 years ago. There is an awful lot more emphasis on partnership these days. I started off working with adults with learning disabilities and there was a distinct mentality of 'we know best' on the part of some social workers at that time. It was something I felt very uncomfortable with, but it was quite normal in those days – although, thankfully, not everybody took that approach.

Sally, the manager of a disability resource centre

Professionalism needs to be differentiated from bureaucracy. In a bureaucracy, employees are expected to follow instructions and are not required necessarily to have an understanding of the issues they are dealing with. Clearly, this is not workable for social work situations. What we deal with is so complex that to adopt a simplistic bureaucratic approach of following procedures in an unthinking way would be disastrous (Payne, 2000). This is one of the things that reflective practice has taught us: that social work needs to be a mindful practice based on a clear professional knowledge base (Thompson and Thompson, 2008a). It is therefore important that we reaffirm professionalism, but without returning to elitism. Duyvendak, Knijn and Kremer support this point when they argue that:

> Caught between the demands of clients movements' for free choice and a greater say on the one hand and governmental demand for reduced expenditures, professionals in public services face a prisoner's dilemma – an exit option is not available. Raising their voice through self-confident reprofessionalisation may help reclaim professional discretion on behalf of those clients who need their support.

(2006a , p. 32)

The alternative to professionalism is bureaucracy. In a social work context, bureaucratic processes are not only far too inadequate for dealing with the subtleties and intricacies of the situations we encounter; they also represent an approach that devalues the knowledge, skills and values of actual practitioners. It is also unfair, given that, if anything should go wrong in a social work situation, we would be treated as professionals, in the sense that we would be called upon to account for our actions and the decisions underpinning those actions. Someone working in a genuinely bureaucratic setting would be able to say quite legitimately that they were simply following orders or procedures. For a social worker, this would not be seen as a legitimate reason for behaving in a particular way. We would be regarded as negligent if we were not able to show that we intervened in people's lives in an ethical, well-informed way and may be in breach of our conditions of professional registration. I would therefore strongly argue that social work has to be a professional undertaking, rather than a bureaucratic one. We shall explore these issues in more detail in the chapters that follow.

Practice focus 13.2

Cassie was a social worker in an older people team. She took her work very seriously and was very committed to older people's rights. She was also doing an MA in Professional Ethics on a part-time basis.

All was going reasonably well until, one day, her line manager told her that several of her clients would be having their services reduced or stopped altogether as a result of budget cutbacks. Cassie pointed out that this should not be done without a reassessment. We haven't got time for that, her manager retorted, and more or less ordered her to draw up a list of the people least likely to be at risk if their services were withdrawn or curtailed.

Cassie was extremely unhappy about this, and, because she saw it as an ethical matter, she raised the issue at an MA teaching session. She was pleased with the level of support she got from her fellow students. She was also delighted when the tutor pointed out that she could be in breach of the conditions of her professional registration if she carried out her line manager's instruction. She realized that she would need to find an opportunity to raise this issue with him and calmly but firmly tell him that she was not prepared to put her professional registration at risk. What gave her confidence was that she knew she would get the full support of the team on this.

The problem of medicalization

While the activities of social work practitioners often overlap with the work of medical professionals and those in professions allied to medicine, social work is clearly not a medical profession or health care profession in its own right. What we offer is subtly and significantly different and may at times bring us into conflict with health care colleagues. However, at one time, social work dealt with such conflicts in what we can now see, with hindsight, was a simplistic and inappropriate way. This involved adopting a medical model of social work, and so for many years social work acted as a form of paramedical undertaking. For example, medical terminology was widely used (diagnosis and treatment, rather than assessment and intervention). There are also still some hospital social workers practising today who remember the days when social workers wore white coats in health care settings. While this seems strange today, it was considered the norm at one point.

Tew discusses the problems of medicalization in the mental health field:

> In recent years, despite a growing interest in alternative approaches within men-
> tal health, social work education has yet to clarify the parameters of what may
> be meant by a social (or psychosocial) model of mental distress. The domination
> of biomedical approaches to mental health has so far offered little space for the
> articulation of more holistic alternatives. Within interdisciplinary contexts, there
> has been a tendency to conflate a social perspective (and social work) with just the
> practical issues that may impact on a person's life, such as benefits and housing
> – and this conflation may still be found in the recent framework that has been
> proposed for education and training in mental health across disciplines (Sainsbury
> Centre, 2000).

(2002, p. 143)

These comments reflect a significant problem for social work in relation to mental health, although the detrimental effects of medicalization, as we shall see below, are not restricted to this field. Medicalization is unhelpful because it involves taking one aspect of the client's situation (the biomedical) and making it primary, rather than seeing it as one aspect among many: the psychological, sociological, political, economic, spiritual and so on. The opposite of this is a holistic approach – that is, one that looks at the overall picture, rather than just one aspect of it. Tew's comments are again helpful:

> A holistic approach demands a much deeper engagement with the many layers
> of feeling and meaning, concerning a person and their social experience, that
> may be bound up in their expression and acting out their distress. It also entails
> a shift from discourses of 'treatment', which place the professional in the role
> of expert, in control of any healing or caring processes, to ones of recovery and
> empowerment, which locate people themselves as in charge of navigating their
> own particular journeys. Such a shift away from the discourse of the medical
> model does not mean an abandonment of what medicine may have to offer in
> terms of managing people's specific experiences, just a process of reclaiming the
> whole person from the partiality of a purely medical definition.

(2002, pp. 146–7)

4

Voice of experience 13.2

I was amazed to find out how medicalized social workers used to be. One of my clients was a social worker in the 1950s and I learned a lot from her. Mind you, although we've moved on a lot, you still see lots of medical model influence on social work, even today.

Anna, a social worker in an older people team

Medicalization can be seen to be problematic in a number of ways, and it is important to give some thought to these:

> A medical model basis for practice is a top-down paternalistic approach, and is therefore not consistent with the partnership ideals of social work. There are ethical reasons why partnership is to be preferred to paternalism, but there are also pragmatic reasons, in so far as we know from experience that paternalistic approaches do not work.

> An atomistic (or individualistic) approach gives minimal consideration to wider social factors. Medicalization has been quite significant in contributing to this form of atomism, as most aspects of a medicalized approach do not pay heed to these wider social concerns. As the comments from Tew mentioned above help us realize, medicalized approaches are not sufficiently holistic to act as a realistic basis for doing justice to the complexities of social work.

> Following on from this, a medicalized approach can be quite oppressive, as it involves discrimination by default. What I mean by this is that, if we are not tuned in to the significance of discrimination in people's lives, we can easily be reinforcing it and therefore acting unwittingly in an oppressive way.

> Medicalization can also be disempowering because, with it, comes a tendency to pathologize individuals – that is, to see the problem as being within them, as if it were an aspect of some form of unacceptable 'essence' that makes them inadequate or otherwise blameworthy. Of course, this is not consistent with social work values, especially a commitment to empowerment and social justice.

There is clearly a lot wrong, then, with social work approaches that adopt such a medical model. There has been an ongoing critique of health care professionals adopting such approaches and being insufficiently holistic (DoH, 2001), and so, for a socially based profession to do so is particularly inappropriate. For the most part, we have seen, over the last decade or two, a significant move away from medicalization. However, we have not resolved all the difficulties involved.

Practice focus 13.3

For almost four years June was the only social worker in a small hospice. She was very skilful in forming effective working relationships with colleagues from other disciplines and was very good at making sure that the psychosocial aspects of the lives of the dying and grieving people she worked with were not forgotten.

When the team manager post for the family support team at a much larger hospice in a neighbouring town was advertised, she saw this as an opportunity to take her career a step forward. When she succeeded in obtaining the post, she was sad to be leaving her old team, but looked forward to the new challenge. However, she was surprised to find that, in her new team, there was very little emphasis on social issues. The whole ethos was very strongly medically dominated. The social work input was very narrowly focused, and this gave June considerable cause for concern. She had not realized that such medicalized approaches to practice were still alive and well. She wondered whether to tackle the issues with the whole team – for example, at a team meeting – or individually through supervision. Either way, she knew that she would have to make a lot of changes.

It is quite clear that there is still a significant legacy of traditional forms of professionalism, especially when it comes to medicalization. Consider the following examples:

- **Childcare.** Although social work in general has moved away from medical terminology, the use of terminology like 'the diagnosis and treatment of abuse' are still widespread. How it is possible to 'diagnose' an assault, for example, is unclear and precisely what 'treatment' involves is also lacking in clarity, but the medical connotations of the use of this terminology are clearly highly problematic.
- **Mental health problems.** There is a large and growing body of literature that offers quite a strong critique of medical models of mental health distress. It is claimed that psychosocial problems are conceptualized as symptoms of an illness. The work of Foucault (2001) has been significant in this regard, but there are other traditions of thought that are equally scathing of a simplistic, uncritical acceptance of mental health problems as symptoms of an illness (Rogers and Pilgrim, 2003). The reality, of course, is far more complex.
- **Disability.** The development of the social model in relation to disability studies and practices has been a major step forward in terms of moving away from medicalized understandings of disability that conceived of social, political and psychological factors almost exclusively in biomedical terms (Swain et al., 2004).
- **Loss, grief and trauma.** These are also significant issues in people's lives that have had a tendency to be treated in medical terms. For example, the

4

well-known theorist in relation to loss and grief, Colin Murray Parkes, has described grief as an illness (Parkes, 1986). Similarly, the growing literature on the study of trauma continues to use medical terminology and to present such complex multifaceted issues in primarily biomedical terms (Rothschild, 2006; Ziegler, 2002).

⋗ **Alcohol and drug misuse.** The idea that addiction is a medical issue, rather than a psychosocial one continues to be the dominant thinking, although it is increasingly being challenged from a variety of different angles. The idea that alcoholism is a disease, for example, has become well established, not only in professional circles, but within general public understandings. Such is the power of a medical discourse in relation to what are primarily social problems.

Voice of experience 13.3

When I moved into the alcohol abuse field I was amazed to find how medicalized it was. I find all this talk about alcoholism as a disease quite strange, but I've found that, despite this medical model stuff, colleagues are quite open to listening to what I have to say about the psychosocial aspects of the work we do.

Bel, a social worker in a multidisciplinary alcohol misuse team

These examples should leave us in no doubt that, while great progress has been made in terms of developing fuller, more sophisticated understandings of social problems that do justice to the psychosocial elements, medical understandings continue to feature as part of the social work world, even in those areas that are clearly not directly of medical concern.

One important point to recognize is that a critique of medicalization is not a criticism of medical staff. To decry the existence of medicalization in social work is not to say that we should in any sense declare war on medical staff or other health care colleagues. That would be naive, unfair and unhelpful. Indeed, as a basis for multiprofessional working, it is essential that we are able to work constructively with colleagues, whose perspectives may be different from our own, without allowing ourselves to become judgemental or unfairly critical of other people's contributions. Social work does not operate in a professional vacuum, and so there is a very strong need for effective multidisciplinary working.

While there continue to be doubts about the appropriateness of dominant models of medicine and calls for more holistic approaches continue to be heard more frequently and more loudly, our concern is not with that area primarily but, rather, with the clearly inappropriate application of a medical model to psychosocial concerns.

While this movement away from medicalized solutions continues apace, there is an interesting tendency for some authors, for example Bentall (2004), to be critical of offering medical solutions to, for example, mental health problems, but who continue to conceive of the problems in medical terms. There is clearly a logical disjunction here, but I see it as a reflection of just how powerful medical discourses are that even people who are critical of medicalized approaches to social problems continue to describe those problems as if they were medical in origin. We still clearly have a long way to go before we can leave behind this unfortunate legacy of medicalization.

This means that social workers now have a significant challenge of working within what are often medically oriented systems, but in doing so without: (i) alienating colleagues who have some degree of adherence to a medical perspective; and (ii) abandoning social work values. Clearly, medicalization is inconsistent with so many aspects of social work values, and so the challenge of developing effective practice and good working relationships with colleagues is quite a significant one as we attempt to develop approaches to social work that are far removed from the problems of medicalization.

Practice focus 13.4

June spoke to each member of the team individually in supervision about her wish to move away from a medical model perspective towards a broader social focus. This seemed to go reasonably well, and so it gave her the confidence to raise the issue at a team meeting. At the meeting she tried to be as constructive as possible, as she did not want the team to feel 'got at'. Thankfully, nobody seemed to take her comments as a personal criticism, but she was surprised at how much resistance she encountered. However, it all made more sense when Sylvia, one of the most experienced members of the team, said: 'But we get on really well with the medical staff and we don't want to fall out with them.' June then went on to explain that adopting a psychosocial perspective should complement the medical perspective and there was absolutely nothing to fall out about.

She tried to get across the point that, if the social work staff adopted a medical perspective too, then the patients would not have the benefit of an holistic understanding. 'Holistic' seemed to be the key word, as the discussion then focused on the importance of this idea, and thereafter, resistance to putting the social back into social work began to wane. Once the team understood that moving away from a medicalized approach to social work did not involve any hostility towards medical colleagues, they became more open to June's suggestions as to how the team should move forward.

When it comes to understanding the significance of professionalism, Jordan's comments are instructive:

> The law provides the framework of rules under which social workers operate; policy provides an interpretation of these rules, and a commentary on their purposes. But there would be no point in using social workers to do these tasks if laws and policies could be precisely and unambiguously stated; it is because situations are complex and susceptible to a number of interpretations that the judgement, discretion and skill of a trained person are required. As Harris and Webb have remarked, 'professionals do not create discretion; rather the inevitability of discretion creates the need for professionals'.

(1990, pp. 3–4)

Conclusion This chapter has shown that professionalism is an important issue for social work, and has criticized the alternative in terms of bureaucratic understandings of social work. However, the chapter has also been critical of traditional, medicalized approaches to professionalism. These are clearly not suitable as a basis for rising to our current challenges. We shall be exploring how we can deal with these challenges in Chapter 15, where our subject matter is that of developing empowering forms of professionalism. However, before we get to that point, we first need to explore the historical aspects of professionalism in a little more detail because, in response to traditional professionalism, we saw a movement based on anti-professionalism. This, too, has unfortunate legacies for present-day professional concerns, and so, before we look at how professionalism can be further developed, we need to look at this other aspect of what has stood in the way of developing empowering professionalism. It is to this legacy of anti-professionalism that we now turn.

See page 221 for some questions about what you have just read.

See page 229 for some pointers to useful further reading.

14

The legacy of anti-professionalism

Introduction

In this second of four chapters addressing the significance of professionalism in social work, we examine how reactions against traditional professionalism came about as a result of dissatisfactions with the earlier scene. We explore how a number of problems have arisen because of this, and how they are still with us today – problems that have held us back in many ways by undermining our professional credibility in the eyes of those we are seeking to help; other professionals we work alongside; and the general public.

The chapter is divided into two main parts. In the first of these, we examine what I refer to as 'the radical critique'. This is concerned with how the movement known as radical social work was, in its day, highly critical of professionalism and how this led to an era that I shall be referring to as 'anti-professionalism'. By this I mean an approach to social work that rejects professionalism as a legitimate basis for practice. In the second part, we explore the problems that have arisen because of such an anti-professional approach.

The radical critique

As was noted in Chapter 13, traditional forms of professionalism were premised on elitism. In the days when such an approach was dominant, it was simply taken for granted that people with professional knowledge were in a position to decide on what should be done and how it should be done. There is, of course, a strong element of judgementalism in this, in so far as it involves assuming that social work clients are not in a position to make decisions for themselves. This is hardly a basis for partnership and empowerment, and therefore contrary to social work's direction. Radical social work was therefore quite right in criticizing this elitism and the patronizing approach that it was premised on. This type of disempowering paternalism should have no place in social work.

With similar concerns on mind, Knijn and Selten provide a clear account of why traditional professionalism was not a sound basis for practice:

> The Dutch philosopher Hans Achterhuis (1979) argued that welfare professionals were not solving or reducing social problems, but were actually creating a new market, which he called 'The market of welfare and happiness' and was also the title of his book. Professionals were more interested in keeping their jobs than

in sorting out the problems of clients and more guided by self interest than the public good. This assault received unexpected support from both workers in the field and left-wing writers (Duyvendak, 1997). Professionals, it was argued, simply reinforced the passivity and helplessness of their clients.

(2006, p. 125)

This passage illustrates nicely the concerns that were raised about traditional forms of professionalism and why there was a need to change the arrangements. The emergence of radical social work as a challenge to existing approaches would prove to be a key development in this regard.

Radical social work was a movement that began in the late 1960s, it developed further into the 1970s and continued to have some sway in the 1980s. It never became a mainstream approach to social work and was always regarded as something of a minority appeal, but it was none the less a highly influential social work movement. It was premised on a political analysis of social work themes and issues and rejected the traditional emphasis on individual psychology in favour of a more sociological approach that took more account of wider social issues, such as poverty and deprivation. Early forms of radical social work placed great emphasis on a class analysis and were informed by marxism (albeit an oversimplified version of marxism in many cases). Later forms of radical social work broadened out to include discussion of such important issues as racism and sexism, and therefore incorporated elements of feminism and anti-racist theorizing alongside a basically marxist analysis.

As a movement, it brought about significant changes in social work, some positive, some not so positive. In terms of positive benefits, radical social work was a pivotal factor in terms of the development of critical perspectives and the emergence of anti-discriminatory practice through showing that so much of the life experience of social work's clientele was shaped by unequal power relations and processes of discrimination that produce oppressive consequences. Radical social work was able to show the inadequacies of an atomistic approach that focused attention primarily, if not exclusively, on individual factors, with inadequate attention being paid to the wider sociopolitical issues. One of the main factors that radical social work criticized was the tendency for an individualistic approach to pathologize the individual – that is, to locate the problem within him or her, rather than within the uneven and often oppressive social arrangements that continued not to feature in traditional social work practices.

Practice focus 14.1

Nick was a student on placement in a community social work team. His practice teacher placed a lot of emphasis on anti-discriminatory practice and was keen to make sure that Nick developed a good understanding of the issues involved. Nick, for his part, was keen to learn, but found it all very confusing. In working with a particular individual or family he felt comfortable in focusing on the specific circumstances of the case. He didn't really understand what the wider social issues of discrimination and oppression had to do with the particular case. In effect, he saw social work as a psychological process of helping, and did not see the relevance of wider sociological concerns. One day in supervision he said to his practice teacher: 'What if I were dealing with a black woman? I can't take away the racism and sexism. All I can do is help her the best way I can.' His practice teacher said she could understand his point of view, but then went on to explain how that was exactly how social work used to be before radical social work came along and criticized the individualistic approach for being too narrow in its focus. We are all unique individuals, she agreed, but emphasized that we are individuals in a social context, and we can miss out on some key issues if we lose sight of that. She recommended some reading on radical social work that she felt might help him to understand the importance of the social and political as well as the personal.

In terms of the negatives associated with radical social work, one very significant factor was reductionism. This refers to the tendency to reduce complex multi-level issues to the level of a single issue – to try and explain complex factors in a simple way. This was done in the context of radical social work by placing almost exclusive emphasis on a class analysis to begin with. Even when issues to do with race and gender were incorporated at a later date, there was still a tendency towards a dogmatic oversimplification of complex issues. This had the effect of leaving us less well equipped to deal with the issues we faced in those days, and the legacy is still with us, in so far as tackling the problems of managerialism (to be discussed in Chapter 15) is not helped by a simplistic analysis that fails to do justice to just how many factors shape a particular situation.

Although radical social work was very helpful in introducing a theoretical base informed by sociology and political analysis, the theory base itself lacked sophistication in many ways. What added significantly to this problem was the fact that many people oversimplified the theory in trying to apply it, thus exposing its weaknesses even more. To a certain extent, there was a 'missionary zeal' that carried people forward in ways that left little scope for dealing with the subtleties and complexities involved. While a commitment to social justice was something to be welcomed, where this was carried through without an adequate understanding of the issues being addressed, the result was always going to be problematic.

Pease and Fook comment in particular on how theoretical ideas relating to radical social work were handled in simplistic ways:

> This phenomenon is similar to what I term a 'commodification' of theory, as if radical theory consists of a material set of ideas which can be transferred from one person to another. A person becomes radical if they can take on all the right ideas – they have thus become converted. This way of thinking, however, is potentially disempowering, since it assumes that the source of radicalism comes from 'outside' the person and lies solely in the acceptance of certain beliefs. There is a danger that the experience of the 'unconverted' will be devalued and discounted, and there is therefore potential for radicalism to be experienced as disempowering (by those who by definition don't have it).
>
> (1999a, p. 5)

This contributed to a large extent to an 'us-them' mentality, in the sense that many of those who were committed to social justice tended to see themselves as set apart from those who were yet to see the light. Part of this was a certain authoritarianism that could be seen to creep in at times – in effect, replacing one structure of elitism with another. As Healy comments: 'Poststructural theories call into question the authoritarianism that lies, often unrecognized, in emancipatory practice theories' (2000, p. 38) – although it is not necessary to adopt a poststructuralist approach to recognize the problems associated with dogmatic reductionism.

One particular aspect of this that has caused considerable confusion has been the tendency for power issues to be dealt with in very simplistic ways. As Fook explains:

> A critical reflective approach should allow social workers to interact with and respond to power dynamics in situations in a much more flexible, differentiated and therefore effective way. By making less 'blanket' assumptions about power, the critically reflective practitioner should be able to engage with the specific power dynamics of situations in more relevant and effective ways.
>
> (2002, p. 157)

Unfortunately, this problem of a blanket approach to power issues that neglects the complexities involved has continued to be a problem to this day (see Thompson, 2007a, for a discussion of this). Radical social work emphasized the need for a critical perspective, but in many ways was not sufficiently reflective and thereby suffered from superficiality in some respects. Reflective approaches (the work of Schön, 1983, for example), by contrast, have emphasized the importance of analysis and depth of knowledge, but have tended to lack a critical perspective (Thompson and Thompson, 2008a). What is needed, then, is an approach that combines the benefits of critical and reflective approaches (Fook and Gardner, 2007), as discussed in Chapter 5.

Radical social work was therefore a mixed blessing, bringing some very clear positives that have stood the test of time and are still, so many years later, a major part of the social work value base. However, there is clear evidence to show that some of the negatives associated with radical social work remain with us. In particular, this approach to practice created an ethos of anti-professionalism. This is because what radical social work did was to reject professionalism itself, rather than to reject the elitism inherent within traditional forms of professionalism. Professionalism came to be seen as a bad thing in its own right, rather than as something that, in its traditional form, brought both strengths and weaknesses. It would have been possible to reject the weaknesses without losing the strengths but, unfortunately, that is not what happened.

Voice of experience 14.1

I remember the days when professionalism was considered a dirty word. I never did like the 'holier than thou' attitude of a lot of professionals, but I think we went too far in seeing professionalism itself as a bad thing. It has left a lot of people confused about whether we are professionals or not – and what that means. That hasn't helped us when it is a matter of coming across genuinely as credible professionals.

Paul, a policy development officer

The problems of anti-professionalism

The anti-professionalism that has emerged from the radical critique has created a number of problems for us. By throwing out the baby of professionalism with the bathwater of elitism, we also lost the benefits of professionalism, the four elements identified in Chapter 13: knowledge, skills, values and accountability. In particular, it can be seen that, in rejecting professionalism, we have paid the price in the following ways:

- **Confidence.** This can be seen to apply in two ways or at two levels. First, there is subjective confidence, and by this I mean the level of confidence each social worker has in his or her own ability to make a positive difference. Without the backing of professional knowledge, skills and values, we are left relatively ill equipped to deal with the very challenging situations we are likely to encounter in social work practice. However, the other side of the coin is the confidence that others may have in us – how much faith or trust they are prepared to credit us with. It is very difficult for people to have any degree of meaningful confidence in us if we do not have any basis in professional knowledge, skills and values. Without the respect and credibility that such professional factors bring, we are in a very weak position to influence others and to bring about positive outcomes. It has to be recognized that a significant part of social work activ-

187

ity involves influencing others and so, if we weaken our position in terms of how much confidence people have in us, then we seriously undermine our capabilities and limit how much we can achieve. Indeed, this is an important part of multiprofessional working. If we are not able to establish our credibility with members of other professional groups, we will be in a weak position to influence how events unfold. Kremer and Tonkens describe the situation well when they comment to the effect that:

> Social professionals frequently depend on the political and public consensus concerning the necessity of social interventions. They will receive little endorsement from public opinion, are rarely applauded in public and their professionalism is often questioned. In turn, the mistrust of outsiders translates into a low level of professional pride and low self-esteem (Gradener 2003; Spiers, Veldboer and Peters 2003).

(2006, p. 165)

➤ **Pride and identity.** To some, professionalism is seen as a matter of perks and privileges, but that is not what I am referring to here. Social work is generally a demanding occupation and, without having some degree of pride in what we do, and a sense of positive identity as professional social workers, we will struggle to develop and sustain the commitment and motivation needed to carry us through the series of challenges that we will encounter over time. It is very easy to become disheartened in the pressures of the job if we do not have some notion of professional pride and identity to fall back on. This is not a proposal for a return to elitism, far from it, but rather a recognition that social workers do an important job and, for the most part, do it well. These are all important factors in having a professional identity that is based on a commitment to high standards of practice and not to elitism.

Practice focus 14.2

Caitlin completed her social work degree at a university that emphasized the importance of professionalism as a basis for good practice. However, when she took up post as a newly qualified worker, she found her new team had no real commitment to professionalism – in fact, they seemed to regard it as something to be avoided.

One day, in discussion with two of her colleagues, she asked about why there was so much negativity in the team about professionalism. One colleague responded that the team was committed to equality and regarded professionalism as an obstacle to that. 'Yes', said the other colleague, 'we don't want to return to the days of looking down on our service users. We prefer to work alongside them.' Caitlin was quite surprised by this, as they clearly had a very different understanding of professionalism from hers. She mulled the situation over for a few days and came to the conclusion that they were equating professionalism with elitism. She then started wondering whether she should try and explain to the team that it is possible to be professional without being elitist or, alternatively, think about looking for a job in a team whose idea of professionalism was more akin to her own. She realized that, if she was to do the latter, she would need to do so quite quickly before she became too settled in the team.

Challenges to bureaucracy. An oft-heard complaint in recent years in the social work world has been the increase in bureaucracy: so many forms to fill in, so many statistics to contribute to, and so on. There has also been a move to increased proceduralization of social work with more and more aspects being described in terms of step-by-step processes. As a group of professionals, we are in a position to challenge this but, if we deny the value of professionalism, as indeed the radical social work movement did, then we are weakened in our efforts to challenge increasing bureaucracy. Webb offers important comment in this regard:

> There is a not entirely inappropriate perception that current social work has sunk into a 'managerialism' that is increasingly afraid of the complexity of risky situations and has become highly defensive. The latter has resulted in increasing dependence upon adherence to more and more elaborate rule systems, procedures and rule following. Thus there is a reduction of scope for social workers to develop competences of judgement, ethical insight, and holistic forms of practice. In effect social work is under threat of becoming a de-skilled profession.

(2006, p. 1)

The overemphasis on risk is a topic we covered in more detail in Chapter 11 and managerialism is an important topic for the discussions in Chapter 15. But, for present purposes, we should note that the movement away from professionalism that radical social work instigated paved the way for greater bureaucracy.

There are clearly significant costs involved in the rejection of professionalism, and so we can see that, while radical social work was to be welcomed in many ways, it was not an entirely positive development, and this has caused us significant difficulties. Radical social work, as already noted, was a major feature in the development of anti-discriminatory practice, and for that we must be grateful. However, the particular approach of radical social work as conceptualized at the time by the people involved has left us with some difficulties in this regard. This is because the issues were in some ways dealt with in what we can now see, with hindsight, was an oversimplified manner. For example, once anti-discriminatory practice grew out of the roots of radical social work's emphasis on class and poverty, racism took over as the major focus of concern, and what this meant was that one form of reductionist analysis was replaced by another. Approaches to anti-racism varied from well-theorized understandings that were well placed to shape practice appropriately (see, for example, Solomos, 2003) to highly oversimplified approaches that justified being referred to as what Penketh (2000) describes as 'the excesses of anti-racism'.

There was also a relative neglect of other forms of discrimination and, for some years, there was a lack of clarity about how different forms of discrimination interacted and had so much in common. It was as if different political and theoretical camps existed that supported their respective positions on discrimination and oppression, but paid relatively little attention to how these combined in highly significant ways to shape people's life experiences. It was only later that the efforts needed to integrate aspects of these different schools of thought produced a more holistic understanding (see Thompson, 2003a, for a discussion of these issues).

Voice of experience 14.2

As a black woman I have been aware of how racism and sexism interact. From this I have been able to develop a better understanding of problems like ageism and disablism, and how all these link together as part of a person's experiences. But it worries me that so many people seem to think of different forms of discrimination as separate, unconnected entities. They seem to have little appreciation of how these things all link together.

Sylvie, a social worker in an older people's team

The early stages of anti-discriminatory practice were also characterized by a reductionist approach based on a simplistic understanding of the many complex issues involved. It was just not appreciated at that time how involved the issues are that people were trying to deal with. An example of this would be in terms of language use. It was recognized that, in many ways, language can reinforce discrimination and can therefore be oppressive – for example, by reinforcing stereotypes or reinforcing relations of dominance and the inequalities associated with them. However, in trying to challenge such uses of language, a reductionist and dogmatic approach was adopted. Instead of having an educational approach that was premised on helping people understand how language can either help and empower or hinder and disempower, it was rejected in favour of an approach that simply sought to ban the use of certain terms and replace them with others. This, and other related aspects, can be dealt with in quite a confrontational approach, quite aggressive in some ways, and it is therefore not surprising that this created a culture of fear. So many people tried to avoid the issues because they were just seen as 'too hot to handle' and were therefore understood to be best avoided. The result of this was that very many people did not learn any more about these issues, they did not develop their understanding further because they had been put off by such a dogmatic and confrontational approach. It is a great pity that this occurred as it is understandable that, in those circumstances, people would back off and not engage positively with the issues. This unhelpful development we can now recognize as having been a significant problem, as it invited the dismissal of some very important issues as simply 'PC nonsense'.

Practice focus 14.3

Cathy was a social worker in a general hospital, working mainly with disabled or older people in need of rehabilitation. Her job involved working closely with a range of professional disciplines, both within the hospital itself and in the wider community. She felt quite comfortable with her colleagues in the hospital, as they had regular team meetings and were very supportive of one another. She had had the opportunity at one team meeting to explain the role of the social worker and the values on which it is based, including anti-discriminatory values. This had gone down well and colleagues told her they had found her explanation helpful.

However, Cathy found working with community-based colleagues much more difficult. She often encountered a lot of resistance to her efforts to make sure patients were being dealt with in anti-discriminatory ways. She got the distinct impression at times that some people thought that what she was saying was 'all a load of PC nonsense', but it was actually a social work team manager – somebody who most certainly should have known better – who actually came out and said it on one occasion. Cathy was quite amazed, and this incident made Cathy realize that we still have a long way to go to get beyond the oversimplified and dogmatic ways discrimination issues were dealt with at one time.

Alongside the problems of a dogmatic reductionism associated with early approaches to anti-discriminatory practice, we have had de-professionalizing tendencies linked to an increasing emphasis in the political sphere on what is known as neo-liberalism. This political discourse is based on a commitment to the importance of the market and individualism, both strongly opposed to the roots of anti-discriminatory practice, with its politicized understanding of the social nature of the problems encountered by social work clients (see Chapter 2). These deprofessionalizing tendencies can be understood in terms of an increasing emphasis on procedures – for example, in relation to child protection (Parton and O'Byrne, 2000). Similarly, there has been an immense move towards the use of targets and performance indicators as control mechanisms on the part of central government in trying to ensure that local government (including social work in the statutory sector) is in line with government policies and the ethos of neo-liberalism. This process of central government defining targets for local government has resulted in an atmosphere of mistrust, with a very clear message being conveyed that professionals are not to be trusted. This introduced the notion of 'managerialism', an important topic to which we shall return in Chapter 15.

Voice of experience 14.3

I had been feeling for a while that social work was in danger of losing its people focus – and, let's face it, it was the people side of things that attracted us to the work in the first place. But, what I found really helpful was a discussion on a training course recently on managerialism. For me, it all fell into place, and made me realize that we need to be much clearer about our professionalism if we are to stop managerialism from spoiling everything.

Gemma, a social worker in a children and families team

Also part of this deprofessionalizing tendency has been the increased emphasis on care management. Many social workers were designated as care managers when the NHS and Community Care Act 1990 was implemented. There was nothing in the legislation or its associated guidance that should have led to the abandonment of a problem-solving approach but, unfortunately, in so many ways, a service-led culture has developed from this. This is understandable up to a point, in so far as the terminology of care management (and the use of terms such as 'service user' rather than 'client') lead us into a situation where the primary emphasis would appear to be on providing care. Care, of course, is important, but care can be understood in two senses. First of all, we can go about our business as social workers in terms of addressing unmet needs and their associated problems in a caring way – that is, in a way that is sensitive to people's circumstances and feelings. Care can also be seen to be relevant in terms of being one of the services that can be offered. This can be in the form of home care, day care, respite care or long-term care, but the use of care as a primary term contributes to a discourse geared towards service provision and therefore dependency, rather than to problem solving, empowerment, social justice and well-being.

As we noted in Chapter 11, we have also witnessed a worrying move towards an overemphasis on risk at the expense of other factors, combined with a tendency to oversimplify risk issues in general. Webb writes about how a 'calculative' mentality has come to play an important role, displacing to a certain extent the holistic approach traditionally associated with good practice:

> Social work in the last 15 years, damaged by successive child abuse scandals has embraced the language of risk and accountability much as have other public institutions. Targets, performance measures and lists of procedures issuing from

central government have offered a 'calculative technology' for the assessment and constraining of risky situations. Of course the further burdening of already over-worked social care personnel leads to the opening up of more risk.

(2006, p. 3)

Without a basis in professional knowledge, skills, values and accountability, we are in a very weak position to resist and counteract such a potentially damaging tendency.

Anti-professionalism has given us no basis for challenging these negative developments in social work, nor for preventing further erosions. It leaves us prey to increasing bureaucracy and increased managerial control over what should be predominantly professional domains. Hence, there is a strong need to reaffirm professionalism, but without returning to elitism.

Practice focus 14.4

Caitlin had deided that, rather than move on so soon, she would stay in her team and try to help convince colleagues that professionalism and elitism are two different things, and that it is perfectly possible to have the former without the latter. She therefore raised the issue with her team manager at a supervision session. Barry, her supervisor, was very experienced and could remember the days of traditional professionalism, and he had been glad when radical social work came along and challenged it so successfully. This led on to an interesting discussion in which Caitlin was able to explain how professionalism had been presented on her course as a positive thing to develop – provided that this did not involve elitism being re-introduced. Barry was very impressed with the eloquent way she had expressed these ideas and asked her to make a short presentation to the team about the subject at one of their forthcoming team meetings. This made Caitlin feel very nervous, as she didn't like public speaking. However, it did dawn on her that, if she was to take professionalism seriously, it was part of her professional responsibilities to help others learn, and so she agreed to do it.

Conclusion   In Chapter 13, we saw how traditional professionalism had been problematic and how the legacy of those problems is still with us in various ways, particularly in the form of medicalization. In this chapter, we have taken those issues a step further by showing how the reaction against traditional professionalism took the form of anti-professionalism, and this too has created significant problems for us, many of which are still to be found today. Although it is appropriate to think of anti-professionalism in the past tense, as we are increasingly entering an era of new professionalism and multiprofessional working, it would be naive not to recognize that the influence of anti-professionalism is still with us in many ways. In the next chapter, we are able to see how there is the potential for overcoming the difficulties that both traditional professionalism and anti-professionalism have left us with. This is to be understood in terms of the development of empowering forms of professionalism, and it is to these that we now turn.

| See page 221 | for some questions about what you have just read. |
| See page 229 | for some pointers to useful further reading. |

15 Developing empowering professionalism

Introduction

 Having reviewed in Chapters 13 and 14 some of the historical developments that have stood in the way of effective professionalism in social work, the time has now come for us to consider how the emerging 'new' professionalism can be a significant step forward for social work. In this chapter we therefore look at how social work can make a positive contribution to empowerment, not by rejecting professionalism, nor by returning to elitism, but by developing a new form of professionalism – one that builds on the strengths of traditional professionalism, but without the weaknesses.

 We begin by reaffirming professionalism and seeing how professionalism is beginning to be seen as an important set of issues again. From this, we proceed to explore how we can make a contribution to the new professionalism through our own professional practice as social workers.

Reaffirming professionalism

We have already seen that much was wrong with traditional professionalism as applied to social work. We have acknowledged that radical social work was correct in critiquing it, but wrong to reject professionalism altogether. We are now at a crucial time historically in terms of social work professionalism, as we are seeing signs of a reaffirmation of professionalism. For example, within the United Kingdom in recent years, we have seen the introduction of professional registration, which means that there are stronger controls over who enters the profession and who is allowed to remain within it. There is now the possibility within British social work for a social worker who behaves inappropriately to be 'struck off', something that has not occurred before. Linked to this is the protection of title. This means that it is now a criminal offence within the UK for anybody who is not formally registered as a social worker (with the General Social Care Council, the Northern Ireland Social Care Council, the Scottish Social Services Council or the Care Council for Wales) to describe him- or herself as a social worker. Prior to the introduction of this measure, anybody could legally refer to him- or herself as a social worker, even if they had no qualifications in social work and were totally unsuited for such work.

4

These have been significant steps forward in terms of putting British social work on a professional footing. There has also been the increased investment in social work education by developing the educational foundations of practice from a two-year diploma to a three-year degree in social work, making social work a graduate profession in the UK for the first time. It is also no coincidence that the British Association of Social Workers publishes a monthly magazine entitled *Professional Social Worker*. This is all part of this process of the reaffirmation of professionalism.

The challenge we now face is to build on these positives of professionalism, without allowing the elitism of traditional professionalism to creep back in. We therefore need to keep a clear focus on our professional values, particularly those of partnership and empowerment that will act as deterrents to any tendency towards an elitist or top-down approach. We shall return to these points below.

Practice focus 15.1

When the day came for Caitlin to make her presentation, she was very nervous, but she had done a lot of preparation, so she was quietly confident that all would go well. She talked about the importance of professional knowledge, skills and values, as well as the need for professional accountability. She then went on to say that all this could be used in partnership and with a view to promoting empowerment. She also pointed out that none of this needs to be done in a top-down, 'we know best' way. In other words, she stressed, we can have professionalism without elitism.

This produced a great deal of discussion, and the team were quite taken by the ideas. In particular, they felt that the issue of professional skills needed to be given a lot more attention, as they felt the breadth and depth of their skills were often not appreciated. Caitlin added that they should also not underestimate the significance of their professional knowledge and values. Barry also added that accountability was crucial too, as public services – including social work – are part of a democratic society, and therefore have to be accountable. Caitlin was delighted with how things had gone, and was so glad she had decided to pursue the issue rather than move elsewhere.

Although, as we have noted, there are encouraging signs of a reaffirmation of professionalism, we also need to recognize that managerialism is still alive and well. This is a term that refers to the process by which central government has controlled local government through such processes as setting targets and performance indicators which lead to the awarding of a star status. That is, each local authority can gain or lose stars in their rating, depending on their performance in relation to these targets. Where a star is withdrawn, then this has significant budgetary implications. The introduction of this system has therefore been a key factor in moving away from the traditional idea that central government concerns itself with central issues, allowing local government to focus on how local needs may differ from the national picture. In place of this traditional model, managerialism has produced a very strong top-down approach, with central government being very controlling towards local government. While, at the time of writing, there are the beginnings of green shoots of what could be called a post-managerialist approach – that is, a movement away from these strict controls – there are still strong elements of this controlled approach in place.

Voice of experience 15.1

Social work has been in the doldrums for some time now as a result of managerialism, but we're beginning to get a more positive feeling coming through now. We've got signs of the pressures easing a bit, but also, we are starting to see people bounce back a bit – some encouraging signs of good old social work resilience. Let's hope it carries on in that direction.

Hannah, a training and development officer in a voluntary organization

The net result of managerialism is unfortunately a message conveyed to the effect that professionals are not to be trusted. Indeed, it could be argued that the emphasis on professionalism these days is in large part in response to the restrictions imposed by managerialism and the implicit lack of trust that devalues what professionals have to offer. Webb paints a similarly worrying picture:

> Social workers are increasingly held accountable for their interventions and decisions in mechanistic ways. Within this accountability culture the high expectations of service users, management and government require social work to specify the limits and define the boundaries of intervention in a coherent way. Indices, rules and precision techniques are sought after as part of the legal and moral responsibility of social work in a society saturated by and obsessed with risk. The effectiveness, evidence-based, risk management and 'what works' movements in social work can be partly understood as a rational set of responses to these demands.

(2006, p. 7)

There is a parallel here with the development of reflective practice which also can be seen as a significant reaction against the rigid approach of managerialism. Similarly, in terms of management, we have also seen the development of a major emphasis on leadership in recent years and this, too, can be understood as part of a reaction against the restrictions. This movement involves trying to get away from managerialism with its 'push' factors (that is, giving people instructions and setting targets *for* them, rather than *with* them), as opposed to the 'pull' factors associated with leadership. That is, a leader is seen as a person who is able to motivate and even inspire his or her staff, to pull them along with him or her, rather than to be in a coercive position of having to push people into doing things reluctantly or with resistance (Gilbert, 2005). As Payne so aptly puts it: 'Managerialism neglects motivating people in favour of control' (2000, p. 29).

Practice focus 15.2

Mike was a social worker in a mental health team. He was also a senior steward for his trade union. He was concerned about the number of people in social work who were suffering from stress, and he related this to the low level of morale in his department. One day he attended a conference organized by the union for its representatives. One of the speakers at the conference gave a talk about what he called post-managerialism. The speaker argued that the Government's emphasis on targets, performance indicators and managerial control had stifled professionalism and had led to a crisis of morale as a result of the lack of trust that is central to managerialism. He went on to argue that what was needed was an affirmation of the new, democratic professionalism, as the rejection of professionalism in public services had left us ill equipped to deal with the ravages of managerialism. Mike was very impressed with this line of argument and felt quite enthused by it. He began to wonder how he could take the issues forward, how – as both a social worker and a trade unionist – he could make a positive contribution to promoting partnership-based, empowering forms of professionalism.

What this all adds up to is a situation of clear indications of a reaffirmation of professionalism, but also signs that this is not a simple and straightforward matter; there are still forces at work in society that are weighed against professionalism. What happens in the coming years will in large part depend on political developments at national and international levels, but we should not underestimate the part that actual professionals can play in banding together and reasserting the importance of professionalism and the value of what we do as professionals. Duyvendak, Knijn and Kremer offer a similar view in making the point that:

> The most striking evidence for the change in climate is the fact that a leading critic of professional power, Eliot Friedson, published in 2001 a book in defence of professionalism, *Professionalism: The Third Logic*. He describes two dominant logics that have now overruled the logic of professionalism: bureaucracy and consumerism. What worries Friedson is not so much the restriction of the knowledge monopoly of professionals, but the fact that professionals are no longer supposed to be the moral protectors of this knowledge. If they can no

longer decide how and where this knowledge is to be put to use, professionalism itself is at stake.

(2006a, p. 8)

Professionalism therefore needs to be reaffirmed so that we can reclaim the moral responsibility for our professional knowledge base and ensure that it is not used unethically or destructively. We must not allow the deprofessionalizing tendencies of managerialism and consumerism to reduce us to bureaucrats, with professional accountability reduced to following orders.

Towards a new professionalism

What should be clear now is that there is a need to revisit professionalism and to reaffirm it without reintroducing elitism. My argument here is that this can be done through an emphasis on partnership and empowerment. These have been reinforced by the rise of the user involvement movement, with its insistence that people who are receiving social work help and other related services should have much more of a say in how these processes occur, the policies on which they are based, and so on (Kemshall and Littlechild, 2000; Shaping Our Lives National User Network, 2003). A partnership approach to professionalism can be seen as the direct opposite of an elitist approach. It is not a case of 'we know best', but rather 'We know things that may be of benefit to you. You know things about your situation that we cannot possibly know, so let us work together to pool our knowledge to develop an alliance that should be quite strong in enabling us to move together towards shared goals'. Lloyd sums the position up well when she argues that: 'The new professionalism implies a two-way sharing of knowledge, expertise and strength (Lloyd et al., 1996; Tanner, 1998a)' (2002, p. 164). Similarly, McDonald, referring to the work of Healy and Meagher (2004), comments that:

> New professionalism, they argue, is that which acknowledges professional expertise while promoting active collaboration with other groups of service providers and with service users.

(2006, p. 152)

This emphasis on partnership as a key part of the new professionalism has implications in terms of how we work, and the skills that we use, in terms of communication, negotiation and so on – all aspects of social work that this book has presented as bread and butter issues.

There also needs to be a renewed emphasis on empowerment. This can act as an antidote to the service mentality that managerialism has pushed so many people into. Webb's comments once again prove insightful:

199

It is argued that social work is abandoning a holistic approach to working with clients in order to rationally align itself within the dominant politics of neo-liberal managed care. Thus social work is less concerned with addressing deeply rooted psychosocial problems than with the re-construction and re-generation of clients' life strategies.

(2006, p. 7)

The point has already been made that there is a considerable irony that a focus on service provision reinforces dependency and is therefore disempowering, while a focus on empowerment can, in many cases, mean that we are able to help people gain greater control over their lives, so that, in very many (but clearly not all) circumstances, they will be in a position to resolve their own difficulties without the need for ongoing services.

Empowerment is an important part of anti-discriminatory practice and, as Payne convincingly argues:

anti-discriminatory and anti-oppressive practice needs to incorporate a concern for anti-bureaucratic practice. This is because bureaucratic behaviour can sometimes offer a way of concealing discrimination and oppression behind a veil of legal and proper behaviour.

(2000, p. 80)

Tackling discrimination and oppression, primary concerns for social work, therefore needs to be premised on professionalism rather than bureaucracy. If the main concern of practitioners is following procedures, rather than genuinely engaging with human need and problems, then anti-discriminatory practice becomes a pipedream, and social work becomes dangerous as a potential source of oppression.

Approaches to professionalism that do not take account of partnership and empowerment as central features therefore run the risk of returning to the days of traditional professionalism and all the problems we can associate with that.

Voice of experience 15.2

Having read about how traditional professionalism in social work used to be, and having seen how it still is in some professions today. I want to make sure that we don't go back to that sort of approach. We have made a lot of progress in terms of user involvement and empowerment, it would be a great shame to go back on that.

Joanne, a hospital social worker

Partnership and empowerment are, of course, also important ethical issues, as they are part of the social work value base (Moss, 2007). Hugman draws out one of the key ethical dimensions of professionalism when he comments that:

Professionalism in this sense can be seen as 'ideas in conversation with context' (James, 1995, p. 161). Values are the language of this conversation and fluency requires that such language is capable of grasping the complexities faced in practice. It is for this reason that decontextualised formal ethical codes are no longer seen as sufficient.

(1998, p. 77)

What this means is that professionalism needs to be understood as a value-based set of activities, linked to critically reflective practice, rather than simply following a set of rules, whether these are bureaucratic procedures or formal ethical codes disconnected from actual practice situations

In terms of these key concepts of partnership and empowerment, it is worth exploring in a little more detail how we can move forward in promoting good practice in these areas and guarding against poor practice (see Table 15.1). We shall now, then, explore each of these in turn, beginning with partnership.

Table 15.1 Examples of good and poor practice

Good practice	Poor practice
Listening to people's point of view because we recognize the importance of consultation and involvement.	Not listening to people. Or only superficially, with no real commitment to working in partnership.
Recognizing that our own perspective is only part of the situation.	Trying to force our perspective on others.
Valuing other people's contributions.	Disregarding other people'scontributions.

Partnership

Knijn and Selten make an important point about how knowledge can be shared constructively in partnership-based forms of practice:

> Sennett proposes that the client acknowledges the superiority of the professional's knowledge in terms of diagnosis and treatment, while the professional should acknowledge the superiority of the client's knowledge in terms of how it feels to live with a demented husband or to live on welfare for years. Note that the boundaries here between expert and lay do not become blurred at all. On the contrary, they remain quite clear, but there is a new balance as to who is the expert and who is lay in a particular area.

(2006, p. 132)

While 'diagnosis' and 'treatment' are not terms I would want to apply to social work, this passage is an important illustration of how professionalism and partnership can go hand in hand.

Having seen how significant partnership is in terms of good practice versus poor practice, we can now repeat this exercise in relation to empowerment as this, too, is a key issue when it comes to developing the new professionalism.

Empowerment

An important point in relation to empowerment is the recognition that it is not an unattainable ideal (Table 15.2). Lloyd gives us an encouraging message that empowering practice is indeed possible, even in these managerialist times:

> Recent studies focusing on the carrying out of care management, rather than the overall implementation of the community care reforms, claim evidence of social work practice surviving and proving its value. For example, Hardiker and Barker (1999: 421) claim that social workers demonstrated 'skilled methods and proactive descision-making' adopting advocacy roles and identifying 'empowerment' as a method to enable service users to negotiate around limited choices. The case studies showed utilisation of 'a wider range of individualised, imaginative solutions' (p. 425).
>
> (2002, p. 163)

Table 15.2 Using power

Good practice	Poor practice
Using own power to empower others	Using own power to retain dominance.
Sharing information and promoting shared knowledge.	Jealously guarding knowledge and information.
Encouraging people to make their own decisions and supporting them in doing so.	Making decisions for people.

Lloyd's example is a good one, as it is too easy to be defeatist and assume that empowerment is a word for the textbooks, but not something that can happen in reality. It shows that defeatism is not justified (indeed, defeatism and cynicism can be seen as 'symptoms' of the managerialist malaise).

Finally, before drawing this chapter to a close, I would like to present some ideas about what I see as a firm foundation for empowering professionalism. It is something that I shall refer to as the three Rs, for reasons that will become apparent. Let us consider each of these Rs in turn:

> **Resourcefulness.** What is called for is not a mechanistic, service-driven approach far removed from the creativity associated with reflective practice. We need a resourceful approach that is consistent with I-Thou

involvement rather than I-it relationships. Reso'
the creativity and the breadth of vision to be at
promise of the human encounter. If we see
crats who fill in forms and ration resources,
resourceful. If we see ourselves as skilled professiona.
knowledge base to draw upon, plus a value base that ensure
practising ethically, then we have the potential to be extremely rese
ful individuals who can offer a great deal to people who are encountering
difficulties in their lives. Resourcefulness, then, is not simply about having
access to resources through budgetary means, but rather being able to
draw on our personal resources as creative, intelligent, well-informed and
committed individuals who can play a significant part in bringing about
positive change in people's lives, not in all circumstances, but certainly in
very many.

Practice focus 15.3

Simon was a social worker in a family support team. In working with the Stevenson
family, he kept encountering obstacles. The sort of thing that tended to work well with
other families, for some reason did not work at all well with the Stevensons. For a while
he was feeling very discouraged and wondered whether he should close the case, as he
clearly wasn't being much help to this particular family.

However, at his next supervision session, his team manager, Suki, asked him how
things were going in relation to the Stevenson family. Simon was honest enough to say
that he had run out of ideas, as the usual things he relied on didn't seen to apply to the
Stevensons. Suki was pleased that he had been honest, but was concerned about his
apparent lack of resourcefulness. She therefore tried to get the point across – gently and
constructively – that Simon should be using his imagination more and not just relying
on a stock set or repertoire of practice tools. She also tried to get him to realize that,
in drawing on his own resourcefulness, he should be looking at how he could help the
family to build on their own strengths, resources and imagination. Simon could see that
he was going to find this quite a challenge, but he was pleased that he was going to have
Suki's support in developing his skills in this area.

Robustness. The point has been made already that social work is not
for the faint-hearted. It is an occupation characterized by very many challenges as well as dilemmas and conflicts. A social worker therefore needs
to be fairly robust in the sense of not falling at the first hurdle, not falling
apart when the pressure is on. There are, of course, limits to how much
pressure any individual can take and nobody should be put in a position
in which those pressures overspill into harmful stress, but it is important

that we recognize that a certain degree of robustness or hardiness is an essential part of the effective social worker's repertoire. However, we should make sure that we do not equate the term robust with macho or unfeeling. We do not want to return to the masculinism of traditional professionalism. Being robust means having certain strength of character; it does not mean having notions of undue toughness and being uncaring or unfeeling. These are clearly incompatible with social work although, unfortunately, not entirely absent from the profession. A robust social worker, then, is not a tough guy or gal, but rather a professional who has a certain strength that he or she can draw upon as part of their professional pride and identity.

▶ **Resilience.** This is a term that refers to the ability to 'bounce back' from adversity, to recover from the setbacks that are part and parcel of social work practice and, indeed, of life in general. Social work will throw up all sorts of challenges and problems, as we have seen, and sometimes we will be able to take these in our stride but, at other times, we will find it difficult, and we may experience an adverse reaction to some of the things that we encounter. For example, dealing with somebody who is grieving may temporarily open up old wounds of our own concerning a significant loss we have had in the past. It is only human to have such a reaction and is certainly not a problem. But, what is very important, is that: (i) we are not macho about this and are prepared to seek support as and when we need it; and (ii) that we have the skills and resilience to be able to bounce back from any such difficulties, so that, while they may knock us out of our stride temporarily, we are able to get back on course and resume our role as a supportive professional at the earliest reasonable opportunity.

Voice of experience 15.3

Being able to bounce back after adversity is what resilience is all about. We need to promote it in others and in ourselves whenever we can. We also need to be able to recognize it when we encounter it, so that we can make the most of it.

Kate, a social worker in a children and families team

All three of these – resourcefulness, robustness and resilience – are highly significant in relation to partnership and empowerment. First, to be resourceful is a sound basis for engaging with clients and others. It gives a basis for their being able to have confidence in us. This, in turn, is very useful in terms of promoting empowerment. Being resourceful ourselves can act as a useful role model for others in terms of helping them to gain greater control over their lives. By contrast, if we lack resourcefulness, we are in a very weakened position when we are trying to encourage others to be more personally resourceful and less reliant on external sources of support, such as ongoing services.

In terms of robustness, partnership is not always a smooth ride and there may be conflicts and tensions that arise. If we fall apart at the first sign of such things, clearly we are not well equipped to deal with the challenges of partnership. Being robust, without being macho, is therefore a great advantage when it comes to working in partnership. Similarly, being robust can help in terms of promoting empowerment. This is because we can again act as a role model in terms of helping people to recognize that, while their difficulties may very well be painful and distressing, we all have inner strengths that we can draw upon from time to time. This is closely linked with the idea of 'power from within', as discussed earlier.

In relation to resilience, we can see that this, too, is important for partnership and empowerment. For partnership, the same comments in relation to robustness apply, in so far as there will be setbacks in many of the issues we deal with, and we may be called upon to bounce back from such adversity whenever we can, as soon as we can. Similarly, showing others how it is possible to bounce back from difficult situations can be a useful way of helping them to construct a more empowering narrative of their lives, and thus move away from the influence of forces in their previous circumstances that have perhaps had the effect of disempowering them.

Practice focus 15.4

Shelley was a very experienced mental health social worker who was seconded to a trauma response project. She was really looking forward to the work and felt that she had a lot to offer as a result of having worked in mental health services for over five years. However, she had not anticipated that she would come into so much conflict with her new team mates. What the conflict stemmed from was that Shelley adopted a very supportive, nurturing approach that had many benefits, but there was little or no emphasis on empowerment in her work. The team's philosophy, by contrast, put empowerment at the heart of their work. They emphasized the potential for post-traumatic growth, linked to the idea of resilience. That is, their primary concern was with helping traumatized people to 'bounce back' and to capitalize on the positive potential of the crises they had experienced. 'Looking after' people was part of this up to a point, but it was not enough on its own. The team were therefore keen to get Shelley to 'tune in' to their approach, as they were sure she had what it took to make a success of the job. Shelley, for her part, felt a bit 'got at' to begin with, but she was beginning to see the wisdom of the team's approach.

The three R's then, are by no means a cure-all for the challenges of promoting the new professionalism based on partnership and empowerment, but they do clearly have much to offer as a useful framework to help us make sense of the challenges and to give us tools for moving forward in the right direction.

Conclusion

The comments of McDonald reflect well the basic message I have been trying to put across in this chapter:

> Jones proposes the development of a new form of professionalism, a renewal which has several dimensions. Social work must become an *engaged profession*, participating as politically significant actors in the social institutions shaping the contemporary environment. It cannot (and must not) sit outside the arenas of power. Social workers may also work towards the development of alternatives, but not as a substitute for engagement in the context and processes shaping contemporary and future practice. It must become a *sustainable profession*. Social work must pay attention to such time-honoured concerns of traditional professionalism in attempting to protect the conditions of autonomous practice, favourable public opinion, commitment to community service, creation of new opportunities for practice, and promoting the general interests of its clients. However, it must take a proactive stance in that it must continually look to new and emerging opportunities for professional practice.
>
> (2006, pp. 149–50)

This gives us a clear picture of what is required of us if we are to rise to the challenge of developing a new professionalism that is truly partnership based and empowering. This chapter has not offered easy answers; there are clearly major challenges involved in developing empowering forms of professionalism, but we have seen how significant professionalism is and how weakened we are without it. It would be a tragedy to return to elitist notions of professionalism, and so it is to be hoped that our discussions here of how professionalism can flourish without elitism (through a significant focus on partnership and empowerment) will be able to give us the strength and encouragement we need to continue in the direction of helping people address their needs and problems and, in so doing, make a contribution to social justice and well-being through the processes of problem solving and empowerment.

See page 221 for some questions about what you have just read.

See page 229 for some pointers to useful further reading.

16

Professionalism in practice

In this final chapter, we provide an overview of how professionalism can be put into practice. In doing this, we are providing a concluding chapter not only to Part 4 but also, in effect, to the whole book. We therefore draw on a range of themes and issues that have featured in each of the chapters that precede this one.

In focusing on professionalism, it is important that we revisit the basis of professional practice. We therefore begin with a discussion of the four key elements of professionalism.

The building blocks of professionalism

We have identified four key factors that underpin professionalism. These are each important in their own way and link together to make a significant whole as an underpinning for professional social work practice:

> **Knowledge.** As we have seen, social work is a demanding occupation that involves a need for understanding a wide range of significant issues. To attempt to practise without at least the basics of that knowledge base puts us in a significantly disadvantaged position in terms of how effective we can be, and also introduces an unnecessary level of risk in relation to the harm that we can do to others and, indeed, to our own careers by trying to practise beyond our knowledge. Efforts to develop our knowledge base are therefore key underpinnings of professionalism in practice. Gradener and Spiers (2006) recognize the importance of knowledge when, in citing from the work of Osmond and O'Connor (2004), they argue that: 'in the current environment, an incapacity to articulate what we know places us at a considerable disadvantage' (p. 165). It is, then, not only a matter of developing our knowledge base, but also of recognizing its significance, valuing it for what it offers and being able and willing to articulate it when we need to. In this way, we can enhance our credibility in ways that run counter to the tendency for social work to be devalued by people who lack a sufficient understanding of it or awareness of its capabilities. We do ourselves and the people

4

we serve a significant disservice if we hide our professional knowledge base under a bushel.

▷ **Skills.** A professional social worker has a wide range of skills to draw upon. These are generally extremely helpful in enabling us to carry out our duties to a high standard and to be able to stand a reasonably good chance of achieving the outcomes we are working towards. We should therefore not underestimate the significance of our skills base. Nor should we make the mistake of assuming that, once we have the basics, everything will be fine. Social work is a hugely challenging enterprise, and so it is very much in our interests and the interests of those people who rely upon us for support and, indeed, of our profession as a whole, to continue to develop those skills throughout our career. If there is something we are already good at, then that is a good starting point, but we can get even better by making sure that we continue to hone our skills. A professional is not somebody who rests on his or her laurels but, rather, someone who makes a positive contribution to continuous professional development.

▷ **Values.** In working alongside people who are often vulnerable for a variety of reasons, or otherwise in distress or experiencing difficulties, there is considerable scope for us to abuse our position and to practise unethically. The value base therefore helps to ensure that we have a framework that will give us a good starting point for reflective practice – one that allows us to make sure that what we are doing is consistent with such values as treating people with dignity and respect and promoting social justice. Mullaly emphasizes in particular the importance of seeing the wider social justice picture and thereby avoiding pathologizing individuals:

> Progressive social work scholarship represents a rich and diversified body of literature that challenges the hegemony of traditional, mainstream social work theories and practices. In calling for fundamental social transformation it rejects the notions that social problems are caused by individual deficiencies or that minor social reforms will overcome the inherent inequalities of a society that fall along lines of class, race, gender and other forms of dominant-subordinate relationships. As part of a critical social theory tradition, however, it is incumbent upon those of us who subscribe to the ideals and values of progressive social work to reformulate our theories and practices in light of changed and changing social, economic, political, cultural and intellectual conditions. To do otherwise is to become irrelevant.

(2001, p. 316)

▷ **Accountability.** This is closely linked to the question of ethics again, as accountability is the process through which we have the opportunity to check (and indeed others also have the opportunity to check) that we are practising in ways that we can justify by reference to the goals of our professional activity and the ethical principles on which they are based.

Practice focus 16.1

After Caitlin's presentation at the team meeting and the lively discussion that followed, the team were keen to make professionalism a much stronger feature of their work. Barry, the team manager, therefore went to talk to the manager of the Workforce Development Unit to ask about possibilities for training on professionalism to be provided. From that meeting he came away with the idea that a team development day on the subject would give more scope for learning than a formal training course. In particular, it had been suggested that the day be divided into four sections, with each one covering one of the four aspect of professionalism

- professional knowledge
- professional skills
- professional values
- professional accountability.

Barry was enthusiastic about this idea and decided he would propose it at the next team meeting.

At that meeting his proposal was warmly welcomed. As there were 12 members of the team, Barry suggested that subgroups of three members each be set up. His plan was that each subgroup would take responsibility for one of the four sessions and decide how best to use the time available. Barry was pleased that they were able to make such good progress on these important issues.

Having reviewed, albeit briefly, these four elements of professionalism, we can now look closely at how the key themes and issues arising earlier in the book can be linked to this important challenge of putting professionalism into practice – making it a reality rather than just a rhetorical statement of commitment.

Key themes and issues

There are various ways in which we can understand social work. This book has not attempted to close the debate or be in any sense definitive; rather, it is a matter of laying down foundations for future development and understanding, so that we can all play a part in trying to make sure that standards of practice are as high as they possibly can be in the circumstances. In order to help with this, I shall now give a brief summary of some of the key themes and issues that have emerged in our discussions in the earlier chapters. It is to be hoped that this will help to give a clear picture of how the different elements covered in different chapters fit together into a coherent whole.

Needs and problems

The key point to emphasize here is that we must make sure that our primary focus is not on the services that we may possibly be able to offer but, rather, on the unmet needs and associated problems that are likely to have brought such services into existence in the past. Our fundamental aim in social work is to promote social justice and well-being. We do that through empowerment wherever we reasonably can. To make a positive contribution to empowerment, we need to be clear about what unmet needs are holding people back, what problems people are experiencing, what is making justice and well-being something they cannot currently attain.

It is perhaps helpful to distinguish between social care and social work. Social care (in the sense of the range of caring services that are potentially available to support people in circumstances where they cannot be fully independent) is what comes into play when social work problem-solving efforts have not been successful, when attempts to avoid the need for services have proven ineffective on this particular occasion. To opt for a social care approach without first exploring social work options is to confuse ends with means. Social work is primarily concerned with needs and problems (as a means of promoting social justice and well-being). Services become an issue when there is no other way of addressing the concerns identified. Making service provision our primary concern creates situations in which we are promoting dependency rather than empowerment. Services have a very important role to play, but they must not be allowed to distort our vision of what social work is all about.

Voice of experience 16.1

When I first took over as team manager I was disappointed by how service oriented things had become. I had no worries about individual staff – they were all great – but the culture was not good. I had to work hard to get them to adopt a problem-solving mentality, but we got here in the end, and they could see how much more empowering that was.

Pauline, manager of a community care team

The social context

When we are dealing with individuals in distress or experiencing other such problems, it is very easy for our focus to be narrowed to look specifically at that individual or the particular family we are working with at the time. While this is understandable, it is not helpful. This is because, as we have seen, we need to understand an individual's problems in a much wider context of society and the various social processes and institutions that can play such a significant part in not only defining the problems people experience, but also in shaping how they are experienced or even, in some circumstances, of actually causing those problems. Tew emphasizes the need for a holistic perspective – that is, one that sees the importance of the 'big picture', including the sociopolitical aspects. He argues that a holistic approach:

> demands a reclaiming of expertise in interpersonal work – the art of staying with and responding to the content of people's distress – that has tended to be lost to social work practice in recent years. However, conventional models of counselling may not always be appropriate here, as they may not encourage a sufficiently social orientation, tending towards an individualisation of distress and a neglect of wider contexts of power, oppression and abuse – the realities of everyday living.

> (2002, p. 152)

What is needed, then, is an approach that recognizes the specifics of the situation for the individual concerned, but also takes account of the wider social picture that has such a bearing on the problems encountered and the potential solutions.

Promoting and preventing change

In trying to achieve our goals, we will often be involved in processes of trying to bring about positive change. In some circumstances, the emphasis is more on preventing change in the sense of preventing deterioration in somebody's circumstances. What is particularly important here is the need for clarity – to be clear about what changes we may need to bring about or what changes we may need to prevent, or at least slow down. Without this clarity, we may be going in the wrong direction and could end up being more of a hindrance than a help.

The significance of change in social work (whether we are promoting positive change or resisting negative change) can be helpfully linked to the significance of grief. This is because a powerful grief reaction can be experienced in response to any change in a person's situation, whether or not death is involved. As we have noted, it is a significant mistake to restrict the notion of grief to situations involving death. Trying to deal with change situations without taking account of the highly significant role of grief in people's lives (and cumulative and disenfranchised forms of grief in particular) is to take on a very difficult task without the necessary level of understanding. This is clearly not a wise approach to the challenges of social work, so we would do well to keep the significant role of grief in mind.

Working in partnership

The basic idea behind this important theme is that we are working *with* the people we seek to help, not doing things *to* or *for* them. We have extensive practice experience that shows that trying to bypass partnership is very unhelpful. For example, trying to impose change on people without trying to get them involved in the process rarely, if ever, works and can create such strong resistance that the whole enterprise becomes fruitless. It can also do significant damage to working relationships, with the result that future work becomes jeopardized in the process.

Highly respected social work author Malcolm Payne encapsulates partnership in his vision of the future of social work:

> The future for social work, then, is:
> - ∴ *citizen-responsive*, concerned to respond to citizens with an interest in the public role of social work;
> - ∴ *user-involved*, where social work collaborates with clients, service users and the user community, and
> - ∴ *multiprofessional*, collaborating with related colleagues.
>
> (2000, p. 85)

This spells out very clearly the basis of partnership as a fundamental social work value – in terms of both: (i) worker-client relationships; and (ii) multiprofessional working. Both of these depend on our ability to communicate effectively; to work constructively with differences; to show and earn respect; and to demonstrate a commitment to putting the client and his or her needs and problems at the heart of our endeavours without allowing professional rivalries to get in the way.

Reflective practice

Here, the emphasis is on going beyond routinized, habitual practices based on uncritical acceptance of situations and what people want or expect from us. A critically reflective practitioner is somebody who does not take things at face value, who does not fall into the trap of atomism (and thereby neglects the wider social aspects of the situation) and who draws on a professional knowledge base and value base in such a way as to maximize the potential for success. Critically reflective practice is therefore the fundamental basis for putting professionalism into practice.

The approach adopted by Hamer fits nicely with the ethos of reflective practice. He comments that: 'Social work process is a creative flow. We have a "menu" of tools and resources at our disposal, but how we use them and fit them together is entirely up to us' (2006, p. 12). Reflective practice is not a matter of looking for 'the answer'. Rather, it involves being creative and imaginative in using the tools and resources available to us, matching them to the circumstances as best we can.

Practice focus 16.2

Martina was a student on placement at a day centre for older people. She was enjoying the placement, but felt under pressure as an essay was due to be submitted shortly. The theme of the essay was the importance of putting professionalism into practice, and she wasn't sure how best to frame her answer to the question. However, as a student on placement in that particular local authority, she was given the opportunity to attend an in-service training course on reflective practice. She found the day both very interesting and very useful. It really made her think about the links between theory and practice and the importance of values.

What was particularly useful was that the day gave her an insight into how reflective practice could be used as a foundation for professionalism. She could see that reflective practice would be very useful for maintaining a focus on working in partnership and promoting empowerment. She understood now that reflective practice and the new professionalism have in common a focus on the importance of knowledge and values – and both recognize the importance of accountability. Martina now realized that she could use reflective practice as a foundation for her essay on professionalism.

Social work as education

The key principle here is that of 'empowerment through learning'. Social workers often encounter people who are experiencing difficulties partly or wholly as a result of how they understand their circumstances. Changing that understanding, helping them to develop more appropriate, better understandings of their situation can be immensely important and very effective in bringing about much needed change in many circumstances. Unfortunately, many people neglect this aspect of social work practice and so we need to make sure that we do not fall into that trap.

The educational dimension of social work offers considerable potential for:

- Reducing anxiety, tension and distress
- Boosting confidence and self-esteem
- Identifying barriers to progress and potential ways of removing or circumventing them
- Bringing people together with shared concerns, interests and potential
- Giving people hope.

The importance of emotion

It has been established here that social workers need to have a good grasp of rationality and be clear thinkers. However, this is not to deny the importance of emotion. On the contrary, a professional social worker needs to be able to balance head and heart, to be able to recognize the significant reasoning underpinning a situation, but also the significant emotionality involved too. It is not a case of 'either … or', but rather 'both … and'.

Jordan's work on the important linkages between social work and well-being is very interesting in this regard. He draws a distinction between the material economy (the financial world) and the 'interpersonal' economy, which relates to the value generated by relationships, care and concern. He comments to the effect that:

> The difference between the material economy producing goods, and the interpersonal economy producing feelings (including morale, team spirit and solidarity) and culture (ideas, images, science, art, music and drama) is that the latter produces something intangible and difficult to measure. But what the interpersonal economy produces is *real*.
>
> (2007, p. xi)

Making a positive contribution to the interpersonal economy is certainly a traditional role for social work and remains an important challenge for us – especially in these managerialist days of a greater emphasis on targets and performance indicators than on meaningful involvement in people's circumstances in ways that enrich their experience of life and promote their well-being. Jordan's focus on relationships is vitally important and once again shows the importance of being able to work effectively at an emotional level, as the success or otherwise of interpersonal relationships depends very much on the quality of emotional exchange involved.

Voice of experience 16.2

The thing I find really interesting – and really challenging too – about social work is that it all hinges on getting the right balance of head and heart. You need to be clear thinking and able to weigh up complex issues, but you also need to be able to deal with all the feelings involved – your own as well as other people's.

Margo, a social worker based at a medical practice

The importance of meaning

Each individual understands his or her own circumstances in a way that is distinctive, a way that is specific to him or her. This is because we all have to make sense of our experience. It is not presented to us on a plate. We have to integrate what

we encounter through our senses on a daily basis in a way that makes s[...]
so that as we come up against new experiences, we are able to relate thes[...]
existing frames of meaning. Sometimes, it is such meanings that need to ch[...]
in order to help people move on, and this can be done through the process [...]
'co-constructing a more empowering narrative' – as it is known in the narrative
therapy literature (Crossley, 2000; Dallos, 2006). This involves helping people to
identify what aspects of their interpretation of their circumstances are problematic, and supporting them in making any necessary changes to that understanding
by reworking the narrative (the 'story' that acts as a linking thread to give meaning and coherence to our fragmented experiences) on which it is based.

A vitally important part of meaning making is spirituality. Unfortunately,
it has commonly been the case that much social work practice has neglected
the spiritual dimension of people's lives. Without taking account of what gives
people's lives meaning, what gives them a sense of purpose or direction and
what enables them to feel 'connected' to other people and the wider world,
we are likely to be working on a very superficial understanding of the person
concerned and therefore to be in a very weak position to help him or her. This
is not to say that we need to develop an in-depth understanding of the spiritual concerns of each person we seek to help, as that would be unworkable.
However, it does mean that, where we are trying to form a clear picture of a
person and their needs, we must take care to ensure that such a fundamental
issue as spirituality is not omitted (Moss, 2005).

Self-management

Everything we do in social work, we do through the vehicle of our self, our
identity. If we do not take care of that most precious tool, then we take serious
risks, with potentially very damaging consequences to ourselves, to the people
we are trying to help and to the organizations that employ us. Self-care and the
wider issues of being a well-organized manager of our pressures is therefore a
crucial part of effective professional social work practice.

Self-management is something that many people are very good at as a result
of their upbringing and general life experience. Others may have a lot to learn
in this regard, in which case it is very important to make sure the lessons are
learned, as the price for poor self-management can be quite high in terms of
stress, burnout, poor health and other such problems.

 Practice focus 16.3

Barbara was a social worker in an older people team. She was very committed to doing
the best she could for the older people she served. She found it difficult to accept that

le were not eligible for services, and so she kept cases open while she tried ther ways of helping wherever she could. The result of this was that she was ng herself. What made it worse was that, when she wasn't working, she found possible to relax. This created a vicious circle: the more tense she got, the und it to manage her workload; the less she achieved, the more guilty she about not being able to meet everybody's needs; and so the more tense and worn out she felt. This culminated in her being off sick with stress for six weeks. During this period of absence she began a course of counselling provided by her employers' employee-assistance programme. The counselling helped her to understand that she could not be all things to all people, that she had to recognize the limitations of what social services in general can do and what any specific individual in particular can achieve. She was beginning to learn the important lessons of self-care, recognizing that she would be in no position to look after anybody else if she did not look after herself.

Managing processes, tasks and outcomes

We are called upon in social work to carry out a wide range of tasks that involve various processes, all geared towards what should have been identified in the early stages as the desired outcomes. However, there is much that can happen to distract us from these issues. It is therefore important that we are clear about what is involved in managing processes, tasks and outcomes and take our professional duties in this regard very seriously, not allowing drift or other such problems to get in the way of success in this vitally important area.

In some respects, managing processes, tasks and outcomes links closely with self-management, in the sense that the challenge of managing a heavy workload is partly a matter of being effective at managing the processes, tasks and outcomes involved, and partly self-management in terms of being able to set priorities, keep a clear focus on what we are doing, be assertive in not allowing other people to overload us, and so on.

Managing risk and resources

As far as risk is concerned, there is a balance to be struck in terms of not trying to be overly defensive and focus primarily on eliminating risk, as this has been shown to create significant problems for people, but nor should we be reckless about risk issues, as that clearly has potential disaster beckoning. Being able to find that balance can be difficult at times, but it is important that we adopt a sophisticated approach to issues of risk so that we do not fall into the trap of oversimplifying some very complex issues. This also is a matter of self-management to a certain extent, in so far as it involves keeping our anxiety about risk under control, so that we can adopt a well-reasoned and balanced approach to the subject.

There is also a need to strike a balance in terms of resources. There will always be limitations on availability of resources, and so it is important that we are not wasteful of those we have available to us and make fully sure that they are appropriately targeted. However, what we should not do is allow resources to become our primary focus and thereby lose sight of our professional goals and values.

> **Voice of experience 16.3**
>
> One of the things I learned at University was that supply is finite, but demand is potentially infinite. So, dealing with a shortage of resources is par for the course. What worries me, though, is that, if we place too much emphasis on what we haven't got, we don't do enough to make the best of what we have got, and we end up being very negative about things. We see the glass as half empty, rather than half full.
>
> **Carol, a senior practitioner in a looked-after children team**

Managing expectations

Social work tends to start from a low base point when it comes to other people's understanding of what we can and cannot do. It is therefore very important that we have the skills and commitment to make sure that we manage such expectations effectively, that we do not allow people to have unrealistic expectations that can cause problems for them and for us, and that we also do not allow unclear expectations to persist. If we are lax in this regard, the result can be the creation of great difficulties, when we are trying to go in precisely the opposite direction –that is, to address existing difficulties rather than create additional ones.

It is also important that we successfully manage our own expectations of ourselves. This is because, in the caring professions in general and in social work in particular, it is very easy for us to give ourselves unrealistic expectations – in effect, to lose sight of a very important ingredient of social work: humility. It is essential to recognize that we cannot meet everyone's needs all of the time. If we forget this important insight, the result can be considerable stress and heartache.

Managing to be a professional in difficult circumstances

This point captures what Part 4 of the book has been all about: the importance of professionalism matched with the difficulties in practising professionally as a result of the historical constraints on this (both traditional professionalism and the problems of medicalization on the one hand and the difficulties arising from anti-professional attitudes linked to radical social work on the other). Social work is about making the best of difficult circumstances, and this applies

to professionalism too. We now have the opportunity to develop empowering partnership-based forms of professionalism without returning to elitism. This is an important challenge that we need to rise to with all our capabilities.

An important point to recognize is that professionalism fits well with the emphasis in recent years on leadership. This is for two reasons. First, professionalism is best cultivated and supported by managers who adopt a leadership approach, as this encourages creativity, autonomy and reflective practice – precisely what are needed to deal with the complexities of human problems we encounter in social work – rather than a top-down, bureaucratic approach that demotivates and spells a very strong message of mistrust. Second, professionalism can, in itself, be seen as a form of leadership – a way of identifying where we need to get to and exploring options together for how best to reach our destination. Partnership-based, empowering professionalism has much in common with leadership, while traditional professionalism is parallel with bureaucratic styles of management that are top-down and thereby create resistance and mistrust,

Practice focus 16.4

Vee was a team manager in a team serving adults with a learning disability. She was very busy, trying to support a highly pressurized team of social workers and support workers. To make sure a huge backlog did not build up, she had to keep the team under close supervision. High levels of staff sickness added to those pressures, so she felt she couldn't afford to let up. So, when she was told that she had to attend a mandatory two-day course on leadership, she was none too pleased.

However, she changed her view after the course. She learned that leadership is about 'pulling' people (that is, motivating and inspiring than) rather than putting them under further pressure by 'pushing' them. In particular, it struck a chord with her when the point was made that a 'push' approach can overload people, lead to higher sickness absence rates and thereby be counterproductive. She realized that this was exactly what had happened in her team.

She was therefore able to use the course as an opportunity to think about how she might change her approach and make it one based more on principles of leadership. She decided to begin by using the next team meeting to get the team to acknowledge that they were overloaded and to explore strategies for dealing with this.

Conclusion

Putting professionalism into practice is not an easy option but, when we consider the alternatives, it soon becomes clear that it is an *essential* option. It is to be hoped that the summaries of key issues provided in this chapter will help to provide an overview of the messages I have tried to convey throughout the book. How well we collectively rise to the challenge of the new professionalism remains to be seen, but there is no doubt that we should make every reasonable effort to make sure that we are successful in this crucial endeavour. So much depends on it.

| See page 221 | for some questions about what you have just read. |
| See page 229 | for some pointers to useful further reading. |

Conclusion to Part 4

What Part 4 should have made clear is that 'professionalism' is a very important word in contemporary social work, and that it is also a very 'loaded' term, in the sense that it has meant different things at different times in our history. We are now at an important point in that history, in so far as we are showing distinct signs of moving out of a period of relative confusion about what professionalism means and establishing a much clearer picture of the 'new' professionalism – that is, a professionalism founded on principles of partnership and empowerment.

We have also seen that professionalism refers to a complex set of issues, and so we need to have some clarity and a degree of sophistication in our understanding of the issues involved, as oversimplification is a very real danger. There are no simple, straightforward 'answers' to the challenge of professionalism – indeed, that is why we need professionalism: because what we deal with in social work is far too complex and sensitive to be dealt with in a simple, straightforward or mechanistic way. Our work requires a much more considered, well-informed and flexible approach that does justice to the complexities involved. We put ourselves in a very dangerous position if we do not recognize the significance of this and invest in professionalism accordingly.

Points to ponder

- In what ways could traditional professionalism be described as elitist?
- What are the four elements of professionalism identified in this chapter?
- What do you understand by the term, 'holistic approach'?
- What is meant by the idea of 'the medicalization of social concerns'?

- What distinguished radical social work from the forms of social work that had gone before?
- In what ways did radical social work criticize professionalism?
- What negative consequences of anti-professionalism can you identify?
- What is meant by 'dogmatic reductionism'?

- What do you understand by the term, 'managerialism'?
- In what ways can this be detrimental to social work?
- How can partnership contribute to good practice?
- What are the three Rs associated with the new professionalism?

- How might you distinguish between social care and social work?
- What, according to Payne (2000), is 'user involvement'?
- What does Jordan (2007) mean by 'the interpersonal economy'?
- How is this relevant to the 'new' professionalism?

Exercises

Imagine yourself in a situation where you were being helped by a 'traditional' professional – that is, someone who acts in a top-down way and does not involve you in decision making. What feelings is this experience likely to generate in you? Would these feelings be helpful in addressing your problems, or would they serve as an obstacle to progress? What lessons can you learn from considering these issues in this way?

Think carefully about the idea of 'anti-professionalism'. In what ways do you think the development of social work may have been held up by the dominance of this notion at one stage in our history? What lessons might we learn from this in terms of the future development of professionalism in social work?

Look at the examples of good and bad practice in relation to partnership and empowerment in this chapter. For each of these items, think carefully about which pole your current practice lies nearer to? Does this give you any ideas about how you may improve your practice in the future, whether by building on strengths or addressing areas for development?

Revisit the four elements of partnership discussed near the beginning of this chapter. Consider how each of these relate to an aspect of your practice base (assessment, record keeping, conflict management or whatever) and identify how each of these four elements relates to it. Finally, think carefully about whether this gives you any ideas about how you may strengthen the professional basis of your work.

4

Guide to further learning

Introduction

In this section of the book you will find basic details about a wide range of possible sources of information to guide your future learning. For each of the four parts of the book you will find details of suggestions for further reading. Some of the topics covered in the book have a bigger literature base than others. There will therefore inevitably be some degree of imbalance across the different sections.

Social work is a vast subject, and so you are strongly advised to make full use of the signposting provided here to wider and more advanced sources of literature and information. For a more comprehensive guide to learning in relation to social work, see Thompson and Thompson (2008b).

Introduction

Carol, J. (2004) *Journeys of Courage: Remarkable Stories of the Healing Power of Community*, Notre Dame, IN, Sorin Books.

Coyte, M. E., Gilbert, P. and Nicholls, V. (eds) (2007) *Spirituality, Values and Mental Health: Jewels for the Journey*, London, Jessica Kingsley.

Cree, V. and Davis, A. (2006) *Social Work: Voices from the Inside*, London, Routledge.

Gelfand, D. E., Raspa, R., Briller, S. H. and Schim, S. M. (2005) *End-of-Life Stories: Crossing Disciplinary Boundaries*, New York, Springer.

Goldman, C. (2002) *The Gifts of Caregiving: Stories of Hardship, Hope and Healing*, Minneapolis, MN, Fairview Press.

Lustbader, W. (1991) *Counting on Kindness: The Dilemmas of Dependency*, New York, Free Press.

Malone, C., Forbat, L., Robb, M. and Seden, J. (2005) *Relating Experience: Stories from Health and Social Care*, London, Routledge.

Mullender, A. and Hague, G. (2003) *Is Anyone Listening?: Putting the Views of Survivors of Domestic Violence into Policy and Practice*, London, Routledge.

Part 1 The social worker as problem solver

Deurzen, E. van and Arnold-Baker, C. (eds) (2005) *Existential Perspectives on Human Issues*, Basingstoke, Palgrave Macmillan.

Doel, M. and Shardlow, S. M. (2005) *Modern Social Work Practice: Teaching and Learning in Practice Settings*, Aldershot, Ashgate.

Horwath, J. (2001) *The Child's World: Assessing Children in Need*, London, Jessica Kingsley.

Jordan, B. (2007) *Social Work and Well-Being*, Lyme Regis, Russell House Publishing.

Langan, M. (ed.) (2001) *Welfare: Needs, Rights and Risks*, London, Routledge.

Thompson, N. and Thompson, S. (2005) *Community Care*, Lyme Regis, Russell House Publishing.

Thompson, N. and Thompson, S. (2008) *The Social Work Companion*, Basingstoke, Palgrave Macmillan, Chapter 2.3.

Watson, D. and West, J. (2006) *Social Work Process and Practice: Approaches, Knowledge and Skills*, Basingstoke, Palgrave Macmillan.

Bauman, Z. and May, T. (2001) *Thinking Sociologically*, 2nd edn, Oxford, Blackwell.

Blakemore, K. (2003) *Social Policy: An Introduction*, 2nd edn, Buckingham, Open University Press.

Burr, V. (2003) *Social Constructionism*, 2nd edn, London, Routledge.

Carabine, J. (ed.) (2004) *Sexualities, Personal Lives and Social Policy*, Bristol, The Policy Press.

Gruber, C. and Stefanov, H. (eds) (2002) *Gender in Social Work: Promoting Equality*, Lyme Regis, Russell House Publishing.

Ife, J. (2001) *Human Rights and Social Work: Towards Rights-Based Practice*, Cambridge, Cambridge University Press.

Jordan, B. (2006) *Social Policy for the Twenty-First Century: New Perspectives, Big Issues*, Cambridge, Polity Press.

Jones, C. and Novak, T. (1999) *Poverty, Welfare and the Disciplinary State*, London, Routledge.

Kallen, E. (2004) *Social Inequality and Social Injustice: A Human Rights Perspective*, Basingstoke, Palgrave Macmillan.

Lister, R. (2004) *Poverty*, Cambridge, Polity.

May, M., Page, R. and Brunsdon, E. (2001) *Understanding Social Problems: Issues in Social Policy*, Oxford, Blackwell.

Parekh, B. (2006) *Rethinking Multiculturalism: Cultural Diversity and Political Theory*, 2nd edn, Basingstoke, Palgrave Macmillan.

Powell, F. (2001) *The Politics of Social Work*, London, Sage.

Powell, F. and Geoghegan, M. (2004) *The Politics of Community Development*, Dublin, A. & A. Farmer.

Scott, J., Treas, J. and Richards, M. (eds) (2007) *The Blackwell Companion to the Sociology of Families*, Oxford, Blackwell.

Sibeon, R. (2004) *Rethinking Social Theory*, London, Sage.

Smale, G., Tucson, G. and Statham, D. (2000) *Social Work and Social Problems: Working Towards Social Inclusion and Social Change*, Basingstoke, Palgrave Macmillan.

Swain, J., French, S. and Cameron, C. (2003) *Controversial Issues in a Disabling Society*, Buckingham, Open University Press.

Thompson, N. (2003) *Promoting Equality*, 2nd edn, Basingstoke, Palgrave Macmillan.

Thompson, N. (2005) *Understanding Social Work*, 2nd edn, Basingstoke, Palgrave Macmillan.

Thompson, N. (2006) *Anti-discriminatory Practice*, 4th edn, Basinsgtoke, Palgrave Macmillan.

Thompson, N. (2007) *Power and Empowerment*, Lyme Regis, Russell House Publishing.

Thompson, N. and Thompson, S. (2008) *The Social Work Companion*, Basingstoke, Palgrave Macmillan, Chapter 2.2.

Thompson, S. (2005) *Age Discrimination*, Lyme Regis, Russell House Publishing.

Healy, K. (2000) *Social Work Practices: Contemporary Perspectives on Change*, London, Sage.

Healy, K. (2005) *Social Work Theories in Context: Creating Frameworks for Practice*, Basingstoke, Palgrave Macmillan.

Heron, J. (2001) *Helping the Client: A Creative Practical Guide*, 5th edn, London, Sage.

Johnson, K. and Williams, I. (2007) *Managing Uncertainty and Change in Social Work and Social Care*, Lyme Regis, Russell House Publishing.

Jordan, B. (2007) *Social Work and Well-Being*, Lyme Regis, Russell House Publishing.

McDonald, C. (2006) *Challenging Social Work: The Institutional Context of Practice*, Basingstoke, Palgrave Macmillan.

Tew, J. (2002) *Social Theory, Power and Practice*, Basingstoke, Palgrave Macmillan.

Thompson, N. and Thompson, S. (2005) *Community Care*, Lyme Regis, Russell House Publishing.

Thompson, N. and Thompson, S. (2008) *The Social Work Companion*, Basingstoke, Palgrave Macmillan, Chapter 2.1.

Trevithick, P. (2005) *Social Work Skills: A Practice Handbook*, 2nd edn, Maidenhead, Open University Press.

Watson, D. and West, J. (2006) *Social Work Process and Practice: Approaches, Knowledge and Skills*, Basingstoke, Palgrave Macmillan.

Beresford, P. (2003) *It's Our Lives: A Short Theory of Knowledge, Distance and Experience*, London, Citizen Press in association with Shaping Our Lives.

Folgheraiter, F. (2004) *Relational Social Work: Towards Networking and Societal Practices*, London, Jessica Kingsley.

Harrison, R., Mann, G., Murphy, M., Taylor, A. and Thompson, N. (2003) *Partnership Made Painless*, Lyme Regis, Russell House Publishing.

Kemshall, H. and Littlechild, R. (eds) (2000) *User Involvement and Participation in Social Care: Research Informing Practice*, London, Jessica Kingsley.

Leathard, A. (ed.) (2003) *Interprofessional Collaboration: From Policy to Practice in Health and Social Care*, Hove, Brunner-Routledge.

Murphy, M. (2004) *Developing Collaborative Relationships in Interagency Child Protection Work*, 2nd edn, Lyme Regis, Russell House Publishing.

Social Care Institute for Excellence (2004) *Position Paper 3: Has Service User Involvement Made a Difference to Social Care Services?* London, SCIE – downloadable from: www.scie.org.uk

Shaping Our Lives National User Network (2003) *Shaping Our Lives: What People Think of the Social Care Services They Use*, York, Joseph Rowntree Foundation.

Sullivan, H. and Skelcher, C. (2002) *Working Across Boundaries: Collaboration in Social Services*, Basingstoke, Palgrave Macmillan.

Weinstein, J., Whittington, C. and Leiba, T. (eds) (2003) *Collaboration in Social Work Practice*, London, Jessica Kingsley.

Part 2   The social worker as thinker

Bolton, G. (2001) *Reflective Practice*, London, Paul Chapman.

Christensen, T. (2001) *Wonder and Critical Reflection: An Invitation to Philosophy*, New Jersey/London, Prentice Hall.

Cottrell, S. (2005) *Critical Thinking Skills: Developing Effective Analysis and Argument*, Basingstoke, Palgrave Macmillan.

Dolan, P., Canavan, J. and Pinkerton, J. (eds) (2006) *Family Support as Reflective Practice*, London, Jessica Kingsley.

Fook, J., Ryan, M. and Hawkins, L. (2000) *Professional Expertise: Practice, Theory and Education for Working in Uncertainty*, London, Whiting & Birch.

Fook, J. and Gardner, F. (2007) *Practising Critical Reflection: A Handbook*, Maidenhead, Open University Press.

Gould, N. and Baldwin, M. (eds) (2004) *Social Work, Critical Reflection and the Learning Organization*, Aldershot, Ashgate.

Hamer, M. (2006) *The Barefoot Helper: Mindfulness and Creativity in Social Work and the Helping Professions*, Lyme Regis, Russell House Publishing.

Johns, C. (2004) *Becoming a Reflective Practitioner*, 2nd edn, Oxford, Blackwell.

Martyn, H. (ed.) (2000) *Developing Reflective Practice: Making Sense of Social Work in a World of Change*, Bristol, The Policy Press.

Murray, M. and Kujundzic, N. (2005) *Critical Reflection: A Textbook for Critical Thinking*, Montreal and Kingston/London, McGill-Queen's University Press.

Redmond, B. (2004) *Reflection in Action: Developing Reflective Practice in Health and Social Services*, Aldershot, Ashgate.

Rolfe, G., Freshwater, D. and Jasper, M. (2001) *Critical Reflection for Nursing and the Helping Professions,* Basingstoke, Palgrave Macmillan.

Schön, D. A. (1983) *The Reflective Practitioner: How Professionals Think in Action,* London, Temple Smith.

Taylor, C. and White, S. (2000) *Practising Reflexivity in Health and Social Welfare: Making Knowledge,* Buckingham, Open University Press.

Thompson, N. (2000) *Theory and Practice in Human Services,* 2nd edn, Buckingham, Open University Press.

Thompson, N. (2006) *Promoting Workplace Learning,* Bristol, The Policy Press, see Chapter 3.

Thompson, S. and Thompson, N. (2008) *The Critically Reflective Practitioner,* Basingstoke, Palgrave Macmillan.

Doel, M. and Shardlow, S. M. (2005) *Modern Social Work Practice: Teaching and Learning in Practice Settings,* Aldershot, Ashgate.

Freire, P. (1972) *Pedagogy of the Oppressed,* Harmondsworth, Penguin.

Freire, P. (1972) *Cultural Action for Freedom,* Harmondsworth, Penguin.

Thompson, N. (2006) *Promoting Workplace Learning,* Bristol, The Policy Press.

Thompson, N. (2006) *People Problems,* Basingstoke, Palgrave Macmillan.

Thompson, S. and Thompson, N. (2008) *The Critically Reflective Practitioner,* Basingstoke, Palgrave Macmillan.

Barbalet, J. (ed.) (2002) *Emotions and Sociology,* Oxford, Blackwell Publishing.

Bendelow, G. and Williams. S. J. (eds) (1998) *Emotions in Social Life: Critical Themes and Contemporary Issues,* London, Routledge.

Bolton, S. C. (2005) *Emotion Management in the Workplace,* Basingstoke, Palgrave Macmillan.

Cooper, R. and Sawaf, A. (1997) *Executive EQ: Emotional Intelligence in Business,* London, Orion Business.

Fineman, S. (ed.) (2000) *Emotion in Organizations,* 2nd edn, London, Sage.

Fischer, A. H. (ed) (2000) *Gender and Emotion: Social Psychological Perspectives,* Cambridge, Cambridge University Press.

Goleman, D. (2004) *Destructive Emotions and How We Can Overcome Them: A Dialogue With the Dalai Lama,* London, Bloomsbury Publishing.

Goleman, D. (1996) *Emotional Intelligence: Why It Can Matter More Than IQ,* London, Bloomsbury Publishing.

Huffington, C., Armstrong, D., Halton, W., Hoyle, L. and Pooley, J. (eds) (2004) *Working Below the Surface: The Emotional Life of Contemporary Organizations,* London, Karnac.

Jordan, B. (2007) *Social Work and Well-Being,* Lyme Regis, Russell House Publishing.

Mervelede, P. E., Bridoux, D. and Vandamme, R. (2001) *7 Steps to Emotional Intelligence*, Carmarthen, Crown House Publishing.

Parkinson, B., Fischer, A. H. and Manstead, A. S. R. (2005) *Emotion in Social Relations: Cultural, Group and Interpersonal Processes*, Hove, Psychology Press.

Payne, R. L. and Cooper, C. L. (eds) (2001) *Emotions at Work: Theory, Research and Applications for Management*, Chichester, John Wiley & Sons.

Thompson, N. (ed.) (2002) *Loss and Grief: A Guide for Human Services Practitioners*, Basingstoke, Palgrave Macmillan.

Thompson, S. and Thompson, N. (2008) *The Critically Reflective Practitioner*, Basingstoke, Palgrave Macmillan.

Williams, S. (2001) *Emotion and Social Theory*, London, Sage.

Chamberlayne, P., Bornat, J. and Apitzsch, U. (2004) *Biographical Methods and Professional Practice: An International Perspective*, Bristol, The Policy Press.

Dallos, R. (2006) *Attachment Narrative Therapy*, Maidenhead, Open University Press.

Deurzen, E. van and Arnold-Baker, C. (eds) (2005) *Existential Perspectives on Human Issues*, Basingstoke, Palgrave Macmillan.

Milner, J. (2001) *Women and Social Work: A Narrative Approach*, Basingstoke, Palgrave Macmillan.

Moss, B. R. (2005) *Religion and Spirituality*, Lyme Regis, Russell House Publishing.

Myers, S. (2007) *Solution-Focused Approaches*, Lyme Regis, Russell House Publishing.

Neimeyer, R. A. (ed.) (2001) *Meaning Reconstruction and the Experience of Loss*, Washington, American Psychological Society.

Parton, N. and O'Byrne, P. (2000) *Constructive Social Work: Towards a New Practice*, Basingstoke, Palgrave Macmillan.

Vetere, A. and Dowling, E. (2005) *Narrative Therapies with Children and Their Families: A Practitioner's Guide to Concepts and Approaches*, Hove, Routledge.

Part 3 The social worker as manager

Clutterbuck, D. (1998) *Learning Alliances: Tapping into Talent*, London, Chartered Institute of Personnel and Development.

Hawkins, P. and Shohet, R. (2001) *Supervision in the Helping Professions*, 2nd edn, Buckingham, Open University Press.

Honey, P. (2003) *How to Become a More Effective Learner*, Maidenhead, Peter Honey Publications.

Honey, P. (2007) *Continuing Personal Development*, Maidenhead, Peter Honey Publications.

Morrison, T. (2000) *Supervision: An Action Learning Approach*, 3rd edn, Brighton, Pavilion.

Thompson, N. (1999) *Stress Matters: A Personal Guide*, Birmingham, Pepar Publications.

Thompson, N. (2002) *People Skills*, 2nd edn, Basingstoke, Palgrave Macmillan, Part 1.

Thompson, N. and Thompson, S. (2008) *The Social Work Companion*, Basingstoke, Palgrave Macmillan.

Brechin, A., Brown, H. and Eby, M. A. (eds) (2000) *Critical Practice in Health and Social Care*, London, Sage.

Coulshed, V., Mullender, A., with Jones, D. and Thompson, N. (2006) *Management in Social Work*, 3rd edn, Basingstoke, Palgrave Macmillan.

Fook, J. (2002) *Social Work: Critical Theory and Practice*, London, Sage.

Jordan, B. (2007) *Social Work and Well-Being,* Lyme Regis, Russell House Publishing.

Marsh, P. and Doel, M. (2005) *The Task-Centred Book*, London, Routledge.

Milner, J. and O'Byrne, P. (2002) *Assessment in Social Work*, 2nd edn, Basingstoke, Palgrave Macmillan.

Myers, S. (2007) *Solution-Focused Approaches*, Lyme Regis, Russell House Publishing.

Parton, N. and O'Byrne, P. (2000) *Constructive Social Work: Towards a New Practice*, Basingstoke, Palgrave Macmillan.

Payne, M. (2005) *Modern Social Work Theory*, 3rd edn, Basingstoke, Palgrave Macmillan.

Sheldon, B. and Chilvers, R. (2000) *Evidence-Based Social Care*, Lyme Regis, Russell House Publishing.

Thompson, N. (2002) *People Skills,* 2nd edn, Basingstoke, Palgrave Macmillan.

Thompson, N. and Thompson, S. (2005) *Community Care*, Lyme Regis, Russell House Publishing.

Thompson, N. and Thompson, S. (2008) *The Social Work Companion*, Basingstoke, Palgrave Macmillan, Chapter 2.1.

Trevithick, P. (2005) *Social Work Skills: A Practice Handbook*, 2nd edn, Maidenhead, Open University Press.

Trinder, L. and Reynolds, S. (eds)(2000) *Evidence-Based Practice: A Critical Approach*, Oxford Blackwell.

Watson, D. and West, J. (2006) *Social Work Process and Practice*: *Approaches, Knowledge and Skills*, Basingstoke, Palgrave Macmillan.

Coulshed, V., Mullender, A., with Jones, D. and Thompson, N. (2006) *Management in Social Work*, 3rd edn, Basingstoke, Palgrave Macmillan.

Denney, D. (2005) *Risk and Society*, London, Sage.

Harding, T. (2005) *Rights and Risk: Older People and Human Rights*, London, Help the Aged.

Kemshall, H. (2002) *Risk, Social Policy and Welfare*, Birmingham, Open University Press.

Langan, J. and Lindow, V. (2004) *Living with Risk: Mental Health Service User Involvement in Risk Assessment and Management*, Bristol, The Policy Press/Joseph Rowntree Foundation.

Martin, J. (2007) *Safeguarding Adults*, Lyme Regis, Russell House Publishing.

Pritchard, J. (2001) *Good Practice with Vulnerable Adults*, London, Jessica Kingsley.

Webb, S. (2006) *Social Work in a Risk Society: Social and Political Perspectives*, Basingstoke, Palgrave Macmillan.

Budjac Corvette, B. A. (2006) *Conflict Management: A Practical Guide to Developing Negotiation Strategies*, New York, Prentice Hall.

Institute of Leadership and Management (2007) *Managing Conflict in the Workplace*, Oxford, Pergamon.

Jordan, B. (2007) *Social Work and Well-Being*, Lyme Regis, Russell House Publishing.

Murphy, M. (2004) *Developing Collaborative Relationships in Interagency Child Protection Work*, Lyme Regis, Russell House Publishing.

Thompson, N. (2002) *People Skills*, 2nd edn, Basingstoke, Palgrave Macmillan, see Chapters 14 and 16.

Thompson, N. (2006) *People Problems*, Basingstoke, Palgrave Macmillan.

Thompson, N. and Thompson, S. (2008) *The Social Work Companion*, Basingstoke, Palgrave Macmillan.

Part 4 The social worker as professional

Batsleer, J. and Humphries, B. (2000) *Welfare, Exclusion and Political Agency*, London, Routledge.

Bracken, P. and Thomas, P. (2005) *Postpsychiatry: Mental Health in a Postmodern World*, Oxford, Oxford University Press.

Crossley, M. L. (2000) *Introducing Narrative Psychology: Self, Trauma and the Construction of Meaning*, Maidenhead, Open University Press.

Duyvendak, J. W., Knijn, T. and Kremer, M. (eds), (2006), *Policy, People, and the New Professional: De-professionalisation and Re-Professionalisation in Care and Welfare*, Amsterdam, Amsterdam University Press.

Gilbert, P. (2003) *The Value of Everything: Social Work and its Importance in the Field of Mental Health*, Lyme Regis, Russell House Publishing.

McDonald, C. (2006) *Challenging Social Work: The Institutional Context of Practice*, Basingstoke, Palgrave Macmillan.

Payne, M. (2000) *Anti-Bureaucratic Social Work*, Birmingham, Venture Press.

Pease, B. and Fook, J. (eds) (1999) *Transforming Social Work Practice: Postmodern Critical Perspectives*, London, Routledge.

Thompson, N. (2007) *Power and Empowerment*, Lyme Regis, Russell House Publishing.

Thompson, N. and Thompson, S. (2008) *The Social Work Companion*, Basingstoke, Palgrave Macmillan.

References

Achterhuis, H. (1979) *De Markt van Welzijn en Geluk*, Baarn, Ambo.

Adams, R. Dominelli, L. and Payne, M. (eds) (2002) *Critical Practice in Social Work*, Basingstoke, Palgrave Macmillan.

Afshar, H. (ed.) (1998) *Women and Empowerment: Illustrations from the Third World*, Basingstoke, Macmillan – now Palgrave Macmillan.

Argyris, C. and Schön, D. A. (1974) *Theory in Practice: Increasing Personal Effectiveness*, San Francisco, CA, Jossey Bass.

Argyris, C. and Schön, D. A. (1978) *Organizational Learning*, Reading, MA, Addison-Wesley.

Asch, D. and Bowman, C. (eds) (1989) *Readings in Strategic Management*, Basingstoke, Macmillan – now Palgrave Macmillan.

Barnes, G. G. (2004) *Family Therapy in Changing Times*, Basingstoke, Palgrave Macmillan.

Barnes, M. and Bowl, R. (2001) *Taking Over the Asylum: Empowerment and Mental Health*, Basingstoke, Palgrave Macmillan.

Bateson, G. (1973) *Steps to an Ecology of Mind: Collected Essays in Anthropology, Psychiatry, Evolution and Epistemology*, St Albans, Paladin.

Bauman, Z. and May, T. (2001) *Thinking Sociologically*, 2nd edn, Oxford, Blackwell.

Beck, U. (1992) *Risk Society: Towards a New Modernity*, London, Sage.

Beckett, C. (2006) *Essential Theory for Social Work Practice*, London, Sage.

Bentall, R. P. (2004) *Madness Explained: Psychosis and Human Nature*, London, Penguin.

Blumer, H. (1969) *Symbolic Interactionism*, Englewood Cliffs, NJ, Prentice Hall.

Bracken, P. (2002) *Trauma: Culture, Meaning and Philosophy*, London, Whurr.

Bracken, P. and Thomas, P. (2005) *Postpsychiatry: Mental Health in a Postmodern World*, Oxford, Oxford University Press.

Brandon, D. and Brandon, T. (2001) *Advocacy in Social Work*, Birmingham, Venture Press.

Brearley, P. (1982) *Risk and Social Work*, London, Routledge.

Brechin, A. (2000a) 'The Challenge of Caring Relationships', in Brechin et al. (2000).

Brechin, A. (2000b) 'Introducing Critical Practice', in Brechin et al. (2000).

Brechin, A., Brown, H. and Eby, M. A., (eds) (2000) *Critical Practice in Health and Social Care*, London, Sage.

Brewin, C. R. (2003) *Posttraumatic Stress Disorder: Malady or Myth*, New Haven, CT, Yale University Press.

Buber, M. (2004) *I and Thou*, 2nd edn, London, Continuum (originally published 1958).

Butt, T. (2004) *Understanding People*, Basingstoke, Palgrave Macmillan.

Buzan, T. and Buzan, B. (2003) *The Mind Map Book*, 2nd edn, London, BBC Worldwide.

Calhoun, L. G. and Tedeschi, R. G. (1999) *Facilitating Posttraumatic Growth*, Mahwah, NJ, Lawrence Erlbaum Associates.

Carr, A. (2000) *Family Therapy: Concepts, Process and Practice*, Chichester, Wiley.

Christenson, T. (2001) *Wonder and Critical Reflection: An Invitation to Philosophy*, London, Prentice Hall International.

Clutterbuck, D. (1998) *Learning Alliances: Tapping into Talent*, London, Chartered Institute of Personnel and Development.

Clutterbuck, D. (2001) *Everyone Needs a Mentor: Fostering Talent at Work*, 3rd edn, London, Chartered Institute of Personnel and Development.

Crossley, M. L. (2000) *Introducing Narrative Psychology: Self, Trauma and the Construction of Meaning*, Maidenhead, Open University Press.

Crossley, N. (1996) *Intersubjectivity: The Fabric of Social Becoming*, London, Sage.

Crossley, N. (2006) *Contesting Psychiatry: Social Movements in Mental Health*, London, Routledge.

Dallos, R. (2006) *Attachment Narrative Therapy: Integrating Narrative, Systemic and Attachment Therapies*, Maidenhead, Open University Press.

Dass, R. (2002) *One-Liners*, London, Piatkus Books.

Davis, A. (2004) 'Foreword', in Folgheraiter (2004).

Denney, D. (2005) *Risk and Society*, London, Sage.

Department of Health (2001) *Valuing People: A Strategy for the 21st Century*, London, DoH.

Dewey, J. (1933) *How We Think*, Boston, MA, DC Heath.

Dewey, J. (1938) *Experience and Education*, New York, Macmillan.

Doka, K. J. (1989) *Disenfranchised Grief: Recognizing Hidden Sorrow*, Lexington, Lexington, MA.

Duyvendak, J. W. (1997) *Waar Blift de Politick? Essays over Parse Politick, Maatschappelijk Middenveld en Sociale Cohesie*, Amsterdam, Boom.

Duyvendak, J. W., Knijn, T. and Kremer, M. (2006a) 'Policy, People, and the New Professional: An Introduction', in Duyvendak et al. (2006b).

Duyvendak, J. W., Knijn, T. and Kremer, M. (eds), (2006b), *Policy, People, and the New Professional: De-Professionalisation and Re-Professionalisation in Care and Welfare*, Amsterdam, Amsterdam University Press.

Ellaway, A., Anderson, A. and Macintyre, S. (1997) 'Does Area of Residence Affect Body Size and Shape?', *International Journal of Obesity*, 5, pp. 38–45.

England, H. (1986) *Social Work as Art*, Hemel Hempstead, Allen & Unwin.

Faubion, J. D. (ed.) (2000) *Power: Essential Works of Foucault 1954–1984*, Harmondsworth, Penguin.

Fineman, S. (2000a) 'Commodifying the Emotionally Intelligent', in Fineman (2000b).

Fineman, S. (ed.) (2000b) *Emotion in Organizations*, 2nd edn, London, Sage.

Fischer, A. H. (ed.) (2000) *Gender and Emotion: Social Psychological Perspectives*, Cambridge, Cambridge University Press.

Folgheraiter, F. (1998) *Teoria e Metodologia del Servizio Sociale. La Prospettiva di Rete*, Milan, Angeli.

Folgheraiter, F. (2004) *Relational Social Work*, London, Jessica Kingsley Publishers.

Fook, J. (2002) *Social Work: Critical Theory and Practice*, London, Sage.

Fook, J. and Gardner, F. (2007) *Practising Critical Reflection: A Resource Handbook*, Maidenhead, Open University Press.

Foucault, M. (2001) *Madness and Civilization: A History of Insanity in an Age of Reason*, London, Routledge.

Freire, P. (1972a) *Pedagogy of the Oppressed,* Harmondsworth, Penguin.

Freire, P. (1972b) *Cultural Action for Freedom,* Harmondsworth, Penguin.

Furedi, F. (1997), *Culture of Fear: Risk Taking and the Morality of Low Expectation*, London, Cassell.

Garrett, P. M. (2002) 'Social Work and the Just Society: Diversity, Difference and the Sequestration of Poverty', *Journal of Social Work*, 2(2).

Gergen, K. J. (1999) *An Invitation to Social Construction*, London, Sage.

Gibson, F. (2006) *Order from Chaos: Responding to Traumatic Events*, Bristol, Policy Press.

Gilbert, P. (2005) *Leadership: Being Effective and Remaining Human*, Lyme Regis, Russell House Publishing.

Goldsmith, H. F., Holzer, C. E. and Manderschied, R. W. (1998) 'Neighborhood Characteristics and Mental Illness', *Evaluation and Program Planning*, 21, pp. 211–25.

Gradener, J. (2003) 'Zinloze Zelfkritiek', *Tidschrift voor de Sociale Sector*, 57(5).

Gradener, J. and Spierts, M. (2006) 'Empowerment of Social Services Professionals: Strategies for Professionalisation and Knowledge Development', in Duyvendak et al. (2006b).

Haffenden, S. (1991) *Getting it Right for Carers: Setting up Services for Carers: A Guide for Practitioners*, London, Harvester Wheatsheaf.

Hamer, M. (2006) *The Barefoot Helper: Mindfulness and Creativity in Social Work and the Helping Professions*, Lyme Regis, Russell House Publishing.

Hardiker, P. and Barker, M. (1999) 'Early Steps in Implementing the New Community Care: The Role of Social Work Practice', *Health and Social Care in the Community,* 7(6).

Harris, R. and Webb, D. (1987) *Welfare, Power and Justice: The Social Control of Delinquent Youth*, London, Tavistock.

Hayward, S. (2005) *Women Leading*, Basingstoke, Palgrave Macmillan.

Healy, K. (2000) *Social Work Practices: Contemporary Perspectives on Change*, London, Sage.

Healy, K. (2005) *Social Work Theories in Context: Creating Frameworks for Practice*, Basingstoke, Palgrave Macmillan.

Healy, K. and Meagher, G. (2004) 'The Reprofessionalisation of Social Work: Collaborative Approaches for Achieving Professional Recognition', *British Journal of Social Work*, 32(2).

Hedderman, C. and Gelsthorpe, L. (1997) *The Sentencing of Women*, Home Office Research Study 170, London, HMSO.

Hendry, J. (1999) *An Introduction to Social Anthropology: Other People's Worlds*, Basingstoke, Palgrave Macmillan.

Howard League (2006) *When Big Brother Goes Inside: The Experiences of Younger Siblings of Young Men in Prison,* London, the Howard League for Penal Reform.

Hugman, R. (1998) *Social Welfare and Social Value,* Basingstoke Macmillan – now Palgrave Macmillan.

Humphries, B. (2003) 'What Else Counts as Evidence in Evidence-Based Social Work?' *Social Work Education,* 22(1).

Hunt, L. (1978) 'Social Work and Ideology', in Timms and Watson (1978).

Itzin, C. and Newman, J. (eds) (1995) *Gender, Culture and Organizational Change: Putting Theory into Practice,* London, Routledge.

Jack, R, 'Strengths-Based Practice in Statutory Care and Protection Work', in Nash et al. (2005).

James, C. (1995) 'Who Learns What?, *Nurse Education Today,* 15(3).

Jones, A. (2000) 'Social Work: An Enterprising Profession in a Competitive Environment', in O'Connor et al. (2000).

Jones, C. and Novak, T. (1999) *Poverty, Welfare and the Disciplinary State,* London, Routledge.

Jones, H. (2001) 'Health Inequalities', in May et al. (2001).

Jones, L. J. (1994) *The Social Context of Health and Health Care,* Basingstoke, Macmillan – now Palgrave Macmillan.

Jordan, B. (1990) *Social Work in an Unjust Society,* Hemel Hempstead, Harvester Wheatsheaf.

Jordan, B. (2007) *Social Work and Well-Being,* Lyme Regis, Russell House Publishing.

Kellehear, A. (2005) *Compassionate Cities: Public Health and End-of-Life Care,* Milton Park, Routledge.

Kemshall, H. and Littlechild, R. (eds) (2000) *User Involvement and Participation in Social Care: Research Informing Practice,* London, Jessica Kingsley.

Knijn, T. and Selten, P. (2006) 'The Rise of Contractualisation in Public Services', in Duyvendak et al. (2006b).

Kotter, J. (1996) *Leading Change,* Boston, MA, Harvard Business School Press.

Kotter, J. and Schlesinger, L. A. (1989) 'Choosing Strategies for Change', in Asch and Bowman (1989).

Kremer, M. and Tonkens, E. (2006) 'Authority, Trust, Knowledge and the Public Good in Disarray', in Duyvendak et al. (2006b).

Levine, D. P. (2004) 'Imagined Realities: Rethinking Needs, Rights and Capabilities', University Lecture, University of Denver, Denver, CO, 12 April 2004.

Lewin, K. (1947) 'Feedback Problems of Social Diagnosis and Action', *Human Relations,* 1.

Le Grand, J. (1997) 'Knights, Knaves or Pawns? Human Behaviour and Social Policy', *Journal of Social Policy,* 26(2).

Lloyd, M. (2002) 'Care Management', in Adams et al. (2002).

Lloyd, M. and Smith, M. (1998) *Assessment and Service Provision under the New Community Care Arrangements for People with Parkinson's Disease and their Carers,* Research Report No. 13, Manchester, University of Manchester.

Lloyd, M. and Taylor, C. (1995) 'From Hollis to the Orange Book: Developing a Holistic Model of Assessment in the 1990s', *British Journal of Social Work,* 25(6).

Lloyd, M., Preston-Shoot, M., Temple, B. with Wuu, R. (1996) 'Whose Project is it Anyway? Sharing and Shaping the Research and Development Agenda', *Disability and Society*, 11(3).

Lovelock, R., Lyons, K. and Powell, J. (eds) (2004) *Reflecting on Social Work – Discipline and Profession*, Aldershot, Ashgate.

Lukas, C. and Seiden, H. M. (2007) *Silent Grief: Living in the Wake of Suicide*, revised edn, London, Jessica Kingsley Publishers.

Lymbery, M. (2001) 'Social Work at the Crossroads', *British Journal of Social Work*, 31 pp. 369–84.

Lymbery, M. (2003) 'Collaborating for the Social and Health Care of Older People' in Weinstein et al. (2003).

Marsh, P. and Doel, M. (2005) *The Task-Centred Book*, London, Routledge.

Maslow, A. (1973) *The Farther Reaches of Human Nature*, Harmondsworth, Penguin.

May, M., Page, R. and Brunsdon, E. (eds) (2001) *Understanding Social Problems: Issues in Social Policy*, Oxford, Blackwell.

Mayon-White, B. (ed.) (1986) *Planning and Managing Change,* London, Harper & Row.

McDonald, C. (2006) *Challenging Social Work*, Basingstoke, Palgrave Macmillan.

Merleau-Ponty, M. (1962) *The Phenomenology of Perception*, Oxford, Blackwell.

Merton, R. K. (1938) 'Social Structure and Anomie', *American Sociological Review*, 3, pp. 672–82.

Milner, J. and O'Byrne, P. (2002) 'Assessment and Planning', in Adams et al. (2002).

Moss, B. (2005) *Religion and Spirituality*, Lyme Regis, Russell House Publishing.

Moss, B. (2007) *Values*, Lyme Regis, Russell House Publishing.

Moss, B. (2008) *Communication Skills for Health and Social Care*, London, Sage.

Mullaly, B, (2001), 'Confronting the Politics of Despair: Toward the Reconstruction of Progressive Social Work in a Global Economy and Postmodern Age', *Social Work Education*, 20(3).

Murray, M. and Kujundzic, N. (2005) *Critical Reflection: A Textbook for Critical Thinking*, Montreal and Kingston/London, McGill-Queen's University Press.

Myers, S. (2007) *Solution-Focused Approaches*, Lyme Regis, Russell House Publishing.

Nash, M., Munford, R. and O'Donoghue, K. (eds) (2005) *Social Work Theories in Action*, London, Jessica Kingsley Publishers.

Neimeyer, R. A. (ed.) (2001) *Meaning Reconstruction and the Experience of Loss*, Washington, American Psychological Society.

Neimeyer, R. A. and Anderson, A. (2002) 'Meaning Reconstruction Theory', in Thompson (2002c).

Nettle, S. (2006) *The Sociology of Health and Illness*, 2nd edn, Cambridge, Polity.

O'Connor, I., Smyth, P. and Warburton, J. (eds) (2000) *Contemporary Perspectives on Social Work and the Human Services: Challenges and Change*, Melbourne, Longman.

Oliver, M. and Sapey, B. (2006) *Social Work with Disabled People*, 3rd edn, Basingstoke, Palgrave Macmillan.

Orford, J. et al. (2005) *Coping with Alcohol and Drug Problems: The Experiences of Family Members in Contrasting Cultures*, London, Sage.

Osmond, J. and O'Connor, I. (2004) 'Formalizing the Unformalized: Practitioners' Communication of Knowledge in Practice', *British Journal of Social Work* 34(5), pp. 677–92.

Parkes, C. M. (1986) *Bereavement: Studies of Grief in Adult Life*, 2nd edn, Harmondsworth, Penguin.

Parton, N. (1996) *Social Theory, Social Change and Social Work*, Routledge, London.

Parton, N. and O'Byrne, P. (2000) *Constructive Social Work: Towards a New Practice*, Basingstoke, Palgrave Macmillan.

Parton, N., Thorpe, D. and Wattam, C. (1997) *Child Protection: Risk and the Moral Order*, Basingstoke, Macmillan – now Palgrave Macmillan.

Payne, G. (2006) *Social Divisions*, 2nd edn, Basingstoke, Palgrave Macmillan.

Payne, M. (2000) *Anti-Bureaucratic Social Work*, Birmingham, Venture Press.

Pease, B. and Fook, J (1999a) 'Postmodern Critical Theory and Emancipatory Social Work Practice', in Pease and Fook (1999b).

Pease, B. and Fook, J. (eds) (1999b) *Transforming Social Work Practice: Postmodern Critical Perspectives*, London, Routledge.

Penketh, L. (2000) *Tackling Institutional Racism: Anti-racist Policies and Social Work Education and Training*, Bristol, The Policy Press.

Perrow, C. (2000) 'An Organizational Analysis of Organizational Culture', *Contemporary Sociology*, 29, pp. 469–76.

Pinkerton, J. (2002) 'Child Protection', in Adams et al. (2002).

Preston-Shoot, M. (1996) 'W(h)ither Social Work? Social Work, Social Policy and Law at an Interface: Confronting the Challenges and Realising the Potential in Work with People Needing Care or Services', *The Liverpool Law Review*, XVIII(1).

Pugh, D. (1986) 'Understanding and Managing Organizational Change', in Mayon-White (1986).

Putnam, R. (2000) *Bowling Alone – The Collapse and Revival of American Community*, New York, Simon & Schuster.

Roberts, A. R. (2006) *Crisis Intervention Handbook: Assessment, Treatment and Research*, 3rd edn, Oxford, Oxford University Press.

Rogers, A. and Pilgrim, D. (2003) *Mental Health and Inequality*, Basingstoke, Palgrave Macmillan.

Rolfe, G., Freshwater, D. and Jasper, M. (2001) *Critical Reflection for Nursing and the Helping Professions: A User Guide*, Basingstoke, Palgrave Macmillan.

Rosen, G. M. (ed.) (2004) *Posttraumatic Stress Disorder: Issues and Controversies*, Chichester, Wiley.

Ross, C. E. (2000) 'Neighbourhood Disadvantage and Adult Depression', *Journal of Health and Social Behaviour*, 41, pp. 177–87.

Rothschild, B. (2006) *Help for the Helper*, New York, W. W. Norton.

Rowlands, J. (1998) 'A Word of the Times, but What Does it Mean? Empowerment in the Discourse and Practice of Development?', in Afshar (1998).

Sainsbury Centre for Mental Health (2000) *The Capable Practitioner*, London, Sainsbury Centre.

Saleebey, D. (2005) *The Strengths Perspective in Social Work Practice*, 4th edn, Allyn & Bacon.

Schacter, S. and Singer, J. (1962) 'Cognitive, Social and Physiological Determinants of Emotional States', *Psychological Review*, 69, pp. 379–99.

Schneider, J. M. (1994) *Finding My Way: Healing and Transformation through Loss and Grief*, Colfax, WI, Seasons Press.

Schneider, J. M. (2000) *The Overdiagnosis of Depression: Recognizing Grief and its Transformational Potential*, Traverse City, MI, Seasons Press.

Schön, D. A. (1983) *The Reflective Practitioner*, New York, Basic Books.

Schön, D. A. (1987) *Educating the Reflective Practitioner*, San Fransisco, CA, Jossey-Bass.

Schön, D. A. (1992) 'The Crisis of Professional Knowledge and the Pursuit of an Epistemology of Practice', *Journal of Interprofessional Care*, 6(1).

Seligman, M. E. P. (1975) *Helplessness: On Depression, Development, and Death*, San Francisco, W. H. Freeman.

Shaping Our Lives National User Network (2003) *Shaping Our Lives: What People Think of The Social Care Services They Use*, York, Joseph Rowntree Foundation.

Shotter, J. (1993) *Cultural Politics of Everyday Life*, Buckingham, Open University Press.

Sibeon, R. (2004) *Rethinking Social Theory*, London, Sage.

Skidmore, R. A, Thackeray, M. G. and Farley, O. W. (1997) *Introduction to Social Work*, 7th edn, Needham Heights, MA, Allyn & Bacon.

Slovic, P. (1999) 'Trust, Emotion, Sex, Politics and Science: Surveying the Risk-Assessment Battlefield', *Risk Analysis*, 19(4).

Smith, P. and Natalier, K. (2005) *Understanding Criminal Justice: Sociological Perspectives*, London, Sage.

Solomos, J. (2003) *Race and Racism in Britain*, 3rd edn, Basingstoke, Palgrave Macmillan.

Spiers, M. L., Veldboer, P. and Peters, F. (2003) 'De Professionaliteit Gesmoord', *Tidschrift voor de Sociale Sector*, 57(5).

Stein, H. F. (2007) *Insight and Imagination: A Study in Knowing and Not-Knowing in Organizational Life*, Plymouth, University Press of America.

Swain, J., French, S., Barnes, C. and Thomas, C. (eds) (2004) *Disabling Barriers – Enabling Environments*, London, Sage.

Tanner, D. (1998) 'Empowerment and Care Management: Swimming against the Tide', *Health and Social Care in the Community*, 6(6).

Tew, J. (2002) 'Going Social: Championing a Holistic Model of Mental Distress within Professional Education', *Social Work Education*, 21(2).

Thompson, N. (1991) *Crisis Intervention Revisited*, Birmingham, Pepar Publications.

Thompson, N. (2000) *Theory and Practice in Human Services*, 2nd edn, Buckingham, Open University Press.

Thompson, N. (2002a) 'Social Movements, Social Justice and Social Work', *British Journal of Social Work*, 32(6).

Thompson, N. (2002b) 'Introduction', in Thompson (2002d).

Thompson, N. (ed.) (2002c) *Loss and Grief: A Guide for Human Services Practitioners*, Basingstoke, Palgrave Macmillan.

Thompson, N. (2002d) *People Skills*, Basingstoke, Palgrave Macmillan.

Thompson, N. (2003a) *Promoting Equality: Tackling Discrimination and Oppression*, Basingstoke, Palgrave Macmillan.

Thompson, N. (2003b) *Communication and Language: A Handbook of Theory and Practice*, Basingstoke, Palgrave Macmillan.

Thompson, N. (2004) *Group Care with Children and Young People*, 2nd edn, Lyme Regis, Russell House Publishing.

Thompson, N. (2005) *Understanding Social Work: Preparing for Practice*, 2nd edn, Basingstoke, Palgrave Macmillan.

Thompson, N. (2006a) *People Problems*, Basingstoke, Palgrave Macmillan.

Thompson, N. (2006b) *Anti-Discriminatory Practice*, 4th edn, Basingstoke, Palgrave Macmillan.

Thompson, N. (2006c) *Promoting Workplace Learning*, Bristol, the Policy Press.

Thompson, N. (2007a) *Power and Empowerment*, Lyme Regis, Russell House Publishing.

Thompson, N. (2007b) 'Spirituality: An Existentialist Perspective', *Illness, Crisis & Loss*, 15(2).

Thompson, N. (forthcoming) *Theorizing Social Work*, Basingstoke, Palgrave Macmillan.

Thompson, N. and Thompson, S. (2007) *Understanding Social Care*, 2nd edn, Lyme Regis, Russell House Publishing.

Thompson, N. and Thompson, S. (2008b) *The Social Work Companion*, Basingstoke, Palgrave Macmillan.

Thompson, S. and Thompson, N. (2008a) *The Critically Reflective Practitioner*, Basingstoke, Palgrave Macmillan.

Thompson, S. (2005) *Age Discrimination*, Lyme Regis, Russell House Publishing.

Timms, N. and Watson, D. (eds) (1978) *Philosophy in Social Work*, London, Routledge & Kegan Paul.

Trevithick, P. (2005) *Social Work Skills: A Practice Handbook*, 2nd edn, Maidenhead, Open University Press.

Van Deurzen, E. and Arnold-Baker, C. (eds) (2005) *Existential Perspectives on Human Issues: A Handbook for Therapeutic Practice*, Basingstoke, Palgrave Macmillan.

Watson, D. and West, J. (2006) *Social Work Processes and Practice: Approaches, Knowledge and Skills*, Basingstoke, Palgrave Macmillan.

Webb, S. A. (2006) *Social Work in a Risk Society: Social and Political Perspectives*, Basingstoke, Palgrave Macmillan.

Weinstein, J., Whittington, C. and Leiba, T. (eds) (2003) *Collaboration in Social Work Practice*, London, Jessica Kingsley.

Ziegler, D. (2002) *Traumatic Experience and the Brain*, Jasper, OR, Acacia Publishing.

Index